Yellowsnake, Son of Prophecy

To Ron and Laura -
Hope you enjoy the
life story of a most
amazing character.

Jake Conrad

Yellowsnake, Son of Prophecy

By

Jake Conrad

ISBN: 1-58721-340-0

1stBooks – rev. 3/23/00

About the Book

When the young Comanche halfbreed was recruited by the U.S. Army Rangers, little did Yellowsnake know where the fortunes of war would take him.

Once Colonel Lincoln spotted Yellowsnake and his survival instincts, their lives would be enjoined for many years to follow. Yellowsnake, under the guidance of his wise Colonel soon wreaked havoc upon the Viet Cong.

After his Viet Nam army tour, Yellowsnake suddenly found himself employed by the CIA, and once again thrust back into the jungle as an invisible operative for the Company.

From the early moments of his life, his spirits and soul were being closely watched over by Shahana, a mysterious Yaqui Medicine Woman.

She had prophesized the terror and danger which would become part of Yellowsnake's life, and before the tragic accident which Shahana had foreseen could claim Yellowsnake's life, the old woman would give her last breath to save him.

After his miraculous recovery, the healing warrior's path crosses that of Jake Montana, an adventure lover and treasure hunter who soon forms a lifelong bond with Yellowsnake.

Their adventurous treasure search takes them deep into the mountains of Arizona in pursuit of one of the fabled Peralta treasure caches.

Yellowsnake's perilous life had seen him working covertly for Daniel Ortega in Nicaragua and for the sinister Manuel Noriega under the close scrutiny of the CIA. However, he knew that with the help of Shahana's watchful spirit he would someday enjoy the company of those he trusted and be blessed with adventure on safer ground.

AUTHOR'S THANKS

My warmest thanks to my Daughter Paula Parshall for her hundreds of hours of tireless assistance.

Special thanks to Pete and Donna Hilgeman for their technical assistance during times of crisis.

Authors E-Mail Address: CJgolddust@aol.com

TABLE OF CONTENTS

Chapter 1

The Prophecy

Albert Einstein once said, "In the middle of difficulty lies opportunity." Little did the brilliant scholar know that he had coined a phrase befitting Yellowsnake's perilous life to come . . .

A flash of lightning lit up the darkened sky straight ahead of him. The rolling black clouds approaching him sharpened his senses even further. Yellowsnake remained motionless, crouched and poised like a coiled steel spring. Two days earlier, he had quietly selected this spot to set his ambush.

He had dug the burrow into the side slope, just large enough to accommodate a warrior his size. It was strategically placed and camouflaged behind a scraggly juniper bush.

Then he heard the soft sound of what he had been waiting for. He watched the dark figure creep past the bush hiding him as he clenched his knife in hand, ready for the kill.

His lean legs catapulted him forward, placing him squarely on the back of the stalker. Yellowsnake wrapped his arm across the neck of his attacker, placing his hand into the armpit of his victim. He hurled him to the ground in one swift move. In a split second, he was looking into the terrified eyes of an enemy who lay helpless on his back. Yellowsnake grasped his enemy's hair with his left hand as he drew his knife and placed its long blade against the stalker's throat. He released a blood curdling cry of victory. "Edward, you're dead again!"

Suddenly, heaven's flood gates broke open, quickly drenching the two of them in torrents of rain. Sadly, their game was over. It was a game he and Edward Red Sky had played many times. This time, it had been Edward's turn to be the tracker. Yellowsnake had been given a fifteen minute head start and was fleeing his enemy.

They were thirteen years old, fine tuning their young bodies while playing the game of life and death, and nearly every time, Yellowsnake was the winner of life. His senses were keen, whether tracking or being pursued. Yellowsnake had become accustomed to winning life's battles. Little did he know of the real battles which lay ahead. He was a 20th century Comanche warrior whose instincts were becoming sharply honed for the days ahead.

His dusty Oklahoma Indian Reservation was only a brief resting place for the young Comanche. He would, in a few short years, find himself en route to Fort Hood. Yellowsnake would soon learn to be all he could be -- an understatement.

If a beginning point is to be marked in this extraordinary life journey it arrived during the summer of Yellowsnake's fourteenth year. The day was miserably hot in 1957 as he sat upon his weathered stoop, meticulously adding final touches to the peacepipe he held carefully in his hands. The pipe's delicately etched signs and symbols were signaling the end of six months hard work.

Two years earlier, at the age of twelve, he had crafted his first peacepipe. His first creation was a tribal mandate to fulfilling a tribal tradition as a prerequisite to manhood. Young Comanche warriors were expected to carve a pipe worthy of being smoked at a Council of Chiefs before they would be recognized as having reached maturity. After several months of painstaking effort, Yellowsnake's pipe had been accepted by the Council Elders.

Yellowsnake was extremely proud of his peacepipe which had been accepted by the Elders. During the long, worrisome months it had taken him to carve and decorate the piece, he had become acutely aware of its real importance. It was not just the pipe which was important. The intense labor and painstaking hours of dedication would soon prove to the council that his body and mind were in sync. The council would, most importantly, know that the young man was ready to face life squarely in its sometimes ugly face. Now, his pride, if nothing else, was forcing him to masterfully carve the second pipe. He knew that by his gifting of the gracefully carved piece, he would be giving something which represented the very best of himself.

2

The treasured object would be embedded with his love, respect, admiration and recognition of the yet unknown person's courageous heart. He could bestow no greater compliment upon any living person. Yellowsnake knew in his heart that the recipient of the peace pipe would not have to question its meaning. The deserving person would know!

Now, on this blistering summer day, the second peacepipe was in many ways even more important to him, for at the moment, it had no home. He glanced up from his work and occasionally scanned the distant skyline around the reservation. It was during these moments that he resembled a hawk on its perch, patiently awaiting the coolness of evening. But beneath his instinctive exercise in patience the young Comanche warrior carried a growing restlessness.

Yellowsnake proudly admired the handsome crop of elk hair hanging gracefully from the Manzanita pipe stem, while reflecting to himself that the elegant ceremonial piece would be safely tucked away until the day it was properly bestowed. It gave Yellowsnake's searing restlessness some ease knowing that the pipe was a compass point to lead him beyond his dull and dusty life on the reservation into a world which awaited his awakening ambitions. It was also on this day that the spirits of his ancestors reached out to unlock the gates to his future. He was feeling the mysterious doors beginning to open.

The emerging warrior was an endless daydreamer, and his mind replayed countless stories told to him by his mother about his blood ancestors of generations past. And her stories were having an explosive effect on his mind as the spirits began to awaken.

Yellowsnake's mind drifted back to his childhood days as he remembered his mother's stories about his warrior ancestors. Hotona's stories were thrilling to the ears of the five year old. As his mother's stories unfolded, her gaze seemed to take her back as if she was there. The youngster sat quietly listening, stuffing his mouth with chocolate chip cookies. Hotona emphasized to her wide eyed son that *Nokona*, who lived more than one hundred years earlier, was the greatest of all Comanche chiefs. Nokona was Yellowsnake's great-great grandfather and he must never forget the importance of his heritage. His mother, in a most gentle tone, explained that Nokona also had many wives. During one of Nokona's raids on the white settlers who were invading *his* Comanche territory, he took a captive white child named Cynthia Parker. Eight years later, she became Nokona's most favored wife and soon after, delivered him a son whom he named *Quanah*.

Hotona wiped the remnants of melted chocolate from Yellowsnake's inquiring face, then continued her story of his Comanche heritage. He listened eagerly as she told him that Nokona was also the father of another son by one of his other wives. The other son was called *Tochoway*. "Tochoway was your great grandfather," she said. "Quanah and Tochoway were very different, much like eagles and doves," she whispered. Tochoway, the defiant one, had inherited Nokona's narrow minded view toward white men. Drive them away at any cost! Tochoway would sooner die than yield to the white invaders. Hotona continued painting the picture with her words. Sometimes she gestured with her hands to shape the event. She told Yellowsnake how Nokona, though a courageous leader, was losing his fight with the white men. And regretfully, he was sick and growing old as he watched his warriors continue to wage war against other tribes intruding on Comanche soil.

He became sicker and sicker, and finally was forced to give up his leadership of the Nation. The dispirited nation soon splintered into smaller, ideologically different tribes. One of the tribes soon adopted the fearful name of **Yellowsnake**, the defiant tribe.

Shortly before he died, Nokona relinquished control of the Comanche nation. Tochoway had positioned himself to become leader of the **Yellowsnake tribe.** Nokona had bequeathed the nation his dying spirit, knowing deep in his heart that its future was bleak, at best. At worst, they would all be dead. Tochoway fearlessly led his tribe with a single minded determination. Wipe out the white trespassers. History would soon reveal that he could not defeat the invading settlers and in the end, he and most of his tribe were killed in battle by the Osage indians.

Hotona interrupted her story to get a glass of cold lemonade to quench the thirst of her five year old listener. She regained Yellowsnake's attention, then continued. "Now then, Quanah was entirely different. He could see that it was useless to continue fighting the white men in battle."

"And besides that," she explained, "Quanah didn't like the idea of having his scalp lifted or going down with a white man's bullet lodged in his heart." Even though he wanted to be a great warrior against the intruders, he knew he had to find a place for his people to live in peace. "Because Quanah was a man of vision, he became leader of all the Comanche tribes," she said. Quanah's good judgment soon endeared him to the white settlers as a chief of wisdom and great vision. The white men named him Quanah Parker, because he was Cynthia Parker's son. "And my little warrior," Hotona said looking into his eyes, "you must never forget that Quanah Parker is your blood ancestor. He is the most famous leader in our Comanche history."

The five year old's ears and eyes were tuned to Hotona's account of the past as he absorbed every word she spoke. Yellowsnake knew his loving mother held Nokona, Tochoway and Quanah Parker in high regard. He would never forget her stories and above all, the bravery of his forefathers. Their blood was his blood!

Deep inside, Yellowsnake knew how his ancestors must have felt about the white man. Whenever his parents took him into the small towns outside the reservation, his feeling of sameness soon disappeared. He could sense the cold, staring looks of the white youngsters. He was seldom treated with genuine kindness and dignity in the outside world. He remembered his parents' conversations about the white man's injustices, especially when it came to bilking the indians out of their money. *"Should I be a white man or should I be an indian in the white man's world?"* he asked himself. His soul searching was short, for he had chosen to be an indian. Yellowsnake's senses had told him at a very early age that someday he would be living in the white man's world. He was willing to accept the challenge, knowing that not all of those he met would treat him with the indignities he had witnessed. He didn't harbor a dislike

for all of them. Only those who treated him as less than equal.
Yellowsnake had vowed to be polite, but be aware!

The once wide eyed child was now staring his approaching manhood squarely in the eye with a feeling of confidence. He was sure the spirit of his ancestors would lead him through life with a watchful eye. The Comanche boy in frayed jeans and cowboy boots ran his fingers through his brown, shoulder length hair as he adjusted his lanky frame to the rickety porch step. Although he had within him a mixture of Scotch and Cherokee blood from his father Jimmy, he was still Comanche, and that would never change. His Christian name meant little to him. His beckoning name from childhood was Yellowsnake, and that too would never change.

Early childhood soon reflected that Yellowsnake had been abundantly blessed with the ageless skills required of an adept Indian Warrior. It was common knowledge among the tribes of the southwest that the Comanches had a special gift for horsemanship. Yellowsnake was no exception and from the age of four, it seemed like he was seen more often on horseback than on his own feet.

Most of the Indian boys in his settlement were fine horsemen. Some were expert with the knife. Others excelled with pistols and rifles, but none mastered them all as well as Yellowsnake. He had inherited the ability to ride with the best of them, rope cattle, bury his knife blade in a stump from fifty feet and pick off jack rabbits from a hundred yards. The bitter wisdom of Quanah had saved the bloodline of one of his few remaining descendants; it was unmistakable in the child warrior.

His body and mind grew during the three years following the completion of his second peacepipe, and his skills became razor sharp. He became regarded as the finest tracker in the tribe. He believed a Comanche who couldn't track animals or men across dirt, sand, smooth rock and river beds, should spend his time working with the women. Yellowsnake knew the Creator had furnished him with a wealth of natural skills and the gift of survival, the same mysterious gift Nokona had carried in his blood.

To this young brave's way of thinking, however, school was a time consuming task which required great endurance. Fortunately, Hotona knew how important her son's education would be to him once he left the reservation, so she persisted. She spent countless hours making sure he absorbed the knowledge he needed to survive in the white man's world. His lessons also caused him to learn that Hotona was indeed of Nokona's bloodline and not one to be dismissed.

The end of spring was approaching during Yellowsnake's senior year when his class was visited by a man in uniform. He was oddly dressed and the stranger's posture and impeccable attire spoke of self discipline and authority. His starched khaki shirt was adorned with colorful ribbons and medals that clinked against one another when he walked.

"Class," his teacher said smiling, "this is Staff Sergeant Sam Robbins from the Army Recruiting Office in Oklahoma City." Yellowsnake was impressed and would have been dumbfounded had he known why the seasoned Sergeant was at his school. Yellowsnake's reputation as a tracker had reached Sergeant Robbin's office. The shrewd recruiter knew of the boy's Indian skills, and in particular his superior tracking prowess. Yellowsnake's skills could prove invaluable to an army about to enter a small Southeast Asian country.

Sergeant Robbins spoke without further fanfare, promoting the virtues of the United States Army and highlighting the benefits enjoyed by those who devoted themselves to their country's defense. Yellowsnake would, in years to come, curse this day and this man more than once.

The small reservation schoolroom emptied out as Sergeant Robbins quickly cornered the boy. He wanted to discuss a "proposition." Both men, the one in uniform and the one about to reach his eighteenth birthday, feigned casualness as they seated themselves on the railing of the covered porch. Yellowsnake was puzzled but flattered by his attention. The man seated next to him represented all the mystery and possibilities of a warrior's life off the reservation. Sergeant Robbins knew he was looking at a special breed of fighter, one in ten thousand.

They talked in polite generalities for a few minutes, and then about life on the reservation, but soon the purpose of Sergeant Robbins' visit became obvious.

"Son, I'm told you're the best tracker on the reservation."

Yellowsnake looked away momentarily. "I suppose I'm as good as any of 'em," he said quietly, a touch of modest pride in his voice.

Sergeant Robbins was a persuasive recruiter. He described the clash about to erupt in a faraway place called Vietnam, and how it would involve the U.S. Military forces. In particular, he described the role of the army. He was certain American Special Forces would be the first to be sent abroad to prepare the way for ground combat troops.

Sergeant Robbins was an honest man. He spoke with a seriousness that sent a chill through Yellowsnake's body. "When our troops get to the Vietnam jungle, the Army will depend on skilled trackers–survival experts–such as you." His brown eyes looked at the boy earnestly. "Would you be interested in joining up with us if I could get you stationed with a Ranger unit?"

Yellowsnake was flattered, and speechless. He had heard of the Army Rangers. Although he'd never grasped the full meaning of their purpose, he listened intently as Sergeant Robbins glamorized their job. "They're an elite, highly trained unit of specialists," he explained, "who possess skills far superior to those of ordinary ground soldiers." Yellowsnake nodded solemnly as the recruiter continued with stories of their accomplishments.

Time flew, and as daylight began to fade, the soldier glanced at his watch and announced, "I've got to leave now." He gave Yellowsnake a level look and said, "How about talking it over with your folks?"

Yellowsnake nodded and smiled. "Yeh. I will."

That evening he shared the Sergeant's invitation with his parents. Hotona's heart sank as she listened to the details. She knew the outcome. Jimmy, Yellowsnake's father, knew the boy had already made up his mind. He resigned himself; perhaps this was what his son was destined to do. He didn't challenge Yellowsnake's decision.

Graduation had come and gone, and summer turned from green to autumn brown. Yellowsnake had replayed the conversation with Sergeant Robbins over and over in his mind, waiting for an answer from within. Now, towering a few inches over the six foot mark, and weighing 180 pounds of solid muscle, he knew he was tougher than he'd ever been; his mettle was ready for anything! Yellowsnake was feeling the spirit of Nokona beginning to stir in his blood again, and he recognized that he had his answer. He knew it was time to break camp and leave the dusty reservation.

Life would not be the same without his folks and the watchful Elders of his tribe. Yellowsnake was saddened by the thought of leaving his horse and faithful dog. Nevertheless, he knew it was time. The only task remaining was a trip to the city to complete his enlistment. But, he had one condition that he had to work out with Sergeant Robbins. It was a consideration of great importance to the young Comanche, and would loom as a deciding factor in his decision to enlist.

When Yellowsnake was a small child, Hotona had explained to him that because he was a blood descendent of Nokona, he was entitled to two honors not afforded all male members of the tribe. First, for as long as he lived on the reservation, he had the choice of being addressed by his given name or a Comanche name of his choosing. Second, he would someday be entitled to sit on the Tribal Council. Politics held no interest for him, so sitting on the Tribal Council was inconsequential. But his name, Yellowsnake, held his soul.

Sergeant Robbins was delighted to welcome the new recruit into his office. They acted like two lawyers finalizing a legal contract, while they discussed the terms of both parties. Yellowsnake asked that it be stated in his enlistment papers that, except in legal matters, the Army allow him to be addressed as "Yellowsnake". The wise Sergeant knew of Yellowsnake's pride in his ancestry and was not at all surprised by the request.

A few days later, Sergeant Robbins shook his hand as he presented him with his enlistment papers along with an attached letter signed by a Recruiting Officer. The letter stated:

INASMUCH AS THIS ENLISTEE'S HERITAGE EMPOWERS HIM TO BEAR A TRIBAL NAME BY VIRTUE OF ANCESTRAL CUSTOM, THIS ENLISTEE RESERVES THE RIGHT TO BEAR SUCH NAME, EXCEPT IN MATTERS REQUIRING HIS LEGAL SIGNATURE.

Only his dog tags would bear his given name, and it was a name he never used! The recruiting officer had shrewdly calculated that this would be a winning proposition all around. If Yellowsnake was captured or killed, his dog tag name would reveal nothing which might pose a threat to the security of the mission. It would be an asset to his function as a tracker, and give his warrior spirit an edge.

His deal with Sergeant Robbins was finalized. He was nearly ready to go! He had only a few days until his departure for boot camp, and a deep seated feeling in his gut told him that before he shoved off, he must make a quick trip to Mexico to see someone special.

When he was a small boy, Yellowsnake's mother had taken him into the heart of Sonora, in old Mexico. There, he had lived for a time with a mysterious old woman, the same woman his mother had spent time with when she was a small girl.

The Comanche, through hundreds of years, had established a permanent peace with the Yaqui nation. The exchange of members between the peace-loving Yaqui and the war-like Comanche had become an important tradition in their respective tribes. It was through this exchange that the young girl Hotona, had been sent to the Yaqui. She had come to know and revere Shahana–a visionary and Tribal Medicine Woman. So Yellowsnake, the Comanche boy, had followed in Hotona's footsteps when he went to visit Shahana.

Yellowsnake treasured his childhood adventure. The Yaqui were a unique tribe of Indians with curious and enigmatic ways. He smiled, chuckling at the recollection of his first meeting with

10

Shahana.

He had been told that she always knew what was going on in people's minds and the young Comanche was real uneasy when he first visited her. However, he was determined to be brave, so he stood tall before her, his shoulders pulled back and his chin out, befitting his Comanche heritage.

Shahana's small, stooped frame belied her presence. Her parched, deeply wrinkled face framed piercing eyes; eyes that had their effect on whomever they rested. Her long gray hair was pulled back and tied with a knot of faded ribbon at the back of her neck. She wore a dusty purple skirt and covered her shoulders with a shawl. The old woman lived alone. Though highly respected, she was also quietly feared by her fellow villagers. She was known to talk with spirits, and to possess visions of things to come.

Although he was only a youngster at the time, Yellowsnake's weeks with Shahana had left their mark on him. Together they moved about the village; he, following like a curious pup watching his master's every move. Her quiet voice always seemed to lift the spirits of those with whom she spoke.

His fear of her receded as she told him stories of her life. At the end of each day, the two would sit near the fire in her two room hut with Shahana filling his ears with stories late into the night.

She told of the Spanish Conquistadors who sailed to Mexico from Spain. They had journeyed by foot and horseback from the Gulf of Mexico, passing through the Yaqui nation. The Spaniards were a cruel and righteous breed. Under the guise of Christianity, they had taken many Yaqui with them as slaves. The Yaqui were forced to work as laborers while the Conquistadors, in their relentless search of gold and silver, ventured further into the unexplored territory of New Mexico and Arizona.

Yellowsnake had more than once recalled Shahana's story about the Mexican explorers who followed the trails of the Spanish Conquistadors many years after the merciless conquerors were driven from Mexico. As a young child, she had watched descendants of the famous Peralta family lead an

11

expedition through her small village. They were searching for gold and were on their way to the vast unknown territory north of Mexico. Many months later, she had listened as the village Elders described how the Mexican explorers were brutally massacred by the Apache Indians. Shahana's descriptions were graphic and unforgettable, and had caused young Yellowsnake to pull his bed covers tightly around him at night, waiting for sleep to come....

As soon as Yellowsnake returned home from the Army recruiter's office, he tossed a few things in a small pack, borrowed his father's pick-up truck, and headed for Sonora. He arrived in the wee hours of the morning, weary but filled with anticipation at seeing Shahana again. The moment he knocked on the door it swung open, the old woman stepping aside to let him in. "Young Comanche, I've been expecting you."

"You knew I was coming?" he asked in bewilderment.

"Why does that surprise you?" she queried. Then, Shahana gestured for him to sit. "You are hungry. I have prepared food for you. We will eat," she muttered in broken English. He had wondered how she would react to the news of his enlistment. Now, it was apparent that she already knew.

After their meal, in the warm semi-darkness of her hut, they sat and talked for many hours. The old woman tapped the contents of her pipe into the embers of the fire, then turned to Yellowsnake and took his hand. She clasped it warmly into her own brown, leathery palms and looked deeply into his blue eyes as if to enter his mind. After a long moment, she nodded and began to speak.

"The spirits have given me the power to see it all, goodness and evil, hardship and joy. Without this guidance, our tribe would never have survived. This power has given me the knowledge to let the tribe know when it was time to move camp. I have seen floods before they arrived. I've been warned of famine. I have seen death foretold in men's eyes, and the joy of birth before it was conceived in the womb.

"There are things that I cannot share with you now, but this I can say: Yellowsnake, your spirit has lived before in your ancestors. This is not the first life you have lived, nor will it be the last life that you will walk on this earth. The life you live now will be perilous and filled with danger, but you will survive to live a long life, with much happiness and good fortune." Shahana stopped talking. Yellowsnake watched her with widened eyes as she lit her pipe and stared into the fire. After some time in silence, her words of wisdom and prophecy continued.

"For many long years, I have helped the members of my tribe. I will do the same for you. Creator, and the spirit of your forefathers will shield you from death. There will be days when your spirit struggles to join those of your ancestors. On those days, I will be with you.

"When you leave my hut, you will see me no more in my world, but I will see you in yours...."

After a long silence, the old woman got up and shuffled off to bed in the adjoining room. Yellowsnake's wondering mind would never forget her words. She had said so much with so few words. He had never doubted her wisdom and powers, and had taken to heart her solemn proclamation.

An eerie quiet took over the dimly lit room as he watched the dancing sparks of the fire vanish into darkness. He was sensing that Shahana's spirit had somehow crept into his spirit while they were talking. Shahana would indeed see Yellowsnake again, just as she said. She alone knew that. She possessed the vision!

Two days later Yellowsnake, flanked by his mother and father, was standing on a dusty road at the edge of the reservation. They were awaiting the arrival of a bus that would take him to Fort Hood and his new life as a soldier. Except for occasional gusts of wind stirring the grasses and whipping up dust devils, there was silence. The three lonely figures were engulfed by their separate feelings, each knowing that life was about to take a turn.

Yellowsnake's knapsack contained only meager clothing and

the bare necessities to make it to Fort Hood for basic training. His prized Comanche knife, with its darkened, leather-bound handle and eight inch highly polished razor edged blade, was among the necessities. While he was cleaning and packing the knife, his mind had flown back to the day Uncle Dete had fashioned the fearsome blade in his blacksmith shop. He watched the sparks jump from the red hot steel then asked, "Will the blade be strong enough to kill the toughest animal?" With a stern look in his eye, Uncle Dete answered him, "This blade will outlive you and all your prey."

His knife and the uncertain years ahead, would tally many death sentences for unsuspecting targets. It's scabbard was imprinted with bright yellow etching and displayed a writhing snake, unmistakably the sign of Yellowsnake, Comanche!

Suddenly, the bus came rumbling over the hill and pulled to a noisy stop at Yellowsnake's feet. He held his father's firm work-worn hands in his own for a moment, then embraced his mother. It was a solemn parting. But as the bus pulled away he pushed his parents to the back of his mind, recalling Shahana's last puzzling words to him.

"You will see me no more in my world, but I will see you in yours."

Strong medicine.

Chapter 2

Vietnam

Inside the dungeon-like quarters of his jungle tent, Yellowsnake was bent double over the edge of his bunk, gently working out the ugly thorn protruding from his leg. Sweat poured down his brow and onto his shirt, and the badly soiled headband he wore was already saturated beyond usefulness.

He was trying to ease the sting of one more puncture to his tough skin, while thinking to himself, *Sergeant Robbins sure had this son-of-a-bitch figured out. Shit, I'm not only here, I'm one of only a thousand American soldiers in this monstrous paradise. What a hell hole this is going to be!*

Vietnam was everything he had heard about while completing his boot training months earlier. There was jungle everywhere. And within the jungle lived the animals, four legged and two legged. The two legged kind were the ones he feared most. They carried guns, knives and rockets and were always ready to take his life. The animals were predictable, the enemy was not. Yellowsnake had accepted Sergeant Robbins' invitation with his eyes open. The jungle had put Yellowsnake to the test. Kill or be killed!

The humidity was oppressive. Wearily, he lay back onto his bunk and closed his eyes. Sleep would not come, so he sought to change the focus of his misery by recalling his days back on the reservation. Then his mind then moved forward through his days of basic training at Fort Hood.

Yellowsnake had thrown himself into the spit and polish life. He had tried to blend in with the other recruits. On the surface, he had. However, during the rigorous field training and maneuvers, his exceptional marksmanship and hand-to hand combat techniques showed him to be a man of exceptional gifts. Even before his training was complete, Yellowsnake was demonstrating some shrewd knife maneuvers for his instructors, techniques they had never mastered. His body was proficient and with swift, catlike moves, he showed them how to gut prey, no matter how many legs it walked on.

Advanced training had hardened Yellowsnake and he had become a soldier in every sense of the word. Now, he lay sweltering on his bunk, reexperiencing the pride he had felt the day he completed advanced combat training. He recalled the celebratory poker game with Walt, Joe and Dinko, and how it was abruptly interrupted by the company clerk summoning him to Headquarters Office.

Yellowsnake was handed an official looking two page document as he entered the HQ that day. He read the pages, discovering that they were his permanent duty orders transferring him to Fort Benning. "Great," he muttered to himself. "Now I can get off this dude ranch!" He had learned all he could learn at Fort Hood and was restless again.

The Company Commander, seated at his desk in the adjoining room, had overheard the young soldier. "Yellowsnake!" he bellowed. "Come in here!" The corners of the officer's mouth turned up in a slight grin as Yellowsnake entered his office and stood at attention.

"At ease, soldier!"

The commander had tipped back in his chair, balancing it on two legs, and said, "Yellowsnake, I think you'll be in your element at Fort Benning. It'll be right up your alley." The officer was fully aware he was losing an exceptional recruit. He held Yellowsnake in his half smiling gaze for a few moments, then leaned forward and handed Yellowsnake his personnel file. "We didn't have any trouble keeping track of you by name in this lash up, did we?", he chuckled. Then all amusement left his face and he bid him farewell, "Good luck soldier."

Fort Benning *had* been his element. Soon after arriving, he'd been assigned the task of teaching jungle survival skills to the relentless flow of incoming troops. The surrounding swamps were tailor-made for teaching jungle tactics. The dry openness and rolling hills of the reservation offered little comparison to the jungle like conditions of Fort Benning. The art of survival applied no matter what surroundings prevailed. Yellowsnake's job was to see that the troops were taught to survive, no matter what the conditions offered. He had spent long days and many cold nights tirelessly grilling the green troops on how to stay alive in the swamps and jungles. If the alligators or snakes didn't get them, soldiers were occasionally lost due to poor judgment brought on by their own panic. Many good men went under the surface of the slimy swamp waters, some never coming up for a second breath. He taught them skills ranging from first aid for snake bite to self-defense against unexpected enemy charges, swinging machetes at their torsos.

The Army's promises had not been empty; there in the harsh Fort Benning training environment, he at last felt comfortable. Yellowsnake had been assigned a permanent home with the rugged 11th Ranger Battalion, and knew he was where he belonged.

Yellowsnake laid on his bunk massaging the spot where the thorn had been extracted, his thoughts moving to the winter day in 1961 in Fort Benning when Sergeant Robbin's prediction about Vietnam had come true. Yellowsnake had just brought his troops back after a long day of sneak attack training when word came down. The 11th Rangers were packing up and shipping out. He, a handful of instructors, and the battalion were being transported to Danang, swiftly and without ceremony.

When they arrived, the instructors had been placed in their own isolated camp in the thick jungle bush outside of Danang. Their assignment was to furnish both weapons and attack training to a new breed of jungle fighter, the South Vietnamese Montagnards. For many years, the Viet Cong had destroyed the Montagnard villages and brutalized their people. These enigmatic mountain inhabitants were fierce, tough, and high spirited. Even though they were experts with the native blow gun and cross bow, they still had to be trained in modern warfare, and proved to be more than willing. Yellowsnake took pride in his assignment. Although more and more American troops were trickling into Vietnam, he was still only one of a few soldiers hidden in the primitive mountainous country. And the montagnards badly needed his help. They needed to learn how to survive the Viet Cong. Yellowsnake made a point of learning from the strange little fighters, as well as teaching them. He

17

was, after all, fighting for his survival on their home turf. After they had completed their tortuous training, the small mountain warriors were well prepared to fight the savagely hated Viet Cong and North Vietnamese Army.

Yellowsnake finally dozed off, his mind mercifully losing its grip on the parade of memories marching through the jungle twilight of his tent. He slept soundly. When he awoke two hours later, his mind snapped into sharp focus. When he perceived no immediate danger, he relaxed again. He stretched his long, aching body and rose from his cot, searching out a towel to wipe the sweat and grime from his face and neck. Then he lay back on his cot, staring blankly at the patched canvas ceiling above his head.

Though the jungle paradise was breathtaking to the eye, it was closer to hell for a plains Indian. The beauty was, for the most part, lost on any man forced to spend most of his attention looking for signs of danger and navigating the unimaginably dense and forbidding jungle. At the same time, Yellowsnake did not regret his decision to join the Rangers. He knew his vitality, self discipline, and self respect would have eroded on the reservation. The Army had been the only way out, and he valued his lessons learned.

He had spent so much time with the Montagnards that the jungle was, in fact, becoming a part of him. He was feeling more at home each day, and had gradually developed an appreciation for its beautiful, though hostile setting.

....

Many months passed. Survival had become a living companion to all his thoughts and perceptions. He was changing. When he was twelve years old, he had put long months into the planning and preparation of his first peacepipe, refining it to the point where it was acceptable to the Tribal Council. Now he was refining his mind and body as a weapon of war. But the intensive training, the heat, humidity, the war, were all taking their toll.

It had been over a year since he had joined the Army. He

18

had passed up his furlough at Fort Benning, and now, in spite of his youth, Yellowsnake was tired. His body was sending him a message. He was burned out and badly in need of a rest. He continued to sleep in painful compromise that night, unable to find a comfortable position for his throbbing leg.

Early the next morning, he was limping slightly as he entered the company clerk's office. "What are the chances of taking a thirty day furlough? I need to go home and get healed." Yellowsnake knew that furlough was seldom granted during tour of duty in a war zone, so he was apprehensive about his request. The clerk passed on his request to the First Sergeant sitting across the office, then returned. "Okay, take off Snake. This is probably as good a time as any. Sarge says things are going to be heating up around here pretty quick."

It took only minutes for him to pack his meager duffel bag. In the jungle, packing light was a given. When he arrived in Danang at dawn, he hurriedly boarded a military aircraft headed back to the United States. By noon the next day, Yellowsnake was back on American soil.

During his long flight home he was surprised to find himself thinking about Maria, a beautiful young girl who lived on his reservation. They had done things together from time to time, sometimes sharing an occasional movie. Most often, they had chosen to ride their horses in the hills outside of town. But now, he felt himself thinking about her in a much different way.

A breathtaking young Comanche woman, Maria was tall and willowy with blue-black hair and sparkling dark eyes. She was a modest, soft spoken young woman who had never pressed him to do anything which made him uncomfortable and, likewise, he had never put her in an awkward situation. That didn't mean he hadn't thought about it though!

He smiled inwardly as he fondly remembered his first mature reaction to viewing her beautiful body. He was thirteen years old. Maria was about his age, but she looked much older.

Her shapely figure never escaped his eyes from that moment on.

"Damn, Snake, wouldn't you love to make out with Maria? She's a beaut," Edward Red Sky had remarked.

"You ain't said shit," Yellowsnake retorted. "Who wouldn't?" After all, he was human and his male hormones were exploding.

He and Maria had shared a mutual friendship and he had often wondered if perhaps someday they could have more. While they were growing into adolescence, opportunities for them to be alone together had been limited because most of her free hours were spent working at her father's General Store. But when Yellowsnake and his friends were together, he would subtly suggest stopping at the store for something trivial. He would do anything for just a glimpse of her.

I wonder if she's still on the reservation, he pondered, staring out the military transport window. *Probably....*

He knew she never had a strong urge to stray too far from the reservation, feeling secure within its confines. She was never one to welcome the white man's world with open arms. In the back of his mind, Yellowsnake knew that this one quality might be the obstacle to the dreams silently growing within him.

When he arrived at the reservation, Yellowsnake was taken aback by how small everything looked after coming from the outside world. It became painfully obvious how sheltered his world had been as a boy. Although everything looked comfortably familiar, he sensed he could no longer call it home.

His thoughts were interrupted by the surprised neighbors who spotted him as he stepped off the bus and had come over to greet him. The unexpected silence was dissolved as dogs barked and children shrieked in delight at the sight of him. He had a moment of confusion as his mind switched to a sudden overlay of a small Vietnam village where war weary children had stared at him in mute fear.

What a sheltered and simple life these kids have got, he silently concluded. There was no fear in their eyes, but their curious admiration was undisguised. Yellowsnake shook the vision from his mind and looked past the familiar faces to see Hotona and Jimmy, hurrying towards him. Hotona was smiling, her eyes dancing as she waited her turn to greet her son. Yellowsnake grinned as he clasped his father's hand, then turned toward Hotona. They embraced, speaking softly with a spicy mixture of Comanche and English words.

Everyone was impressed by the sight of the spit and polish Army Ranger. With some amusement, Yellowsnake noticed the young men of the tribe gawking shyly on the periphery of the spontaneous welcoming committee. He honored them by making a point to greet them each by name. Not so long ago, he had been the one gawking. It felt like a lifetime ago.

Yellowsnake's evening was spent catching up on all the news of the reservation, and he was naturally obliged to describe his own life in far off Vietnam. The next morning, after awakening from a sound night's sleep, he lazily climbed out of bed, slipped on his tattered jeans and followed an inviting aroma into the kitchen where Hotona was cooking breakfast. As he sipped his coffee while they talked, he told her he might ride by the general store to see if Maria was still around.

"Yes," Hotona answered, "she is still around. I see her from time to time and she always asks about you. I'm sure she'd like to see you." Hotona's kind and honest words lifted his spirits tremendously.

"Well then, maybe I'll just wander over there and see if she's in," he said casually.

Yellowsnake had summoned his faithful dog Spike to his side as he wound his way slowly through the trees to the corral. He wanted to see his horse, and he needed time to build up courage before encountering the enchantress who seemed to have taken possession of his heart while he was away in Vietnam. He bridled Hurricane and swung himself onto his dear friend's bare back. When the threesome finally reached town, they clopped along the dusty street, passing the worn, familiar buildings of his childhood. Thoughts of uncertainty tormented Yellowsnake's mind. *What will I say to her? It's been a long time since I've seen her. She may not want to see me.* His stomach tightened at the thought.

He tethered his horse away from traffic to one side of the general store, then took a deep breath before quietly opening the screen door. He stepped inside and paused, letting his eyes adjust for a moment from the bright, early morning sun. He looked toward the old wooden counter and there she was, as straight and beautiful as a Roman statue. But this statue had a gentle smile on its face. Her eyes were shining with a glow he had never noticed before.

"Hey beautiful!" he blurted out. Her head jerked around and she smiled widely almost squealing as she spoke, "Snake! You're back!" Her delight was unmistakable. He walked toward the darkened counter and placed his hands on it's worn edges and leaned toward her. Her smiling eyes coyly darted around the store, then she too leaned over the counter and greeted him with a soft kiss on his cheek. His heart raced as the two stood close to one another, talking in hushed tones. A feeling stirred inside him with an intensity that he'd never felt before. Finally, with his courage at high tide, he spoke.

"Maria, would you like to go out with me tonight?"

There was no hesitation.

"I'd love to," she answered. "Why don't you call me after I get home from work, around six. We'll decide where to go."

"Great", he beamed, gently touching her hand. Then he turned and headed out the door. Six o'clock seemed an eternity away.

That afternoon, he snacked on Hotona's delicious fried chicken and corn bread and then that evening called Maria. He said he would pick her up at eight o'clock for a drive into town. When Jimmy handed Yellowsnake the keys to the old pick up that night, he cautioned his son in quiet tones, "Remember, treat Maria gently and with respect. She is closer to God than most of us."

Until that moment, Yellowsnake had forgotten that Maria had been raised a strict Catholic.

He paced his steps quietly like a cat as he walked up the squeaky steps toward her screen door, only to be startled as Maria pushed open the door, flashing a big smile. "I'm ready to go! Are you?"

"You bet", he said, laughing at his own surprise.

Yellowsnake followed Maria down the footpath to the truck. It gave him time and vantage to admire her flowing skirt and freshly starched blouse. It was impossible to ignore how snugly the blouse was tailored to her feminine torso, and as he looked at every curve of her beautiful body, his blood began to percolate.

While they drove slowly toward town, they soon agreed neither a movie nor bowling sounded exciting and a better choice would be Pablo's Pizza.

They found a booth in a quiet corner of the busy restaurant and settled in. After ordering, they wandered together through the past, laughing about the many adventures and good times they had shared as children.

When they finally noticed the waiter staring at them, Yellowsnake glanced at his watch. He was startled to see that three hours had passed! He leaned across the table top and took Maria's hand in his own, saying "Would you like to take a ride out to Gunsight Hill and see if the spirits are out tonight?"

She was smiling as she looked into his eyes. Without hesitation, she agreed, "Yes, I'd like that."

The air was cool and crisp. Yellowsnake parked the truck on a small knoll that faced a full moon rising. Small cloud tufts caught and held the moonlight, bright stars shone between the clouds set into the black velvet night sky. It was a breathtaking iridescent canopy. Except for the occasional call of a coyote, it was peaceful and eerily quiet. They gazed through the open windows of the truck. Their thoughts were shared, but few words were spoken. He was afraid he would break the magical moment as he awkwardly put his arms around her, drawing her close.

With her warm body pressed tightly against his, he kissed her tenderly, full on the lips, running his fingers through her shiny black hair. His kisses were consciously becoming longer and stronger, and his hand gently roamed across her thigh, up her narrow waist and across her breast. He could feel Maria's heart racing wildly through her cotton blouse.

Maria's strong religious values established a line which no man crossed. With a deep breath, she pulled away from him. "I like you...very much," she whispered, "but I cannot do what you want me to do!"

Yellowsnake wiped away the tears that were welling in her eyes and reassured her. "Maria, you know I'd never hurt you, or make you feel bad. I respect you and your feelings."

She put her arms around his neck and drew him close. She tenderly kissed his cheek and whispered quietly. "Thanks for understanding. It means a lot to me."

Yellowsnake turned the key in the ignition and started the truck. The drive home was silent and he sensed the tender feeling in his heart.

She's a beautiful woman with a very special heart. The man that wins her love better know how lucky he is....

He was struck with the stark realization that the precious weeks of his thirty day furlough were racing by, and he found himself thinking of her more and more. At the same time, he was becoming painfully aware of how sheltered his world had been as a boy. Although everything on the reservation was comfortably familiar, he knew he would never be able to call it home again.

Yellowsnake and Maria spent every evening together, absent of people and distractions. With only nine precious days remaining, Yellowsnake could no longer bear the mounting desire building up inside him. He asked her to marry him.

At first Maria's reaction to his proposal was one of shock and disbelief. She loved him, but knew he must return to the war. She feared Yellowsnake might be killed in Vietnam, and didn't think she could live with that unknown.

They talked for hours. Yellowsnake became increasingly persuasive. He tried to convince not only her, but reassure himself as well that he was well prepared for jungle survival.

"Maria, I promise I will return to you as soon as my one year tour is over. He beseeched her to marry him. "If you are my wife, the army will provide for you. I don't need much. I'll send you money as well. You'd be very comfortable." He added, "And you could continue working in your dad's store; that will help fill the lonesome hours ahead."

The anguish on Maria's face was obvious. Clearly, she was having a difficult time with her decision. He knew she loved him, and he loved her. Although their instincts told them this may not be a wise choice, their hearts counseled otherwise.

The next evening as they sat quietly snuggling in the cold night air, she told him she had spoken to her father and mother about marrying him. As much as they favored her relationship with him, they were not in favor of marriage. They knew, as did she, that Yellowsnake might not return. They couldn't bear to see her grief and heartache if he was killed. She was, however, nineteen years old and capable of making her own decisions. Her parents knew the risk when they finally told her they would respect her decision.

"So yes, I will marry you," she told him gravely. "It may well turn out to be the wrong choice, but I'm listening to my heart. I love you and I'm willing to take that chance."

The sound of her words filled him with joy. She was the missing link in his life. He needed her strength and love, and now it would be his.

Three days later they were married in a simple ceremony in the nearby Catholic Chapel. The brief ceremony was attended by his mother and father, her family, and a handful of friends they had known in school.

The next four days were the happiest of their lives. Their honeymoon was spent at a tiny resort near the Texas border. The quiet surroundings were lush and serene, as if it had all been designed with the newlyweds in mind. He made love to Maria with a passion he hoped would never leave him. They became one as they rocked in each others arms, soaring together as fulfillment rushed into their bodies. Throughout their unbridled passion, there was one certainty. Yellowsnake had placed the seed of Nokona in her body. Neither of the lovers knew if it would bear fruit.

Though they had blocked out the dark moments that lay ahead, the inevitable day arrived, the day he must return to Vietnam. Maria wept quietly. She fought a nagging uneasiness inside; her greatest fear was that the man whom she now held close, might somehow be different when he returned. Tearfully, she kissed him good-bye.

Yellowsnake watched solemnly as Maria and his parents drove away from the military base. His heart was heavy as he walked across the tarmac towards the waiting aircraft. When he boarded, he paused to take one last look over his shoulder. He bathed his senses for a long moment in the simple beauty of the surroundings he was about to leave. His thoughts were of Maria as he fought off the empty feeling of separation.

....

Even before the wheels of the mighty military transport touched down outside of Danang, Yellowsnake began to feel the sweat pour off his brow and trickle down his chest. He was back.

He pulled his duffel bag from the cargo area, hearing the hushed voices of nearby soldiers, "All hell is breaking loose! Danang is being shelled by the Viet Cong."

The war which the French had deserted years earlier in this far off place had become an American war. It wasn't declared, but it was war.

Yellowsnake hung on for dear life as his jeep bumped noisily along the rough road toward his outpost camp. *I wonder if I'll come out of this war in one piece?* His thoughts flashed back to the body bags he had seen as his plane arrived.

His peering eyes looked beyond the guarded gate toward the isolated camp, then he saw the remnants of wispy smoke trails still rising from the jungle–the same jungle he had called home thirty days earlier.

Yellowsnake passed through the gate and bounced along the narrow road into camp, then looked around, his eyes taking in the scorched devastation. His camp had been hit hard by another unpredictable attack from the Viet Cong. He unloaded his bag from the jeep and walked towards headquarters, feeling dismayed when he saw the area where his hooch had been located. All that remained was a gaping crater, large enough to engulf a troop truck.

This, he thought, *is not looking good! There are craters everywhere. This must have been one hell of a raid by the VC.*

Yellowsnake entered the headquarters tent, then greeted a couple of friends and asked where he was to bed down. The First Sergeant heard his voice. "Snake, the shit's hit the fan around here. We'll get you bunked pretty quick, but don't plan on calling this home. The word is we will be moving camp further north.

"Colonel Harlan arrived unexpectedly two days ago," he continued. "He was checking on our progress with the Montagnard troops. While he was surveying the situation, Charlie mounted a massive barrage on the camp. In the midst of the chaos, the Colonel panicked and tried to fly out of here. His chopper took a direct mortar hit and, hell, they hardly found enough of him to bury. Whole thing exploded like a stick of dynamite!" The Sergeant shook his head slightly at the recollection, in lingering disbelief.

His first hour on the ground had slammed Yellowsnake back into the reality of war. He spent the next two weeks methodically ramroding his Montagnard troops through their training at a record pace. When they came out, they were well prepared physically, and mentally toughened. He had done his job.

Then the word came.

"Pack your gear! We're moving out tomorrow morning at first light."

It didn't take him long to again pack his meager bag. He and the other instructors were ordered to rendezvous with the remainder of the 11th Rangers at an unknown location, north of their present camp.

When the instructors arrived at their secret destination, Yellowsnake was surprised to find the new camp was a deserted

English Military compound. The English had abandoned the compound when their small force got hammered badly by the Viet Cong. Yellowsnake could see his new home was even more isolated than the small outpost he'd just left. He watched the main body of Rangers rejoining his group at the compound, when suddenly his attention was distracted by an unexpected incoming helicopter sweeping low over the tree tops directly ahead. The chopper was carrying the new Battalion Commander–a man as remarkable as Yellowsnake. The quiet figurehead inside the chopper would soon become an important force in his life, not only now, but for years to come.

Chapter 3

The Colonel

Yellowsnake watched as the helicopter touched down softly on its pad. Bird Colonel John Lincoln, the new officer, swung easily out of the chopper and was escorted to Headquarters hut. Out of uniform, the square jawed Colonel could have passed as a professional boxer en route to his next match. He stood six feet tall and weighed in at one hundred ninety pounds and his massive forearms told a story of someone unafraid of hard work. His coffee colored hair was neatly trimmed, and his thick eyebrows accented equally brown, intense eyes. They were eyes which would not miss anything that happened under his command.

It was rumored that he was a straightforward and honest officer who placed little value on ceremony. Word was that the Colonel had seen his fair share of jungle encounters in recent months, and had experienced more than one brush with death while in the bush. And word spread quickly among the troops that Colonel Lincoln was a man deserving of honor and respect, since he was not hesitant to be elbow to elbow with his men in the jungle. He wasn't a man to sit behind his desk, especially when there was an important mission to accomplish.

Also, the Colonel made a strong effort to know something about almost every man in his outfit. This was in part, because they were his boys; in part because they were also his weapons of war; and finally, because he knew he may some day have to write a condolence letter to a grieving family.

As soon as Yellowsnake had his gear squared away, he grabbed his towel and headed for the showers. But as he crossed the compound, towel in hand, the company Sergeant shouted at him.

"Yellowsnake, the Colonel wants to see you in his hut."

He was surprised and feeling unprepared as he reflected to himself, *Oh great, now he'll probably jump all over my ass because I look like a long haired bush ape.* Yellowsnake had forgotten to remove the soiled headband before he was ushered into the Colonel's office. A light sweat burnished his copper skin and indeed, he looked bush worn as he stood at attention in front of the Colonel's massive desk and pondered, *What's this guy really like?*

Without looking up from the stack of papers in front of him, the Colonel spoke. "Have a seat soldier, I'll be right with you." Yellowsnake pulled a chair up in front of the Colonel's desk, watching the Colonel shuffle some papers to one side. The commander looked up without a distinguishable smile. "I make it a point to know something about as many of my Rangers as possible. And, frankly, I've been told about you," he said.

Oh no, here it comes, Yellowsnake prepared himself. He squirmed uncomfortably in the hard backed chair as he watched the Colonel studying his personnel file.

"I see you were graded as one of the top trackers back at Hood and Benning. Is that true?" Colonel Lincoln asked.

Yellowsnake replied, "Yes, sir! I did all right while I was there."

The Colonel went on to tell him that his duty at their new isolated outpost would be different than at the camp where he was previously working. Yellowsnake would no longer be training the Montagnard fighters in jungle warfare. The intensity of the Viet Cong attacks on various camps throughout the area had made it necessary to use the most skilled men in the outfit to perform missions which were crucial to the survival of the entire battalion. He needed a man with superior tracking skills, endurance and the ability to survive dangerous and lengthy missions into the jungle. The man's job would be to track the Viet Cong in order to locate their camps and stashes of weapons, ammunition and general supplies.

The Colonel stressed that the assignment would be hazardous duty involving a high degree of personal risk. However, there was no one else in the battalion with Yellowsnake's tracking skills.

"From here on out, you'll be your own man and your own boss. It'll be up to you to survive from day to day when you're on Charlie's trail. You'll need to identify their exact location and path of movement and report back to us nightly. I don't give a damn what weapons you carry to protect yourself, that's your choice. Go to the armory and select all the firepower you want. The one thing you must carry at all times is your radio, so you can report on enemy movements."

Yellowsnake was silently digesting his new commander's directive. *Oh, shit! this job sounds like a real beaut',* he was thinking.

The Colonel, cracking a gentle smile, began probing him about his background and experience. "Do you think you'll be able to survive in the jungle after running out of food and water several days away from camp? This won't be easy duty."

Yellowsnake chuckled. Then he explained that living like a feral animal was nothing new to him. On the reservation, he had lived for many days on meager rations, often relying only on the game he killed while chasing stray cattle.

The Colonel thought for a moment. "I don't know how many enemy you've killed since you've been over here–do you have a problem with killing?"

"No sir, I know it's part of my job," replied Yellowsnake in a level tone.

Colonel Lincoln proceeded to give Yellowsnake the specifics of what needed to be accomplished while he was tracking the enemy. The Colonel emphasized, with unmistakable sincerity, that he would not send Yellowsnake out alone on any mission which was not absolutely necessary. He knew each time Yellowsnake entered the jungle by himself, the odds were more than fifty-fifty that he would encounter the enemy and, perhaps, get himself killed.

The keen eyed Colonel, who didn't believe in bullshit, came directly to the point. "At times, when there is a high level mission to be performed by us and the Montagnards, I'll lead our men to see that our assignment is properly carried out and our troops return as safely as possible." The Colonel had, inwardly, thought about this issue a lot. While making his somewhat gallant decision to be with his men on particularly dangerous missions, his gut had clearly warned him of his own mortality.

Nonetheless, he had made his decision based on the welfare of his men.

Then the Colonel really surprised Yellowsnake. His words and voice carried an unmistakable ring of solemn concern.

"Whenever it becomes necessary for me to lead our men on a special mission, my life is in danger just like the others. I'd like to make a deal with you."

What kind of deal is this guy talking about? Yellowsnake wondered.

There was a grave look in his eyes as the Colonel continued. "If you'll keep me alive through this goddamn war, I'll see that you are taken care of for the rest of your life."

The Colonel is worried about his ass just like everybody else around here! reasoned Yellowsnake. He looked squarely into the Colonel's piercing eyes as he replied, "Yes, sir, I'll do whatever you want me to do, sir."

With that, the Colonel said, "All I am asking is for you to be my second set of eyes. I want you to be looking over my shoulder when I'm directing a mission. You know I'll be busy and distracted at times. You take care of me and I'll take care of you!"

What the hell is this guy up to? Yellowsnake wondered. *None of the officers I've met are like this. They're usually just worried about saving their own hides. They'd much rather stay back where it's safe. He's sure as hell not like the other brass I've met.*

It was now clear that the Colonel had read Yellowsnake's much traveled file, and had reached an early conclusion that the Comanche was an instinctive breed who would prove invaluable to the battalion's survival.

Colonel Lincoln continued to talk...frankly longer than Yellowsnake liked, and Yellowsnake was getting uncomfortable. He was unaccustomed to talking at such length with an officer, especially a Commanding Officer. The Colonel ended their strange conversation by saying the rest of the battalion would, among other things, continue training and leading the mountain Montagnards. They had courage, but lacked the skills to fight as sharpened soldiers against an enemy like the Viet Cong.

The Montagnards, prior to France's departure of Vietnam, had done nothing more than fight off the VC invaders with crossbows and arrows. As soon as the montagnards were properly trained and molded, the mountain fighters would become an integral part of frequent attacks the Rangers would lead deep into VC strongholds.

Yellowsnake stood at attention, about to be dismissed, when the Colonel said, "I'm trusting you will prove to be the man I believe you are and, from here on out, we'll be working together."

He laid on his bunk that evening, his mind slowly dimming into sleep, when suddenly all hell broke loose. "Incoming! Incoming!" voices from outside shouted. In an instant, enemy mortar shells were raining down upon the camp, and within seconds the sky was lit up, reminding him of fourth of July fireworks. The sounds of gunfire came from all directions as he scrambled off his cot, reaching for his Comanche knife and automatic rifle. Before he was able to open his tent flap, an exploding mortar knocked him senseless.

Twenty minutes later Yellowsnake awoke, not fully knowing what had hit him. He had a brutal headache. He picked himself up and pushed back the tent flap, peering through aching eyes at the devastation. The camp had been nearly destroyed. When he looked over his shoulder, he could see headquarters hut still intact. The Colonel was luckier than some, escaping unharmed. Yellowsnake surveyed the craters and strewn camp remains, then was seized with rage. He could see the Montagnards had been hit hard. Five of their troops lay dead, and many of them were seriously wounded by shrapnel. They were a gutty little bunch, and now he understood why they hated the Viet Cong so deeply.

Yellowsnake circled through the camp ruins back to the remains of his own tent. His eyes met those of Colonel Lincoln just as he emerged from headquarters hut. His eyes told Yellowsnake that he was more than just pissed off!

He motioned toward Yellowsnake as he growled, "Snake, get your gear packed. We're going to put an end to this shit! I have a job for you tomorrow morning, so get ready!"

Yellowsnake sensed the Colonel meant what he said. He

hastily packed his backpack and went directly to the armory shack. The armory Sergeant equipped him with a field radio, which he was to carry at all times. He pointed to the arsenal of weapons, telling Yellowsnake he had his choice, "Sounds like you'll be working this one alone, so take your pick."

Yellowsnake grabbed a rifle, then selected a mean looking twenty gauge sawed off shotgun, a pistol, and two extra combat knives to carry on his belt. The Sergeant handed him a supply of hand grenades to fasten to his flak jacket and, aside from his food rations, he was loaded for bear. The problem was, he didn't know how long he would be gone. With the help of the supply clerk, his pack was stocked with rations and he was ready to go.

Yellowsnake was feeling the uneasiness of darkness setting in. He stretched out on his cot inside a makeshift shelter, hoping for a few hours sleep. Suddenly, a soldier burst in. "Snake, the Colonel wants to see you. Come over to headquarters — pronto!" He suited up in his camouflage garb, then joined his leader in headquarters hut. The Colonel was stooped over a dimly lit table on which a map was spread. He looked up only briefly when Yellowsnake entered.

Colonel Lincoln had been studying an area surrounding the compound very intensely and, still hunched over the map declared, "We've got to find out where Charlie is stashing his supplies and weapons. They'll tear us up if we don't act soon. We've got to put the Montagnards on their trail and hit them quick. At first light, I want you to leave camp and comb the northern perimeter. You'll need to pick up the VC trail and start from there. Do you understand? Also, don't forget, I want you to call me each night at 2300 hours sharp with a report. If you return sooner, you can report in person, but if you're on their trail and haven't finished your mission, call me at 2300 regardless."

Yellowsnake didn't sleep well that night, he was nervous. This would be his first real tracking mission in Vietnam. He knew what was expected of him as a tracker, but didn't know what to expect from the enemy once he found them.

Before dawn, he was on his way. He was fully armed and feeling secure with his trusty Comanche knife and machete attached to his belt. Then he disappeared into the jungle and, like a phantom, was out of sight.

He combed the northern perimeter of the camp and soon picked up the trail of the enemy, causing his confidence to rise. To him, it was as easy as tracking a semi truck on a sandy beach. Nonetheless, Yellowsnake knew he must be damn careful not to let his guard down. He was acutely aware that he was alone and had no backup help. It was plain and simple, trackers had one specific mission. Track the enemy. Yellowsnake was not there to kill the enemy unless it became absolutely necessary to save his own life. He hoped this wouldn't be the case.

The heat of morning was intensifying as he hacked his way through the dense jungle undergrowth, heading north. He kept a steady pace, sensing the campsite of the VC was near. In less than an hour, he was at the small clearing where the VC had slept the night before. From the looks of the smoldering ashes, he had missed them by only minutes. He knew he was close; his pulse quickened.

The enemy's trail was becoming fresher and it seemed the squawk of the birds and the scream of the monkeys became louder, making Yellowsnake very edgy. He stopped a few seconds for a drink of water. He felt the sweat pour down every crevice of his body, settling at last into his jungle boots. Suddenly, he heard a noise ahead. He had sensed the enemy was close, but not this close. He felt the surge of adrenaline kick in as he reminded himself to be very careful. A slip up at this point could cost him his life.

Yellowsnake's camouflage smudge began to burn as it pooled around his eyes. The pain caused him to become even more alert. He knew he had to ignore the discomfort and crouching down, he began crawling along the jungle floor with the deftness of a viper. He cautiously hugged the edge of the trail to avoid being discovered, and could see the VC straight ahead. They were wearing their customary black shirts and cooley style hats. They appeared to be unhurried, carrying their weapons casually over their shoulders. He watched their every move, knowing from here on out, he must travel as quietly as the wind.

35

The VC pressed on, resting from time to time, and Yellowsnake likewise stopped and rested quietly, knowing they were not far ahead. It was becoming clear to him where they were headed. Their trail would eventually lead them back to the Ho Chi Minh trail, their main supply route from North Vietnam. Afternoon had vanished into evening before the enemy finally stopped. They had reached their destination for the day. He knew that by now he was miles from camp and would have to spend his first night in the jungle by himself. There was no chance of making it back to camp that night.

He remained deadly silent as he inched forward until he could see them clearly. They had reached a small clearing off the side of the trail and, moving even closer, he could see their tunnel. This was where they were hiding their supplies. At last, his mission was making sense. He was flat on his belly, scarcely breathing for fear of making noise. He reached quietly into his pack for his field glasses to take a better look. He could see every feature of their faces. They scurried like ants, back and forth, in and out of the dark hole. It was obvious they had a large stash of supplies inside the tunnel. He didn't dare move. He watched them remove their weapons, placing them on the ground just outside the tunnel. He could see uniformed soldiers carrying boxes of weapons and ammo into the tunnel from a carefully guarded stack outside.

Soon, the sun was well down behind the tall trees and the temperature was quickly falling. Yellowsnake retreated carefully from the VC campsite and worked his way back along the trail, staying low and quiet. At last he saw what he was searching for; a spot safely away from the Cong in which he could get some badly needed rest and grab a bite of his meager rations.

He settled himself into a small, dense brush-covered area, seeking a tree to lean against. He wearily removed his backpack and selected a can of gourmet cold beans. In the jungle, a stalker would never build a fire for fear of being discovered. Warm food was a luxury awaiting him back at camp.

While he sat quietly under the gnarled, massive tree, trying to keep himself warm, Yellowsnake nervously glanced at his watch between shivers. It was nearly time to call in. He removed the radio from his backpack and carefully adjusted its transmitter. At exactly eleven, he started transmitting his message to Colonel Lincoln's headquarters in whispers. "I'm on the trail of the VC . . . Have located camp and tunnel. . .Map coordinates are as follows." His radio squawked a static filled confirmation from camp. He dearly hoped the VC hadn't heard the noise, for his destiny would be sealed if he was discovered. His message ended with a whispered "I'll leave at first light . . . be back ASAP."

The jungle came alive at night, and Yellowsnake was as nervous as a cat. It seemed an eternity until morning. He was cold, hungry and knew it wouldn't be long before the enemy started moving. He would have to get the jump on them to avoid detection in case they turned back on his trail. If they discovered him, he would be fleeing for his life and, if caught, they would quickly end it. He rested very little that night, and every noise sounded like the enemy approaching. *I don't think I'd better sleep tonight,* was his last thought. The next thing he knew, he was startled. *Damn, I dozed off!* He listened intently, then heard voices. The voices were coming toward him. *Oh, shit! I've got to get out of here!* He quickly grabbed his pack and slung it over his shoulder, checking a second time to be sure his weapons were intact.

He rose cautiously to a crouching position, resisting the urge to stretch out his cramped legs. Yellowsnake crept quietly away from the trail, not knowing where he would pick up another one, hoping he could maintain his cover. He moved slowly and steadily through the thicket, taking care not to rustle bushes which might draw the enemy's attention. A few minutes later, he stopped and listened, trying to discern whether the VC had become aware of his presence. When he peered through the bushes, he saw them moving toward a small water hole. It was morning and they were ready to have their meal of rice before hitting the trail. He breathed a sigh of relief knowing they were not searching for him.

He retreated to a safer distance, sweeping around the trail in an arc wide enough to prevent being detected. He had closed the circle and much to his relief, he reconnected with the trail. It wasn't much of a trail, but it was the trail which had brought him in and he was ready to get out. He wove his way along the crude path, steadily picking up his pace. His senses remained honed as sharp as his knife blade. Now his only fear was an encounter with unexpected VC who might be using the same trail. He kept moving, his eyes focused straight ahead and searching for any sign of unnatural movement. At short intervals he stopped and strained his ears, listening for noises foreign to the jungle. If the enemy was headed his way, the birds and monkeys would surely warn him. They were his friends and his warning beacon.

He kept his body moving along the rugged trail, sometimes fast–sometimes painfully slow. When Yellowsnake finally arrived at the compound, it was a most welcome sight! It was nearly two o'clock in the afternoon and he was thoroughly beat. The emotional strain of thirty-two hours on high alert settled heavily upon him. With his energy drained, he entered the headquarters hut to report in.

Colonel Lincoln turned suddenly as the weary tracker entered the room. His eyes lit up. "Snake, you're back! Good job, boy!" He put his hand on Yellowsnake's shoulder. "Son, I know you were worried, but you did a hell of a good job. You should be proud of yourself." Colonel Lincoln strode across the room and pulled a chair up to his desk, motioning for Yellowsnake to sit. "Now you know what is expected from here on out," he continued in more sober tones. "Each time you go out, it'll get a little easier. I know that's hard to believe, but it will." The Colonel ordered Yellowsnake to rest up. "You've had a mean two days and we don't know when you'll be needed again, but you will, sooner or later. Tonight we're going to send some of our more skilled trained Montagnards out with one of our Rangers to take out that supply tunnel."

Yellowsnake felt rewarded when he heard Lincoln's words. Now he knew his efforts had not been wasted. A search and destroy attack would be directed against the supply tunnel he had located; now he could clearly see the value of this mission and the missions which lay ahead.

His body was dead tired as he returned to his tent, but his

38

thoughts were blanketed with rising confidence. *It's not so bad, being in the jungle by myself. That is, if I use my head. At least I have only myself to take care of. If I stay calm and use common sense, I should be able to make it back in one piece. There's no one else to make a stupid mistake that could cost me my life.*

Yellowsnake soaked in a long hot shower, and then he performed simple first aid on his scrapes and scratches. He was eager as he headed to the mess tent for a well earned hot meal. After he finished his chow, he strolled contentedly toward his bunk, savoring the full feeling in his gut. He collapsed bone tired on his cot, and closing his eyes, felt warmly comfortable and safe. Thoughts of Maria filled his mind. He longed to be with her. He couldn't be with her, but now knew he could keep his promise to stay alive and return to her safely when his tour ended.

He was nearly asleep as he listened to the quiet commotion of the Montagnard troops along with Sergeant Dutro, preparing themselves for a night trek into the jungle on the same trail he had traveled only hours earlier. True to his word, Colonel Lincoln had decided now was the time for swift action.

Yellowsnake's respect for the Colonel grew more and more as each day passed. He was straightforward and a man of his word. Above all, he felt the Colonel could be trusted. He had met few men in his life who could be truly trusted, and the Colonel was one of the few.

It was nearly noon the next day when Sergeant Dutro and the Montagnards arrived back in camp, heavily laden with the treasures of their raid the previous night. They had traveled swiftly through the jungle and had completely surprised the Viet Cong. They had shelled the VC camp heavily with mortars and rockets, killing most of them immediately. A large portion of their weapons, ammunition and food supplies had been abandoned in the tunnel.

When the Montagnards and Sergeant Dutro returned to camp, they were carrying as many Russian made AK 47 rifles as possible, along with boxes of ammunition which were in short supply at the compound. One of the many problems which persisted continually as the war began to escalate, was the

39

difficulty of transporting U.S. supplies from Danang into the nearly inaccessible bush area. The enemy's weapons were plentiful, so anytime the Rangers and Montagnards were able to capture their armament, they did so. By the looks of the stash that Sergeant Dutro's troops were hauling in, the previous night's raid had been very successful. And they had, most importantly, destroyed the enemy's remaining supply of weapons and ammo, thanks to Yellowsnake's accurate report of their position.

Bright and early the next morning, Yellowsnake was summoned to headquarter's hut. When he reached the HQ, he was met by Colonel Lincoln coming out the door with a small duffel bag in hand. Without breaking his stride, the Colonel spoke, "While I'm gone, Major Dawson may have some work for you. I'll be back soon, so stay alive! We have a lot of work ahead of us when I return."

Following the successful raid by Sergeant Dutro's Montagnard band of fighters, Colonel Lincoln had been ordered back to Command center headquarters in Danang. Yellowsnake's personal fear was that the Colonel would be recognized by his superiors as a highly skilled field operations leader, causing him to be transferred to another outfit. This was not a situation he wanted, to be in this hell hole without leadership he could absolutely trust. He squinted upward against the bright sun, watching the Colonel's helicopter lift into the sky. *I hope Charlie will let things stay quiet around here for a few days until we get our camp back in order*, he silently wished as he turned toward his tent for some more shut-eye.

Yellowsnake was relaxed, enjoying a cigarette after breakfast at dawn the next morning, when suddenly he was brought to his feet by the menacing sound of not too distant gunfire. Everyone bolted from the tent to retrieve their weapons as the gunfire continued. It seemed to be coming from the montagnard guard posts just outside the compound. He strapped on his weapons, running across the compound.

From behind, he heard Major Dawson's voice, "Yellowsnake, get with Sergeant Dutro! Take some Montagnards and sweep the perimeter for a look-see." He met up with Dutro and the Montagnard troops.   Yellowsnake instinctively took the point, picking his way through the thicket toward the outer edges of camp.   Their silent arrival at a perimeter guard post soon disclosed the disaster. The Viet Cong had sneaked up in the darkness and positioned themselves near each post along the perimeter; when daylight arrived, they opened fire on the unsuspecting sentries.

When Yellowsnake and Sergeant Dutro searched the perimeter, they found four Montagnard guards had been killed, three of them by gunshot wounds. The fourth had his throat cleanly cut. The guards had returned the gunfire, but it was too late. There was a *lot* of blood. While the montagnards sadly carried the bodies of their dead comrades, the patrol returned to camp.   Sergeant Dutro carefully described the details of the sneak attack to Major Dawson. He was livid!

That afternoon, Yellowsnake again got the call. "At first light tomorrow," the Major said, "I want you to saddle up and try to pick up the trail of those little bastards. Let's cause them some grief of their own."

There was an abundance of AK 47's and ammunition from the recent raid, so he grabbed more than enough full ammo clips and began suiting up for his next pursuit. At dawn, he easily picked up the VC trail. They were heading due west from the compound. He moved swiftly for about three hours without pausing, except to hack at thorny branches in his path. Then, Yellowsnake found what he was searching for. He cautiously approached the enemy camp on his belly, realizing this was not a supply dump, but an overnight camp for the VC attackers. They were gleefully celebrating the small success they had achieved with their attack on the compound sentry posts.

He carefully counted their numbers as he charted their position.   Then suddenly, he became aware of someone approaching him on the trail. Before Yellowsnake could ease back off the trail, a VC soldier appeared not more than forty feet away. The startled tracker silently backed away from the trail. He crouched on his knees and withdrew his Comanche knife from it's scabbard. His enemy was dressed in black, walking directly toward him. And much to his surprise, the soldier

41

passed by him. Yellowsnake seized the opportunity. He sprang to his feet, grabbed the VC by his chin and rammed his knee into the soft tissue of the man's back, dropping him to his knees. Not unlike his warrior forefathers from a hundred years earlier, he grabbed the soldier's hair and pulled his head back, exposing his vulnerable neck area. With a lightening move, he made one swift and fatal slash across the throat. The blood flowed from the lethal wound as he grabbed the Viet Cong's blood soaked shirt and dragged him into the bushes a few yards away. He grabbed the soldier's rifle and slung it across his shoulder, just in case he needed extra firepower.

He was breathing deeply as he crouched down and wiped the drying blood from his knife blade on his pant leg. Then he began making his way back to the edge of the trail. "Shit!" he muttered, "There's another one." He once again dropped to his knees and took position behind a nearby bush, trying to remain motionless. The approaching soldier was on the same trail as his now dead friend, and Yellowsnake knew exactly where he would be walking. The unsuspecting VC nonchalantly swung his machete back and forth, maneuvering along the dense trail. Suddenly, the soldier nervously sensed he was being watched.

Yellowsnake pounced on him like a hungry lion, jerking his arm back, causing the VC to drop his machete. He wrapped his arm like an iron vise tightly around the Viet Cong's neck, silencing his voice, then buried his knife deep in his victim's belly. He knew that as a tracker, killing the enemy was not his job. His mission was to get information back to headquarters. In this case, there was no choice. As soon as he wiped his knife blade clean, he hid the soldier from sight and began his swift retreat to the compound.

He was weaving his way along the trail and had walked for less than an hour when he heard the birds and monkeys creating a commotion ahead of him. He sensed another unneeded problem and silently eased himself off the trail. Straight ahead, paused on the trailside, were nine black shirts.

Damn, if I try to skirt these guys, the squawking birds are sure as hell going to give me away. On the other hand, I can't go straight ahead - they're dead in the middle of my trail!

Yellowsnake's mind raced. He could see the Viet Cong sitting in a tightly grouped circle, apparently eating while en route to their camp. He flattened his body to the ground and peeked through the underbrush; then he decided there wasn't much of a choice. All things considered, his best bet was to go straight ahead.

He quietly removed the hardware he had stolen from the dead soldier and slithered smoothly along the ground, keeping Charlie in clear view. When he got closer, he readied his rifle, double checked his supply of ammo and kept crawling along the ground. All the while, he kept a steady eye on the VC, looking for any indication that he had been spotted. *I'm lucky*, he thought to himself. *No signs of them seeing me yet. I hope like hell I can keep moving without attracting their attention. If they see me, I've got big problems.*

He moved to within fifty feet of the ring of soldiers, knowing his moment to act was at hand. *This is my only chance. I can't screw up because it won't get any better*, he concluded. He tried to collect his thoughts and steady his erratic breathing as he slowly brought his rifle up and aimed a steady bead through the bushes toward the circle of soldiers. He squeezed the trigger, spraying bullets across their circle as the VC scrambled for their weapons. His fire didn't cease as they frantically reached for their weapons. It was too late. He was able to take out every one of them. His rifle barrel smoked as he rammed another clip into his weapon. He could see all of the bodies were still. He cautiously began crawling slowly toward them.

When he was within twenty feet of the lifeless bodies, he stood up and walked slowly. It appeared they were all dead, all but one, that is! He glanced out of the corner of his eye when he saw a bit of movement. The wounded soldier was reaching for his rifle. As soon as he saw the VC's arm move, he tilted the shotgun clutched in his left hand and pulverized the skull of his last attacker. Although he was sensing the menace to his life had ended, a sweaty chill came over him. The impact of killing nine more enemy soldiers made him a little shaky. Now, all he could think about was getting back to camp without being discovered by other soldiers. Even worse, he felt like the bush was crawling with them.

He retreated quickly along the trail, his anxiety peaking. *With my luck, there will be one of those sneaky pricks perched in a tree, just waiting to snipe me. After all I've been through, I don't need that.*

Fortunately, he had taken out his final threat. Yellowsnake was nearing exhaustion when he finally arrived back at the compound several hours later. He reported directly to Major Dawson, telling him the location of the small detachment of Viet Cong troops, and reluctantly thinking it would be best to tell him the whole story. He completed his report, then blurted, "By the way, sir, there are eleven less VC in the jungle now. It wasn't what I wanted, but I did what I had to do."

The Major was flabbergasted! "What? Why didn't you avoid them?"

A highly irritated Yellowsnake fired back. "Sir, I didn't have a choice. If I'd tried to circle them, they probably would have picked me up and I wouldn't be here now to report to you. They'd have skinned me alive!"

The Major scratched his head, then looked at him apologetically. "You did the right thing, son. I'm sorry you ran into them. It doesn't sound like it's worth sending our people out after them. You took care of the job. Hopefully, that won't happen too many times. Get some rest." It was the Major's good fortune that he had not challenged Yellowsnake any further. The bloodied tracker had had a full day!

The days wore on, and he found himself making more and more trips into the jungle, always at the request of Major Dawson. Each trip found him becoming increasingly skilled at avoiding the enemy, and even more dangerously routine in nature. He was always careful to stay well out of the range of the VC, staying low to the ground, watching their every movement and mindful to keep an escape route available.

All to frequently, he encountered more and more booby traps along the trail. That scared the hell out of him. The VC were devious little devils. Today, they might set a pendulum stake trip wire, and tomorrow he was apt to spot a deadly mine buried in the middle of the trail. But his confidence grew with each mission, almost to a point of cockiness. Each time he went on the trail, he schemed to himself, *I'll fix those little bastards. They must think I'm not smart enough to spot their mines. I can hide 'em better than they can.*

He was acutely alert when he traveled the dense trails, and foremost on his mind was the VC's deadly traps. He'd stop and carefully dig up their well-hidden mines, gently lifting them from their resting places and then relocate them to a different part of the trail. He felt warmly gratified by his conviction that the VC would become surprised victims of their own treachery.

The night was typically hot and humid and the rain was pouring down in torrents when Major Dawson summoned Yellowsnake to headquarters. The Major said he was receiving reports from Danang indicating dangerous enemy activity. He explained that the VC, along with a reported troop buildup of North Vietnamese army regulars, had been spotted in an area very near the Ho Chi Minh trail. Yellowsnake's treacherous assignment was to pick up a trail the VC had been using between the compound and the Ho Chi Minh trail, and get as close as possible to observe their strength. Once he sighted the VC encampment, he was to call in to the Major. Dawson emphasized that it was an especially hot area of Charlie's activity, and the mission would be extremely perilous due to troops moving in all directions.

He was drenched by the warm early morning rain when he embarked on the designated trail, heading for what would prove to be a long, hazardous journey. He had equipped himself with his sawed off shotgun, AK 47, a number of grenades, radio, his faithful fighting knife and an extra knife. Once he was on the trail, he kept a wary eye out for booby traps and mines. He hacked through the endless trail brush for nearly two hours before he discovered the death traps. There were five mines strategically scattered in the middle of the trail. His knife blade became his digging tool as he carefully removed them. Then he gingerly repositioned them two hundred yards up the trail from where they had been buried. He made a mental note of their location as he marked the spot on his area map, then pushed his journey deeper into enemy territory.

The hours passed quickly and soon the sun began it's drop behind the thick canopy of trees, but he sensed his destination was near and kept going. Finally, at dusk, he heard the chatter of enemy voices ahead. This had to be the gathering point reported to Major Dawson. He crept closer and soon could make out the images of what he estimated to be over a hundred soldiers, including fifty or more North Vietnamese regulars. He hurriedly made note of their numbers, then disappeared into the protection of the canopy to find a suitable tree in which he could spend the night.

First securing his equipment, he climbed more than twenty feet into the tree before reaching a cluster of thick branches which would serve nicely as his bed for the night. It was 2300 hours and, as customary, he tuned in his radio to call the Major with his report. He spoke in whispered tones as he addressed the officer by his code name. "Big Duke, Big Duke! This is Yellowsnake. Over". He paused. "Big Duke, Big Duke! This is Yellowsnake. Can you read me? Over."

Finally, headquarters responded. "Yellowsnake, this is Big Duke. Over."

He began painting a picture for the Major, describing the number of troops gathered, especially, the number of North Vietnamese army regulars amassed. He said it looked like they were intending to mount some sort of attack because there was a lot of serious preparation taking place. After the Major confirmed receiving his report, he radioed, "Yellowsnake, get out now! Get back here ASAP!" Yellowsnake acknowledged and signed off, then stowed his radio for the night. Wearily, he opened his knapsack and retrieved a can of rations, not relishing another cold meal. He wished he could light a cigarette, but knew better. Before he became too sleepy, he pulled his rope from his pack and tied it around his waist several times, making sure he was secured to the high branches of the tree. All he needed was to fall from the tree during the night and arouse the enemy or, even worse, injure himself. Nonetheless, tree lofts had turned out to be the safest way to sleep in the jungle, and he badly needed some safe rest.

Before daylight, he was awakened by voices approaching in

his direction. As his mind cleared, his thoughts raced, *Oh my God, they're starting earlier than I thought. Damn it! I'm not ready yet. I've got to move!* He frantically unlashed the rope and jammed it in his knapsack. He checked to see if everything was secure, then began his rapid descent. When he had nearly reached the ground, he heard angry voices. They had spotted him and were heading his way.

He was startled and scared because he knew he had been seen. Yellowsnake took off through the thick of the jungle at top speed. It was dense, thorny, tangled underbrush and he couldn't take time to cut a trail. He had to put distance between himself and them if he was going to stay alive. He ran a couple hundred yards, then stopped to listen. The enemy was hot on his trail and he had to figure out how to evade their pursuit. He knew they would not give up their chase until they had caught and killed him. He ran for hours, stopping only briefly to listen for signs of the oncoming threat and each time he stopped, he heard them. They had not given up. It had become a battle of wills.

His course had taken him in a southerly direction from the point at which he was first spotted by the VC. He was sweating profusely after running for three hours when he finally decided to turn his route east and, hopefully, pick up his trail back to camp. He ran until darkness fell over him like a blanket. His body was running out of gas. It was tempting to stop, but he knew he couldn't. Charlie was still hot on his erratic trail. At last, he knew the enemy could no longer pursue him in the darkness, so he located a tree which looked like a safe haven for the night. He was exhausted, but still had to muster enough strength to climb the tree. He was painfully tired, and with a full knapsack on his back, he began his ascent. He reached his selected perch in the branches, pausing once again to listen. The enemy was no more than three hundred yards behind him, apparently content to make camp for the night. He was also aware that it was approaching radio time as he strapped himself into the tree. The limbs and trunk offered him a surface on which he could rest and take the weight off his feet. He quietly called headquarters and upon reaching the Major, he whispered that he had been spotted by the enemy and was running for his life. He'd get out as fast as possible and do everything in his power to evade them.

The darkness didn't afford him any sleep. He knew he must be on his way well before daybreak. Before sun up, he had descended the tree and begun his journey eastward. He paused at intervals to listen for signs of the enemy. He was relieved when he realized he could no longer hear them. He was breathing easier as he watched the sun begin it's rise over the trees, sensing he was nearing his original trail. He knew that once he reached the trail, he would be just north of the location where he had replanted the enemy's land mines. The trail finally appeared out of nowhere and at that moment, he heard what he didn't want to hear. The voices of the enemy were distinct and they were on his trail. Then he heard something ahead of him that chilled his blood. More voices! He made a quick decision, *I'll get off the main trail and keep heading south, and try to avoid whoever is headed toward me. With some luck, maybe I can create some distance from the troops behind me.*

He had carefully circled the spot at which he had reburied the VC land mines and kept a low profile until he made it safely around the area. He was making his way along the trail when suddenly he encountered another threat. The oncoming troops ahead of him on his trail had spotted him. His movement had drawn their attention and they began firing. He took off in a full run again; suddenly, without apparent reason, the gunfire of the oncoming troops stopped. *The dummies must figure they got me,* Yellowsnake reflected with guarded relief. He couldn't expect too many more breaks like this. And he wasn't going to depend on luck to get him out of his mess.

He found himself back on the main trail, and he just kept on running. His frantic pace was startled by a thunderous explosion. It was music to his ears, for what he had hoped for, had indeed happened. He heard the screaming and yelling of the wounded VC, about a quarter mile behind him. Both the oncoming troops who had suddenly stopped firing and the VC who were following him had converged at the land mines, encountering the demise intended for *him*. His scheme had worked, at least for the moment.

He moved another hundred yards or so, then stopped and listened. To his amazement, there were still voices behind him. Only now, it was the few remaining troops who had escaped the blast–mad as hornets. They were following him through the uncut trail he had traveled earlier. Then, he made one of the few mistakes every tracker hopes he will never make. While he had quickened his pace, his thoughts had been focused on the activity behind him. He was not paying close attention to what lay ahead. He had been looking over his shoulder, and when he turned to look ahead, he encountered two VC directly in front of him. The unseen stragglers had caught him by surprise.

They opened fire on him before he could ready his rifle and, like a branding iron, he felt a piercing jolt to the right side of his body. He had been hit. He fought to remain focused as he raised his rifle and began firing, knocking down one of the soldiers running toward him. The other VC moved quickly and, before Yellowsnake had a chance to react, the onrusher lunged wildly, trying to knock him off his feet. He could feel the blood running down his side. He reacted instinctively as he sidestepped the killer while delivering a solid blow to his temple. He knocked the small soldier to the ground and did the only sure thing he knew to end the crisis. His hand reached the handle of his lethal Comanche knife as he pounced on the soldier who lay on his stomach. He raised the VC's head and with an upward motion, slashed his throat so deeply his blade hit the vertebrae.

The bloodied warrior moved in catlike fashion as he grabbed his rifle and jumped to his feet in one swift movement. Now he had to force himself to continue his pace on the trail which would take him nearer and nearer the compound.

If I meet any more VC, I'm dead! I don't know how much longer I can go with this hole in me, Yellowsnake thought grimly to himself. He paused momentarily as he moved off to the side of the trail. His bloody fingers nervously fumbled with his canteen. He took a big drink and then doused his side with the remainder of his water. The wound was an ugly sight as a broad wedge of his flesh was missing. Luckily, the bullet had ricocheted off the edge of his flak jacket and only shallowly penetrated his side. After he confirmed with a fearful glance that it didn't look fatal, he felt relieved.

His greatest fear was another encounter with more unneeded soldiers. His wound was throbbing fiercely, and he was becoming lightheaded from blood loss. He could feel himself getting weaker and, with the sun descending, his pace slowed to nearly a walk. He wasn't sure he could run, even if he had to.

Each minute seemed an eternity before he finally reached the compound. He was staggering toward the sentry post when the Montagnard soldier standing guard spotted him and radioed into the compound, "Yellowsnake is back and he's wounded!" In moments, he was grabbed and shouldered into sick bay. A waiting surgeon quickly cleaned his wound, gave him a shot of pain killer, and began stitching him up. "You're lucky, boy, a few clicks to the right and you wouldn't be here now."

"I know Doc, those bastards were doing their best to kill me," Yellowsnake muttered.

When he was finished with his work the doctor told Yellowsnake he would have to spend few days in bed to let the wound heal. "This is going to hurt like a son of a bitch for awhile," the doctor warned. Yellowsnake didn't care. He was alive, and that was all that mattered.

He was forced to lie quietly in the sterile sick bay, and the discomfort of his stitches and the wound dressing only elevated Yellowsnake's frustration within himself. He lay there seething silently. *How could I have let myself become careless and lose concentration on the trail? I'll never make that mistake again. I was stupid once, and I was lucky.* The price to pay was too high, and next time it could very well cost him his life.

With each day, he felt his strength returning. His wound was healing nicely, and he was itching to get back into the thick of it. Major Dawson, while stopping by daily to check on his progress, told him about the raids by the Montagnards and Sergeant Dutro on the VC stronghold. Sergeant Dutro's fighters had done extensive damage to the troop buildup, while destroying their weapons and ammunition supply. With a little luck, the incoming barrages would slow down.

Early one hot rainy morning the Major stopped by Yellowsnake's bed. "Oh, by the way, Snake, I've got something

for you. This isn't much of a ceremony, but you've earned it."
He reached into his pocket, pulled out a small packet, and
opened it. Inside was a Purple Heart, the medal given to soldiers
wounded in the field. The Major smiled. "I hope this is the last
time I have to give you one of these."

Yellowsnake flinched with irritation as he watched the
doctor carefully remove his stitches. He looked up to see the
bespeckled company clerk making his way through the sick bay
tent. The clerk handed Yellowsnake a letter as he passed and,
without even looking at the handwriting which was obviously
feminine, he could tell who the letter was from. A sweet
fragrance filled his nostrils, one he hadn't smelled since he left
the reservation. It was from Maria. He waited a few minutes
until he thought he was alone before he eagerly opened the letter.
Suddenly, he sensed his world was expanding. Her soft words
caused his throat to tighten with emotion. She was expecting
their child in a few short months. His heart was racing as he
blurted out, "Damn, I'm going to be a daddy!" Without looking
up from his paperwork, the nearby doctor chirped back.
"Congratulations, I know how you feel. I've got two kids of my
own and I'll be out of here in two weeks to see them."
Yellowsnake smiled, for they both felt good.

Yellowsnake bluntly brushed aside the tent flap and stepped
into the brilliant sun. He was feeling as high as he had many
years earlier when the reservation Elders allowed him to smoke
their sweet grass in ceremonial fashion. Yellowsnake, along
with his joy, felt a little distressed that his child would be born
before his tour was complete. The modern day warrior now had
added incentive to return home in one piece.

His keen eyes squinted at dawn's early light breaking
through to the compound floor, then he heard the sound of
chopper blades approaching. He watched the craft settle on it's
pad and the rotor blade begin to slow. The door opened,
revealing the profile of Colonel Lincoln. His boss was back. He
followed the noisy chopper's disappearance behind the trees
once more, then the wounded warrior returned to the solitude of
his tent.

That evening, Yellowsnake sat quietly by himself, enjoying

his coffee and cigarette after chow call. He was feeling good. His thoughts were suddenly curtailed when Colonel Lincoln entered the mess tent. He glanced toward Yellowsnake, grabbed a cup of coffee and joined him across the table. The Colonel looked over each shoulder to be sure they were alone. "Snake, I understand you had a fight while I was gone. Sorry to hear that. Hopefully, you're healing up because I'm going to be needing you soon."

Yellowsnake described his mission into the jungle a couple of weeks earlier, explaining almost apologetically how he had received his wound. "Colonel, that won't happen again. I won't let it. I was careless once, but not twice." The Colonel gave him an understanding smile. He understood Yellowsnake's concern for survival.

The Colonel then offered some details as to why he had been gone so long. He had been in Danang at Battalion headquarters with senior officers, reviewing intelligence reports on the VC and North Vietnamese army activity. Most disturbing was the unusually large build up of troops being observed by reconnaissance flights.

"I'm telling you this in confidence," said Colonel Lincoln. "This information cannot go beyond us. Real soon, we're going to be mounting a major strike on Charlie's stronghold in a small village northwest of Hue. We've discovered a huge buildup of weapons and there are NVA troops coming in daily from across the border. We don't know what yet, but we do know they're up to something big. Get yourself healed up. In a few days, we'll be making this trip and I'll be leading the mission."

The healing tracker spoke with commanding reassurance to the Colonel. "My wound is fine, sir. I'll be ready to go when you are. This gut wound isn't going to slow me down."

A few days later, the mission was on. The choppers arrived at the compound to take Colonel Lincoln, Yellowsnake, the Montagnards and a few selected Ranger leaders into a landing area outside of Hue. They were all aware that the countryside around Hue was heavily occupied by the VC. While the troops assembled, Colonel Lincoln spoke to Yellowsnake. "On this mission, we have our own radio man. You'll be sticking close to me and you know what your job is. Stay close and watch the situation while I'm directing our attack. The moment I see we've done our job, I want to get the hell out of there."

They were heavily laden with all the mortars, rockets and automatic rifles they could carry. The force lifted off and headed toward their landing point. The early morning darkness was turning into light as they arrived at their destination. While the troops were unloading from the choppers, the Colonel extracted his field map, glanced at it briefly and pointed to a spot while motioning to Yellowsnake. "I want you to take the point, here's where we're headed."

The ever wary Yellowsnake was at point when the attack body began it's trek through the jungle. The Colonel and radio man were not far behind Yellowsnake. They worked their way through the unfamiliar jungle, reaching their destination in less than an hour.

The attack force stood on a heavily wooded ridge, looking down at the small village reportedly harboring the build up of VC and North Vietnamese Army troops, along with a large cache of ammunition and weapons. Colonel Lincoln studied his map as he directed the strategic deployment of the Ranger leaders, each of whom was in charge of a group of ten Montagnards. He instructed the Rangers to stay on their radios and listen for his signal. Silently, the Montagnard troops took their assigned positions.

When the time was right, the Colonel commanded them to open fire at will. The barrage of shells began falling on the village below like meteorites. When Yellowsnake looked through his field glasses, he could see chaos everywhere. There were black-shirted Viet Cong soldiers scrambling from hut to hut and among them, North Vietnamese regulars were similarly frantic in an attempt to get to their weapons. For the first time, Yellowsnake could see women and children running for shelter toward the perimeter of the village, and as he watched, his heart quietly took cover. The barrage continued and the village was quickly devastated.

They watched the fire and smoke billow high into the air when Colonel Lincoln ordered the attack groups to cease fire.

The smoke lifted, revealing a village floor gruesomely littered with bodies. There was no movement in the village and scanning the perimeter of the area, the Colonel could see the remaining soldiers had fled, retreating to the protection of the dense jungle. The joyous Montagnards knew they had done their job well as they viewed the blackened remnants of the stronghold.

The saliva in Yellowsnake's throat thickened. Until this moment, his heart had allowed little room for sympathy. Sadly, untimely thoughts going back to his childhood were flashing through his mind. His first view of a kill had occurred when he watched his uncles butcher chickens, hogs and cattle. He had accepted the bloody task as necessary to life. His fleeting thoughts captured his mind's impression of Nokona, greatest of Chiefs. Even Nokona would have been saddened by the sight laying on the village floor.

Yellowsnake was not remorseful about seeing the dead Viet Cong fighters lying scattered about. It was a necessary part of war. And although he was somewhat sympathetic toward the four dead women who were caught in the attack, he knew that often they were equally dangerous warriors. The muscles in Yellowsnake's stomach tightened as he looked at the motionless bodies of two children, neither of them more than eight years old. This was not the war he had envisioned. The children were not the enemy! The war had become extremely ugly, and he knew he would have to toughen his heart even more to survive it. Even though he had not fired a shot at the encampment, he was part of the brutality.

Colonel Lincoln stood motionless at Yellowsnake's side, rubbing his hand across his brow as he peered toward the strewn bodies. He removed his sunglasses which had shielded his eyes from the morning sunrise.

As Yellowsnake turned his head toward the Colonel, the Colonel looked at him with eyes that reflected a deep sadness. And those same eyes were betrayed by the light moisture of tears being valiantly held back. They looked at each other, neither of them needing to speak words to describe their feelings. They were jungle fighters and men of war, but they were human.

Even though Yellowsnake was sure the Viet Cong soldiers and even some of the women were deserving of their fate, he knew that thinking further about the bitter attack would not return the innocent lives of the children.

After the troops received their order to begin their entry, they advanced quickly and quietly through the remains of the village. When they reached the smoldering ruins of what, only moments before, was home to many, the Montagnard troops began searching for the tunnels in which the VC had stashed their weapons and ammunition in preparation for their suspected attack.

Within minutes, two tunnels were located. Colonel Lincoln immediately summoned Sergeant Dutro to his side. "Sergeant, send our moles into the tunnels and set a charge that will blow up the entire cache. We can't carry it all back with us, so we'll have no choice but to blow it up." The moles quickly set timed charges inside the storage areas.

The two warriors watched the tunnels explode with a mighty blast, then the Colonel turned to Yellowsnake and said with a smile, "That ought to fix the sneaky cockroaches for a while, don't ya think?"

The troops were feeling noble at having completed their weighty mission and were assembled for departure. Colonel Lincoln gave the signal, "Saddle up, we're getting the hell out of here now." The Colonel ordered his radio man to call back to the compound, alerting the choppers to be waiting for them at the original landing zone. The attack body moved back along it's trail, Yellowsnake remaining at point with the Colonel close behind. "That was one hell of a good raid, Colonel!" he applauded his leader. "We didn't lose a man. They never even had a chance to fire back at us, so it's been a good day."

They followed the narrow trail through slashed underbrush lying about and hadn't traveled far when violence erupted. Machine gun fire spewed at them from all directions. A VC patrol was returning from an attack on another village further to the southwest. The patrol had obviously heard the explosions at the village stronghold and prepared their ambush. The Rangers and Montagnards hit the ground, spreading out for cover. They could see several VC snipers in the trees ahead of them, waiting like vultures for the kill.

Yellowsnake hastened to the side of Colonel Lincoln as the Montagnards and Rangers opened fire, knocking out some of the snipers lurking ahead. There were unfortunately, many remaining VC troops combing the ground, probably surrounding them at that moment. The radio man signaled each group to begin moving forward, then they were hit by unmerciful gunfire from all sides. There were more VC than they had expected. The Colonel's forces were spotting the VC positions and returning fire heavily, picking off black shirts one by one. Thirty minutes later, the enemy's onslaught was slowly diminishing, but the attack was far from over.

The nearby underbrush catapulted upward without warning, sending the Colonel and Yellowsnake diving for cover. Yellowsnake wheeled with an instinctive move from his prone position, spotting three black clad soldiers with rifles in their hands. He pivoted directly toward them, opened fire, and dropped two of the attackers. The third aggressor attempted to sidestep Yellowsnake's gunfire and, in the process, dropped his rifle. Thoroughly frustrated, the maddened soldier pulled a machete from his belt and charged.

Yellowsnake knew his ammo clip was empty as he effortlessly pulled out his knife, bracing himself against the charge of the enraged man. They collided fiercely as the VC took a mighty swing at him, then metal met flesh. For a brief moment, he felt the piercing rip enter his shoulder, then felt it going numb. A large swath of his upper shoulder had been deeply slashed and he was losing blood fast.

Yellowsnake, with one long stride sidestepped the next swing of his opponent's lethal blade, then grabbed him from behind. His next move nearly decapitated the soldier with the brutal strength of a slash to his jugular vein. The soldier would never move again. The Colonel's reflexes weren't nearly as keen as Yellowsnake's, and he was only now pulling his pistol from his holster as he scrambled to his feet. Yellowsnake glanced back, seeing the Colonel was unharmed.

He dropped his knife on the ground next to the Colonel.

And while he rammed another clip into his rifle, he ordered the Colonel to cut away a piece of his shirt to stop the bleeding. The Colonel regained his composure as he tore off a section of Yellowsnake's camouflage shirt and began wrapping the shoulder as tightly as possible. They both knew unconsciousness would soon overtake Yellowsnake if the flow of blood wasn't stopped.

During the scurry, the fight appeared to have ended. But suddenly the tangled underbrush parted with the intensity of a charging bull. Four more VC, half crouched and with blood in their eyes, broke into the tiny clearing, rifles and machetes in hand. And once again, Yellowsnake's instincts took over. He rolled onto his badly slashed shoulder and grabbed the reloaded rifle at his side. It took one swift move as he positioned the rifle butt on his belly, wedged the barrel between his legs, and opened fire. His rifle didn't stop firing until he had emptied his clip on them. He stood up, cautiously checking each bloodied soldier to make sure they were all dead. Then he realized he was becoming lightheaded from loss of blood. The ambushers had been killed, but not without a price.

The Ranger leaders and Montagnards hastily regrouped and took a head count. Sadly, there had been nine Montagnards and one Ranger leader killed in the attack. They were badly damaged and needed to get out fast. They dutifully gathered up the dead and wounded, then embarked on their forced trek toward the landing zone. It had been the longest hour of their lives when they finally detected the welcome sound of whirling chopper blades awaiting their arrival.

The able men loaded the dead and wounded into the belly of the chopper and once they had reached the safety of the clouds, they were soon back at the compound. The wounded were hastened to sick bay where doctors and medics were standing by, for word of the conflict had arrived long before the choppers. Colonel Lincoln stayed close to Yellowsnake's nearly unconscious body, conscientiously loosening the tourniquet. His bleeding had been stopped for the moment. The doctor was wiping his bloodied hands as he approached the table where Yellowsnake lay. With a familiar half-smile on his face, he said,

"Didn't I just fix you up a little while ago? I told you I didn't want to see your face around here again!" Yellowsnake, although barely awake, nodded. "Yes sir, I didn't expect to be back quite so soon."

The deep machete wound across his shoulder required more than forty stitches. It was an ugly slash but, fortunately, the blade had struck him at a diagonal angle across his flesh. Even though the wound had bled profusely, none of the critical muscles and tendons had been completely severed. His mind told him to feel thankful, and damn lucky. He was terribly weakened from the loss of blood, and was ordered to spend at least four days in bed to recover his strength. He was experiencing a lot of pain, so he welcomed the order.

A short time later, the Colonel quietly reappeared at his bedside, leaned over and looked intently into his protector's half open eyes. "Thank God," he whispered, "you're going to be okay. You saved our ass out there today, and I'll never forget it. Get all the rest you need, and I'll see you when I return." Yellowsnake's ears were hearing the Colonel's undisguised sincerity, eliminating any doubt that the commander was indeed his friend.

Two days had passed before his healing body began awakening in sick bay, slowly alerting him to the sound of an incoming chopper arriving to pick up Colonel Lincoln. The Colonel was airborne minutes later, headed toward Danang to report to his senior officers. Later that morning, Major Dawson stopped by Yellowsnake's bed while making his rounds through sick bay. "The Colonel wants you to lay low until he returns. When he gets back, we'll decide what our next move is." He was still nursing the deep ache in his shoulder, and Yellowsnake welcomed Dawson's words.

The attack on the village, and subsequent destruction of the ammunition and weapons in the enemy tunnels proved to be of great value to the battalion. The raids by the Viet Cong were dropping off dramatically, and there were now fewer and fewer sneak attacks on the compound.

Yellowsnake was absent of any specific duties while the Colonel was in Danang, so he spent his time walking around the compound with his arm in an awkward sling. All the while, he kept observing, instructing and advising the other leaders on techniques and tactics as the training of the Montagnards continued at an intensified pace.

When the Montagnards completed their training, they were no longer primitive mountain fighters. They had become a well organized, tightly knit group which was ready to meet the VC head on. And with the passing of each day, Yellowsnake continued watching the ever increasing flow of Navy intruder jets and Army gunship choppers flying over the compound. Their flights were directed toward the Ho Chi Minh trail and it's countless side trails. The war was escalating, and his job was only going to get tougher.

Yellowsnake taught the eager Montagnards everything he knew about tracking an invisible enemy through the jungle. He realized that the more they absorbed, the easier his job might become. After all, this really was their war. Major Dawson was feeling relieved in knowing the VC attacks were decelerating into minor encounters. He began assigning the more skilled Montagnard trainees on short missions to gather needed information.

Colonel Lincoln's chopper unceremoniously returned to it's pad at the compound many days later, arousing the wounded warrior's desire to get back into action. The unsavory scar across his shoulder was healing nicely, and Yellowsnake was again feeling fit. He had suffered some minor tendon damage in his fight with the VC, but it wasn't anything he couldn't live with. All and all, he was nearly perfect and was even more confident that the Colonel was a man he could rely on.

Even though his admired leader was only twelve years Yellowsnake's senior, Colonel Lincoln had become a father figure to him. The confident commander continued to demonstrate wisdom beyond his years. Yellowsnake remained mystified as he often reflected upon the Colonel's unsolicited promise. *I know I can take care of the Colonel, but what did he mean when he said he would take care of me after we get out of here?*

His trip to Danang had required the Colonel to report on the outcome of the VC village attack in his meeting with command staff officers. Although he had been commended by his superiors, he was also admonished to limit his personal involvement in missions to those deemed of highest priority to the Army.

The next morning found Yellowsnake being summoned to the Colonel's headquarters hut. The Colonel smiled as he rose from his chair, then he walked around his desk and firmly grasped Yellowsnake's hand in both of his own. With no intention of releasing his grip, Colonel Lincoln looked Yellowsnake squarely in the eyes.

"Thanks again for saving my butt out there. I'm glad you were at my side. Someday you'll know how much I appreciate it!" he said. The Colonel had placed a high value on Yellowsnake's actions during the mission, and was ready to bestow upon him the medal he so richly deserved.

"I'm recommending you for the Silver Star, along with your next Purple Heart. Medals don't mean much around here, but its the Army's way of saying thanks. Someday, I'll show you this soldier's real gratitude." As usual, Yellowsnake didn't know what all of this meant, but trusted the Colonel at his word.

As the two men spent more and more time together, fewer and fewer formalities existed between their ranks. They had become friends who needed one another and it didn't matter that the Colonel was a high ranking officer and Yellowsnake an ordinary enlisted man.

The longer the undeclared war dragged on, the more the traditional spit, polish and military rituals had vanished from the compound. Especially as it pertained to Yellowsnake, for now he was wearing his long hair Comanche style, and the headband he wore around his forehead was seldom removed. Since their first meeting, the Colonel had never mentioned military appearance or Army expectations to him. And, without saying so, he made it clear he really didn't give a damn what Yellowsnake looked like as long as he was able to do his job.

A few days later, the Colonel told him of his meeting in Danang, and how his personal involvement in leading missions would be limited. "I would like to use the Montagnard trackers whenever possible for the regular day to day missions, and I want you near me at all times. You never know what's going to happen or when we might need to move quickly. In the meantime, I'd like you to work with Sergeant Dutro and the other instructors on improving the tracking skills of the Montagnards. I know there will probably be other missions for us but, for the time being, the ordinary missions will be left to the Montagnards. You and I each have only a few months left over here and I'd like to see to it that both of us get out alive." His words were profound!

Days and weeks passed following their meeting and most of Yellowsnake's time was spent training the Montagnards. At first he took them on short trips to specified points, allowing them to go alone a short distance further before returning to camp on their own. During each training session, he took the eager trackers further along the trails leading in the direction of the VC. To his delight, he was adding to their bank of skills, giving them scores of tips which might someday save their lives.

He taught them how to disarm deadly booby traps and remove land mines planted along the trails–moving them to locations totally unexpected by the enemy. The Montagnards took great joy in learning this tactic.

Strangely, the VC activity had dropped off dramatically and raids against the perimeter of the compound were occurring with even less frequency. It was rumored they were now targeting villages located near the border of Laos and, gratefully, were no longer a threat to the compound. Colonel Lincoln's trips to Danang became more frequent, and each time he was gone a little longer. But sooner or later, he always returned, and each time the stakes were raised.

Chapter 4

The Beast Within

Late September had arrived when the Colonel returned, and within hours Yellowsnake was once again summoned to headquarters hut.

While the Colonel was away Yellowsnake had, for a second time, been awarded a Purple Heart; this time for the machete slash on his shoulder. But far more meaningful to him was the Silver Star awarded him for saving the Colonel's life when they were attacked by the four VC soldiers. The medal itself was unimportant. However, the personal significance of the medal meant a great deal.

His thoughts wandered back to his childhood. *I know what these medals represent, but they'll never mean as much as when the Tribal Council accepted my peacepipe and recognized my manhood. That award will always be more important than anything and making the pipe is a sacrifice I'd make anytime.* No one but Yellowsnake knew. He would have sooner taken a bullet in the eye than fail his mission with the Elders!

As he crossed the compound to Lincoln's headquarters, Yellowsnake reflected on the Colonel's concern over the high level of danger American soldiers were exposed to each day. The U.S. forces were so few in numbers, and were burdened with the inexperience of the South Vietnamese learning to fight their own war.

The impact of Colonel Lincoln's words lingered in his mind. "Our chances of getting out of here alive would be a hell of a lot better if we had more troops at hand."

When he reached the hut, he was escorted into the drab office where he was soon joined by Colonel Lincoln, Major Dawson and Sergeant Dutro. The Colonel looked tired, and the lines of concern across his face showed a deep weariness; he was in need of some extended rest stateside. As the four warriors discussed enemy activities, the Colonel expressed his foreboding over recent reports from Danang.

He had been informed the VC and North Vietnamese regular army troops had established a very large fuel depot and weapon supply area, both of which were dangerously close to the Ho Chi Minh trail. Reconnaissance missions over the area had revealed that large quantities of fuel and arms were being transported in by highly unusual means, and were being stored in caverns and tunnels deep below the ground. The reports confirmed that the fuel, arms and ammunition were being shuttled in on the backs of elephants, discreetly guided and well-camouflaged.

The Colonel got right to the point. "Our job will be to take out the fuel and arms depot and destroy as much of Charlie's force as possible. First, we'll be choppered in as close as possible to our objective and, from there, we'll have to hoof it with as much armament as we can carry. Hopefully, we'll take them out as cleanly as we did on our last attack. Danang wants me to ride herd on this one."

Two days later, the tense but eager Montagnard troops again boarded the choppers. Their battle plan was finalized, and now they were headed perilously close to Ho Chi Minh's turf. In all, their numbers totaled more than one hundred.

The moment they arrived at the drop-off zone, the Montagnard fighters quickly shouldered their heavy load of firepower and started off through the jungle. The agile and well organized column moved skillfully through the thick undergrowth with Yellowsnake at point. They knew the area was hot with VC, but had no sure way of knowing how much opposition they might encounter.

The column took special care to approach the mission target in silence, then spread out in a skirmish line, positioning themselves on their bellies, while inching cautiously closer to observe the enemy's activity. Yellowsnake had positioned himself behind a tree, shoulder to shoulder with the Colonel. Harboring two automatic weapons and his knives, he waited for further instructions. He watched the Colonel carefully study the target zone through his field glasses while whispering to a young lieutenant crouched behind him. As he squinted through his binoculars, the Colonel's scowling voice reflected his disbelief. "Our reports were right. They're bringing their fuel and equipment in with elephants. Can you believe that shit?"

The keen eyed Colonel turned to redirect his field glasses toward the path the enemy soldiers were following, then spotted the area where the fuel was being transported and stored. That was primary their target. They lay quietly for a while, watching the last of the huge gray swaggering bodies disappear into the jungle, returning to an unknown supply source. Then the Colonel made his decision. "Let's do it!"

The mortars and rockets had been set in place and the troops were ready to fire on command. Colonel Lincoln's order to fire was calculated for the moment he felt there would be the greatest number of enemy soldiers gathered in the cleared area. "Fire at will!"

Having been caught by surprise, the menace fell early. The Montagnard troops had formed a semi-circle around the encampment; mortars and rockets were striking the confused enemy from all directions. By now, the fierce mountain fighters had become highly adept with their weapons, and they saturated the fortress with rifle fire until their clips were empty. The smell of sweet revenge was evident as they took dead aim at the soldiers scrambling in utter disarray without any signs of leadership.

Much like the attack against the VC village just weeks earlier, the fire power and devastation obliterated the stronghold. This time, there was no evidence of women or children in the area. There were uniformed NVA bodies strewn everywhere and, as before, a few remaining troops were seen fleeing for protection of the dense jungle.

The Colonel gave the cease-fire signal and, in minutes, the smoke cleared. A squad of Montagnard fighters hustled into the area to secure it, then radioed back to the Colonel that it was safe to enter the area. When they reached the charred, smoke-filled clearing, everyone knew there was a final, but critical task to complete. They had wiped out the stronghold, now they needed to destroy the fuel and arms supply stored in the large tunnels the VC had dug into the hillside.

Once again the brave Montagnard moles, who seemed delighted to enter the dangerous tunnels, went in to place detonation charges to blow up the arms and fuel horde. The timers were set as the Montagnards and Ranger troops quickly vacated the area and withdrew to a safe distance from the tunnels.

Minutes later, the entire countryside blew up. It was an enormous explosion igniting the fuel supply with such intensity that the sky was filled with rocks, trees and dirt, spreading out in every direction. When the great fireball subsided, nothing remained but a burning inferno inside two deep craters. The scorched holes were all that remained of the storage sites.

The Colonel didn't delay as he assembled his troops and ordered them to begin their perilous withdrawal. The leader's instinct told him there were VC troops scattered throughout the area, and they were heading in his direction. He sensed it was only a matter of time until they confronted some VC soldiers head-on while traveling back to the landing site.

The alarm signal went off in Yellowsnake's head as he moved to the point of the retreating column. He was acutely aware of the increased noise and activity of the birds and monkeys ahead of him. He was particularly alert for snipers who might be perched in the trees. Suddenly screeching birds warned him of danger ahead.

The troops spread out quickly and quietly, readying themselves, while knowing another firefight was imminent. Within minutes, the VC were nearly upon them. The Colonel passed the word. "Use your rifles and grenades as much as possible. It's going to be tough to spot them."

The Montagnards sensed the VC were comfortably in range when they commenced their blind fire fight. They began heaving grenades in the direction of the invisible attackers. There was automatic weapon fire everywhere, with bullets flying aimlessly at the unseen enemy.

The Colonel and Yellowsnake lay shoulder to shoulder

waiting, the resolute commander directing the Ranger leaders through his radio man. Yellowsnake was scoping in a three hundred sixty degree sweep, anticipating trouble headed their way at any moment. Unlike their previous mission, the Colonel had drawn his pistol and held it in a ready position. They turned when they heard the bushes breaking twenty yards to their right, and Yellowsnake's judgment took command.

When he saw the black-shirted attackers break out into a small visible area, he opened fire. He was showering bullets back and forth in a sweeping motion, much like the windshield wipers of his old truck. When his clip was emptied, he quickly inserted another and continued at the same pace. He didn't know how many VC he had hit, but it was becoming very quiet. He had to wait.

The Colonel, with his pistol pointed in the direction of the enemy and lying on his belly with his elbows propped in a firing position, was watching Yellowsnake's every move. Yellowsnake motioned to the Colonel to stay put, indicating he would check to see if the unseen attackers were dead. His knees rose slowly from the ground as he cautiously moved toward the bloodied bodies. Suddenly, a head popped up just ahead of him. Not all of them were dead.

A VC soldier–having been hit, but not seriously–had been lying on the ground playing possum. His body stiffened as he raised his automatic rifle and, for reasons unknown, he swung it toward the Colonel. Yellowsnake alertly dropped to his knees in front of the Colonel, shielding him, and while awkwardly crouched, he opened fire on the not-so-dead VC. With the anger of a trapped varmint, the wounded soldier opened fire on him.

Yellowsnake's body was thrown backward with a violent thrust and searing pains shot through his chest. The intensity of the red hot spears told him he had been hit bad. During the firefight, his flak jacket had loosened up and was wide open in front, doing him little good. When he hit the ground, he rolled over flat on his stomach. As he lay face down with his head tilted to one side, he looked back painfully at the Colonel.

The Colonel could see his eyes were still open. Before unconsciousness could overtake him, Yellowsnake moved his arm gently, motioning his finger toward the soldier who had shot him. He was telling the Colonel to move toward the attacker to make sure he was dead and, if not, to finish him off with his drawn pistol. The Colonel nodded his head, inching carefully toward the murderous soldier who had just shot his Comanche friend. When Colonel Lincoln reached the bullet riddled body, he signaled no more shots were needed. The VC had been hit squarely in the forehead.

When he turned to Yellowsnake, the Colonel could see his companion was critically wounded. He quickly summoned the nearby Lieutenant. "Bring help right away!" Two Montagnard medics arrived in seconds with a stretcher and went to work, knowing their swift actions would determine life or death for their fallen friend. Luckily, Charlie's gunfire had subsided and the shower of Montagnard grenades had done their job on the enemy. Yellowsnake was loaded onto a stretcher, with straps placed across his chest and legs to keep him immobile while his rescuers raced through the jungle. The situation had become urgent, and the Colonel and Lieutenant were only steps behind.

The nervous Lieutenant radioed the order for all of the Montagnards and Ranger leaders to group up and make a dash to rendezvous with the awaiting choppers. The firefight had once again proven costly, as there were thirteen Montagnards dead and several others wounded during the attack. The dead and wounded were gathered up and transported to the landing zone first.

It didn't take the Colonel long to realize it was senseless to waste precious time in the jungle trying to patch Yellowsnake up. He ordered the medics to run with him as quickly as possible to the rendezvous point. He knew that the doctors at the compound were the only ones skilled enough to save Yellowsnake's life. The retreating force had kept their senses alert for unseen snipers as they moved swiftly along the trail, toward the anxiously waiting choppers. There was a collective sigh of relief when the helicopters came into view. They had, thankfully, encountered no more enemy, and most important, the choppers had not been discovered.

The birds of rescue were resting gingerly on the ground with rotor blades spinning wildly, their pilots waiting nervously for the soldiers to board. Within minutes they were airborne, en route to the safety of the compound they called home.

Moments after the choppers touched down, Montagnard medics grabbed Yellowsnake's stretcher and shuttled him to the surgical tent. There was blood everywhere. His shirt was drenched, and fresh blood was trickling down the sides of his stretcher onto the dusty ground. His eyes were mere slits as the Colonel jogged alongside him to the surgical tent. They placed him gently on the operating table. The medical team cut away his battered clothing while the surgeon went to work. "My God, this man has four holes in his chest!"

Yellowsnake was fully sedated and woozy from the tremendous loss of blood, rendering him oblivious to the pain. One at a time, the bullets were extracted from his battered chest and four hours later the doctors emerged from their task. They were drenched in sweat and covered with blood. The bullets had been successfully removed, and one of the orderlies was sent to inform the Colonel that Yellowsnake was hanging on to life by a thread. It was a miracle he had survived the ordeal as long as he had. No ordinary man would have survived the trauma of stretcher movement and chopper transport, let alone the lengthy and intensive surgery. The next few hours would prove critical.

The minutes turned into hours, and Colonel Lincoln kept an uneasy vigil in headquarters tent. Evening had turned to night when the tense Colonel stopped by to look in on the wounded warrior. He was told by a very tired surgeon that he had never seen anything like it. Miraculously, none of the bullets entering Yellowsnake's body had hit vital organs. "He's got some heavy bleeding in one lung that we're watching, but the rest of his organs are intact. He's a very, very lucky soldier."

As the transfusions continued throughout the night, Yellowsnake showed tentative signs of recovery. Towards morning he began to stir...he was coming back. The sedation was wearing off and his eyes slowly opened, signaling to everyone that he was alive! When he tried to force his tired eyes to focus on the familiar surroundings, the watchful doctor grasped his hand. "Son, your tribal spirits sure as hell must have been guarding you. Either that, or you've been blessed with nine lives."

Considering the pain he'd endured, Yellowsnake was beginning to feel a little better and most thankfully, the chaplain wasn't giving him his last rites. The doctors examined his extensive wounds, predicting it would be several weeks before he was back on his feet. His prognosis, however, was for complete recovery and, upon hearing the good news, the weary one closed his eyes, sleeping for what seemed an eternity.

He emerged from his long sleep nearly two days later. At his side was the white-coated surgeon, smiling as he placed his hand on Yellowsnake's arm to greet him. "Welcome back."

The doctor once again reassured Yellowsnake that he would be fine after completing his recovery, then disclosed that the Colonel had left early that morning for Danang. But before Lincoln had left, he had instructed the doctor to give something to Yellowsnake when he awoke.

The surgeon pulled open a nightstand drawer next to the bed and removed a small package sealed in plain white paper. He handed it to Yellowsnake, who had no doubt as to its contents. He was right. Gently grasping it, he removed the clustered Purple Heart. Underneath the medal was a handwritten note with a simple message. "You've done your job for me. Now it's my turn to do the same. See you soon."

He lay motionless on his hospital bed with his wounded and healing body yearning for more deep slumber, trying unsuccessfully to grasp the note's meaning. *What do his words mean? Why in the hell doesn't he just tell me what he has in mind?* Little did Yellowsnake realize that Colonel Lincoln, from the moment he first arrived in Vietnam, had been formulating a well-conceived, long range plan. The carefully calculated path lying ahead included Yellowsnake. The crafty Colonel was a man of direction and courage, deliberate and confident in every aspect of his command. And from the time he had looked into Yellowsnake's blue eyes, he had decided there was a place for Yellowsnake in his future plans. Although he was still woozy, the bullet-ridden Comanche lay thinking, puzzling over the Colonel's short message.

During his weeks that followed in bed, Yellowsnake had plenty of time to think. He thought a lot about Maria, his expectant wife. He was blanketed in warm memories of his parents, his sure-footed horse, and faithful dog. But most of all he wondered about his unborn child's future and quietly asked the spirits to shield his loved ones from harm. The surgeon's timely words to him about the protection of his tribal spirits still lingered in his ears.

The mere mention of Spirits had also rekindled Yellowsnake's vivid memory of Shanana, his Yaqui Medicine Woman friend. She had foretold of many perilous days which would pass through his life. *How could I have survived these bullet wounds?* he pondered. *They should have killed me. I'll never know for sure, but I have the feeling she was there all the time. She said she would be there when I needed her. If she was, I know she'll be with me for the rest of my life.* Deep inside, he knew she was with him. He just couldn't see her.

Several days had passed, and while the hospital orderlies were helping him sit upright in his bed, they paused and listened to the familiar sound of chopper blades approaching the compound.

A half smile crossed his face. *Wonder what Colonel John has up his sleeve this time?* He was feeling a great sense of accomplishment by sitting upright and being able to once again eat his food from a mess tray. The hot meal was beginning to settle to his stomach when the tent flap flew open and Colonel Lincoln entered. "How are you feeling, son?" Even though Yellowsnake was not that much younger than the Colonel, he took no offense in being called "son". In fact, he took it as a compliment. "I'll feel a lot better when I get these damn tubes out of my arms."

The Colonel leaned over slowly, placing his hands on the edge of the bed. "That was a gutsy thing you did out there and, believe me, I won't forget it. I know I owe you my life! I always figured you would do what had to be done but, until that moment, I wasn't sure you would lay down your life for me. Now, I have no doubt."

He grinned as he continued. "You know, you've got bigger

balls than those elephants we saw on our mission." Hearing his words, Yellowsnake broke into laughter, then quickly regained his composure for fear of splitting open the stitches decorating his chest.

On his way out of the tent, the Colonel stopped. He turned abruptly and speaking in a quiet, sober tone he said, "By the way, I'm recommending you for the Distinguished Service Cross for your brave actions." And then he was gone. As he settled back onto his pillow, Yellowsnake had a warm feeling inside in knowing that his leader truly appreciated his sacrifices during the fateful attack.

The following morning, Colonel Lincoln briskly entered sick bay in full uniform. He appeared preoccupied as he picked out Yellowsnake's cot in the dim light and pulled up a chair next to him.

"Got your traveling clothes on again Colonel?" grinned Yellowsnake. Colonel Lincoln gave a short laugh and said, "I've been called back to Danang. It may be a few weeks before I return. Headquarters wants me there until we can formulate a plan for all of the incoming troops. I know it'll be several weeks before you're back on your feet, let alone able to resume your duties. By the time you're fully recovered, both of us will be short timers ready to get the hell out of this madness. When I return, I expect to see you fully healed and feeling a hundred percent, so I've asked Major Dawson to restrict your activities. You won't get any jobs which might cause you to re-injure yourself, so you'll be limited to light duty to make damn sure you go home in one piece with me.

"When you're up to it, I want you to confine your activities to working with the Montagnard trackers. Let them do everything you've done all of your life to sharpen their instincts. If they can become half as good at tracking as you, I'll be happy. But don't take them any further into the jungle than safety will permit. If you suspect Charlie is nearby, return to camp." With his sermon complete, the Colonel departed.

Though Yellowsnake felt relief, he was also beginning to feel a dark sinister force within him which had slowly crept into his spirit. It was giving him some worry. He had tasted war, and it didn't taste too bad. The invasive feeling was beginning to trouble him. He wondered, had he evolved from cautious animal to heartless savage? *Have I become a beast who kills just for the sport of it?* After his first few kills, he had felt no remorse for the brutal execution of his enemy. *Has the river of blood of my enemies darkened my soul?* he asked himself. *Dear God, I hope not! Surely my ancestors high above know that I don't kill just for the fun of it. I've got to fight my enemies, just like they did hundreds of years ago. They fought to survive and to preserve their honor. I have to do the same, only this is now.* Yellowsnake was searching his soul, but the answers were still not clear.

Major Dawson soon entered the sick bay tent for his usual rounds and predictably, he stopped at Yellowsnake's cot. The Major asked him the customary questions about how he was feeling, then he got to the point. "You know, you've received some serious wounds over here. Those bullet holes in your chest can get you out of this place and back to the states. Would you like me to arrange for that?"

Yellowsnake was flabbergasted! Although he was aware of the Army's policy, Yellowsnake had never even considered the option of retreat. He propped himself up in bed and hesitated for only a moment. "No sir, I think I'll stick my tour out, just like everyone else. The way I see it, I could have been one of those poor guys going back to the states in a body bag–without a choice! Thanks, but I think I'll stay."

The days turned into weeks and he was finally on his feet. Although he was standing, his legs trembled with unaccustomed weakness and he nearly collapsed. He was feeling a little discouraged as he reflected to himself, *At least I'm on my feet. It could be a hell of a lot worse.* He knew he'd be feeling stronger each day, and was eagerly looking forward to the Colonel's return.

The jovial company clerk passed through the sick bay tossing letters and packages on the wounded soldiers' beds and threw a box toward Yellowsnake, along with a letter. The box was wrapped in plain brown paper, which easily identified it's source. He anxiously tore open the gift from Hotona to discover a smaller box inside which held his favorite chocolate chip cookies. Though they were stale and hard, they tasted good. He savored the sweetness of the gift, then opened the sealed envelope which had been forwarded to him from Danang.

As he opened it, the words caught his eyes. "Yellowsnake– Congratulations! You are the father of seven pound, four ounce black haired Comanche boy! He's healthy, has all fingers and toes. Maria fine. Came through like trooper." Yellowsnake couldn't resist the urge. He let out a war whoop and laughed so mightily that he almost tore his stitches. "Like to name Nikoma. 'Nik' for short. Thought you'd like that," the message continued.

It sounds like a good comanche name. That's fine by me, he thought. The telegram ended with "See you when tour is over. Stay healthy." and was signed by Maria's parents.

He lit a cigarette and walked slowly toward the mess tent for a cup of coffee. He strutted like a proud peacock. His ancestral bloodline would be carried on by the newborn Comanche. At the moment, life couldn't be any better.

Soon, the Colonel returned from Danang. Only a few hours had passed before Yellowsnake was summoned to his hut. He quietly approached Colonel John Lincoln's desk, then the familiar hard-backed chair spun around to face Yellowsnake. "The Major tells me you didn't have the brains to get out of this place. Is that right?"

"Yes, sir," answered Yellowsnake, smirking proudly. "I figured you might be needing me again and besides, I didn't want to leave before my deal with you was complete."

The Colonel chuckled, then added, "Seriously Snake, I'm happy you're willing to gut it out with me." After checking on the progress of Yellowsnake's nearly healed wounds the Colonel shared with him a few brief details of his recent trip to Danang. Then, changing the subject, the Colonel continued in a different tone, "This son of a bitchin' war is going to heat up soon. My job with command in Danang is nearly complete. You and I are going to be out of here in a few weeks and we're both going to

74

be home by early next year. When we return to the states, command is transferring me to intelligence in Washington, D.C. That's my next assignment."

"As for you," he continued. "I'll see to it that you are transferred to any Army installation in the United States you choose. Just let me know what kind of duty you want and I'll take care of it. For now, that's the least I can do for you. Obviously, you wouldn't want to come to D.C. That's not your kind of place and, frankly, I'm not too anxious to be there myself. But I'm afraid I have no choice."

He was thinking carefully about the offer, and Yellowsnake didn't hesitate to give him his answer. "Colonel, when you and I leave this place, the first thing I'd like to do is go home and see my wife and kid."

The Colonel smiled, "Of course! Congratulations, by the way. I heard you became a father while I was gone!" The Colonel gave him a verbal jab which only a friend would tolerate. "I didn't think you had it in you, fearless warrior."

Yellowsnake laughed as he continued his thought. "Colonel, if I have a choice, I think I'd like to return to Fort Benning and go back to what I was always comfortable with. Teaching hand to hand combat to the troops."

His eyebrows raised and without hesitation, the Colonel accepted his decision. "If you're sure that's what you'd like to do, I'll see that it's taken care of."

With the passing of each war-torn day, more and more American troops arrived at the–now bulging–compound. Meanwhile, Yellowsnake's strength had nearly returned to what it was before his injury. The Colonel's duty order was clear, so he resumed his duties of training the Montagnards in jungle tracking. He also passed along tips to the new Ranger advisors on how best to handle the Montagnards during their training maneuvers. By now, the Montagnards had become a strong contingent force. Their numbers had steadily increased and they had become very skilled fighters. The perimeters of the compound had become a well-manned fortress and skirmishes with the VC were now a rarity.

The Colonel had returned to headquarters in Danang and

would not be seen again by Yellowsnake until his final visit late in 1961. He knew that when the Colonel returned, both of them would prepare to leave Vietnam, returning home to the realities of a sane world. His hair had now grown long over his shoulders, and his headband had become a permanent part of his attire. The warrior chief image he cast was enough to scare any wishful enemy who might attempt to kill him. *I wonder if I'll be able to take this thing off my head and act like a normal man when I return?*, he wondered to himself. Yellowsnake had some serious misgivings, but he kept them to himself. If he harbored a beast within his spirit, it would somehow have to be killed. His deepest thoughts told him that only a person possessing visions of the future might know when the beast would die. His dear and mysterious Medicine Woman friend, Shahana, held the power to slay the beast, if she was still watching over his spirit.

As 1961 neared its end, he became restless, knowing it wouldn't be long before he'd be leaving. In the back of his mind, he still puzzled over the vagueness of the Colonel's words. "You take care of me and I'll take care of you." *Well, the Colonel got me the assignment I requested, but really, any commander could have done the same. I wonder if that's what he meant when he said he'd take care of me? It doesn't seem like much.* Yellowsnake had no way of knowing how he fit into the Colonel's long range plan.

When the Colonel's helicopter arrived at the compound for what would prove to be his final visit, Yellowsnake began his painful transformation. The ordeal was much like a snake shedding it's skin. He visited the camp barber and had several inches sheared off his long brown mane. Reluctantly, he removed his tattered headband, knowing the soiled band of cloth symbolized many months of life and death struggles. He had arrived as a young soldier who had quickly learned to live as the jungle dictated. Now he was a seasoned warrior, engrained with the awakened instincts of a killer animal. For the first time in several months, he prepared to dress himself in a regulation army uniform. Although he was properly dressed in military fashion, he felt uncomfortable knowing that he no longer blended into the lush, inhospitable habitat of the jungle.

The uneasy day of departure finally arrived in early 1962. His battalion had successfully completed it's tour in war-torn Vietnam. Most happily, it was time to return home.

Two hours prior to departure, Yellowsnake was summoned one last time to headquarters. He sauntered into the Colonel's office, his spit shined boots squeaking with each step, Yellowsnake's starched khaki shirt boldly displayed his Distinguished Service Cross, Silver Star and clustered Purple Heart. He approached the Colonel's desk, stood at attention and waited sheepishly for the Colonel's reaction.

"Well, I'll be damned. If you don't look like a poster soldier!" The Colonel's remark broke the tenseness of the moment, and both men laughed quietly. Their chuckles were directed at the unspeakable gulf between the life they had come to consider as normal, and the life of civilization just a few hours away. Only the two of them could appreciate the mad secret that blooded warriors share.

After their amusement died down, they were both silent for a moment, then the Colonel spoke. "Yellowsnake, I know that all during this war, you've never really understood what our deal was about. All I can tell you is there will be some important things happening in the future. I have a strong suspicion that I know what lies ahead for me at the Pentagon. And I strongly suspect those things will include you. They've given me my assignment, and you're orders are taking you to Fort Benning. However, as time passes, the pot will start to boil, and when it does, you'll be hearing from me. I'll leave you my phone number where I can be reached in D.C. And I'm telling you, if you need me, call! I'll be there for you. You've done more than I could expect of any friend, and I wish you a safe and speedy return to the States."

With a hesitation reflecting their unspoken mutual admiration, they shook hands for what Yellowsnake assumed might be the last time. They had become trusted friends and, at the very least, would never forget each other.

Yellowsnake's transport helicopter lifted off its pad and headed toward Danang, causing him to stare into the blue sky with mixed thoughts... *In a way, I'm glad I'll never be seeing this country again. It's been a wild ride on a dangerous roller coaster!*

Chapter 5

Green Berets

Yellowsnake seated his scarred, bullet torn body into a comfortable position, knowing he was aboard one of the huge military transport aircraft carrying the 11th Ranger Battalion back to the United States. He looked out the window and viewed, for what he perceived to be his last time, the green mountain jungle canopy below. The battalion had completed it's one year tour of duty in Vietnam and, with the exception of Yellowsnake, was being transferred to a new assignment elsewhere. He was restful and drifting on the tuneless drone of the aircraft, his thoughts returning to his perilous year in the jungle.

He silently recalled his parade of missions into the jungle tracking the enemy. His flashbacks reminded him that after he had received his first wound, the inbred precautions of a wild animal had fully awakened in him. The change had surprised him at the time, but he told himself, *Being alone in the jungle doesn't allow you the luxury of acting like a human being. You've got to act like an animal or you won't survive.* And, of course, he was right. Fortunately, he was able to sustain a level of acute awareness in the jungle, and the many missions which followed his first wound became almost routine, or so it seemed. But every mission produced results. Because he had dependably called in the location of the enemy, each mission he completed undoubtedly saved the lives of many troops. But he was finding that the acute awareness which had become routine in his jungle survival had become akin to an addiction. Things began to look and feel drab away from the hunt. Although he had never been a social extrovert, Yellowsnake had become increasingly impatient with social niceties.

His mind had become hardened to death, both the enemy's and his own. After his first encounter with the VC, he had no longer felt remorse in killing. The enemy were just merciless savages and deserved to be killed. Or, was he the real savage, and they his undeserving victims? While his aircraft approached its landing point in the United States, he pondered his future, *What will life be like now? I was my own man in the jungle. I was my own animal.* Could he cope in the jungle which lay ahead? He had to.

Ever so gently, the transport touched down and began it's taxi to a stop. Yellowsnake began saying his last good-byes to the members of his unit. Although many of the seasoned veterans had become his comrades, he was still a loner. He departed the aircraft and retrieved his duffel bag. He was again alone, only this time he was alone in a new jungle.

After he checked in with the airfield traffic coordinator, he arranged to hop a short military flight headed to Oklahoma. Within hours, his feet were back on Indian soil. He had not called ahead to inform anyone of his arrival and would simply show up; that had always been his way. His tired body had endured a long, dusty ride as he arrived at the familiar setting of the reservation. He paid the driver and propped his duffel bag against a nearby stone wall, then headed for the general store. He gave the tattered old screen door a gentle kick with his boot, stepping inside the store. The person foremost in his mind stood behind the counter, looking as beautiful as ever.

He walked quietly toward her. Maria didn't look up immediately and then, lifting her head and looking him squarely in his eyes, her eyes became as large as saucers. She moved with the grace of a dancer, rotating her body and sliding through the swinging counter door and, throwing her arms out wildly, pulled Yellowsnake to her. "Thank goodness you're back!" He said nothing as he moved his face close to hers, kissing her gently. Their many months of separation would soon become a fading memory and for the moment, words were not necessary.

They tightly embraced one another as Yellowsnake told her he had just returned and was here to stay. Happy tears spilled from the corners of her eyes as he held her close and, with his callused fingers touching her cheek, he glanced over her shoulder. On the countertop behind her was a tiny bundle. The little blue blanket propped in a small basket was filled with movement. He saw something barely protruding over the edge of the soft blanket. It was a rounded pink shoulder and a small curious head laden with thick black hair sticking out comically in all directions. Without asking, Maria knew what had caught Yellowsnake's eye.

He loosened his grip on her warm, firm body, then walked toward the carefully wrapped nest. The baby's arms flailed wildly at the sight of the strange soldier. It's squeals and gurgling sounds clearly demanded attention. As he neared the unfamiliar bundle, almost crouching to look this new prize squarely in the eyes, Yellowsnake began to smile. The noisy new Comanche in his life also had blue eyes.

Yellowsnake gently lifted Nikoma from his tightly secured seat and placed him on his shoulder. Nikoma's head bobbed awkwardly against his neck. He placed his hand tentatively on the baby's thick, soft bush of hair, thinking to himself, *I like the name. It's not exactly the same as Nokona, my great, great grandfather, but it has a nice ring to it. We'll call him Nik, just like Maria suggested.*

They were a proud and happy couple, standing close to each other with the infant warrior grasping for Yellowsnake's ear. The gentle touch of Nikoma's long fingers tickled him. Yellowsnake and Maria talked excitedly, neither of them saying a great deal before being interrupted by the other, both knowing there would be plenty of time to share their thoughts.

He placed Nik carefully back in his baby seat, telling Maria he would return when she was through working and take her home. Maria had been renting a small home during Yellowsnake's long absence and tonight, her home would be his home. He kissed her as he left her father's store and grabbed his dusty duffel bag thinking, *I'll just hoof it from here and surprise the folks.*

He toted the bulky bag on his shoulder and in minutes he arrived at the door of his childhood home. His mother felt the reverberation of his boots on the worn front steps. Hotona pushed open the screen door and squinted into the bright sunlight to see who had come to visit. She was adorned in her apron, and so startled at his arrival that she dropped the newspaper she was carrying under her arm. She squealed and threw her arms around her returning warrior. "I'm so happy you're home!" Simple words spoken in tones of profound relief.

"It's great to be back." Deep in his badly scarred stomach, however, Yellowsnake wasn't sure his answer reflected his true feelings.

Her wrinkled arms were wrapped around Yellowsnake's long, lean arm as she led him through the house and straight for the kitchen. She caringly sat him down in his customary chair. He watched her happy eyes while she poured him a steaming cup of coffee. He knew he was home.

She listened patiently about the trivial details of his trip home, then asked, "Tell me about you. Are you okay?" Hotona had never been given many details of Yellowsnake's experiences and wounds in the jungle. The army, in its guarded wisdom, had informed both Hotona and Maria that he had suffered serious wounds, but was alive. He relived each encounter which resulted in a wound to his body with great detail. As he spoke, he unbuttoned his shirt and removed it, exposing his undershirt. He lifted his t-shirt, showing her the scar near his stomach which had become his first wound. Then, moving upward toward his shoulder, he peeled back his sleeve and displayed the long, ugly diagonal machete scar which had required over forty stitches.

His graphic description intensified. Hotona's kitchen was transformed into the jungle as he continued describing the details of each encounter. He lifted his shirt entirely over his head, displaying the scarred bullet wounds peppered across his torso. While she studied his wounds and then his face, she said in a mother's serious tone, "I knew the spirits would be watching over you. I knew you'd come back in one piece."

He felt her words were exposing an, as yet, unacknowledged truth. *Perhaps Shahana and the spirits really were with me. Mother is certain they were.* Their dinner hour was approaching when Jimmy arrived home. He kicked his shoes into the kitchen corner, glanced at the table where his son sat bare-chested, then at Hotona and back at the table again with a blank and questioning look on his face. He was dumbfounded. Yellowsnake slid his chair back and walked toward him, gripping his father's strong arms with hands that had slain the enemy. Jimmy wordlessly took in his son's wounds, then he smiled proudly at his healthy Comanche son. Now, for the first time in more than a year, the whole family was again united.

Yellowsnake munched a sweet roll with his coffee, keeping a keen eye on the clock since he wanted to be sure he wasn't late for Maria. He had promised to pick her up at five thirty.

Like so many times before, he borrowed his father's dilapidated pickup truck which had, for the past year, been stored behind their wooden shed.

An hour later he, Maria and Nikoma arrived at the small, light gray bungalow in which Maria had been living the past year, his pulse beating rapidly. Tonight he would be sleeping under a shingled roof for the first time in many months.

When they had finished their evening meal, he accompanied Maria to the small bedroom and watched as she gently placed Nik in his tiny bed, tucking him in for the night.

They softly turned to each other and no further words were spoken. Yellowsnake placed his long arms firmly around her body and pulled her close, knowing that in moments they would again be sharing the same burning emotions which had flamed so wildly during the short few days of their honeymoon. With only the night's cool breeze between them, he ran his hand across her bare, firm breast. She, in turn, tenderly touched his places of woundedness. He silently engulfed her with his passionate love. Their senses were ignited like a raging wildfire.

The long night brought a new awareness to him. As they embraced with their limbs entwined, Yellowsnake felt a sense of peace unlike any feeling he'd ever experienced. In the heat of their passion, he had a sense of conquering his prey, yet feeling himself conquered.

She watched the first rays of morning sunshine enter their bedroom window, then Maria quietly slipped out of bed and looked in on Nik. She whispered to call her mother and father, letting them know that she wouldn't be coming to work until much later. Nik was still sleeping as they sat at the kitchen table, and as with Hotona, Yellowsnake gave Maria a graphic picture of his year in the jungle.

And, in turn, Maria tenderly shared the day to day things she'd done in his absence to occupy herself. Her life, compared to his, sounded so mundane. The words from her lips made it obvious that she had missed him a lot during his long absence. The minutes passed and it was becoming unmistakably clear that while he had been fighting his war, her ties to the reservation and her parents had grown even stronger. Though he knew she had missed him deeply, he realized she had no desire to leave the reservation and become part of the white man's world. He had hoped that while he was gone, she would cultivate a need to explore the world outside the reservation, a world which she had rarely experienced.

Yellowsnake gently reminded her that although he was home on his thirty day furlough, he was not yet out of the army. He was going to be stationed at Fort Benning as he had requested. He wouldn't be returning to the jungle, but he still had to fulfill his obligation to the army. "When I leave here to return to Fort Benning, I'll find a home for the three of us so we can be together while I'm instructing. Then I'll be able to see both of you most every night," he said assuredly.

He watched Maria's eyes, sensing that things were not right. Then she spoke. "I think it would be better if you went to Fort Benning alone. Nik and I need to stay on the reservation. You won't be that far away and you'll be able to visit us on a regular basis, so that will be just as good."

Yellowsnake knew he was not going to win the battle. Her religious beliefs and strong ties to church and family would prevent her from ever leaving the reservation. She had an unmovable conviction in her mind, deciding that his and everyone else's life would be better if she and Nikoma didn't move to Fort Benning. She knew his job would at times require him to be gone for long days and nights, and felt he would have an overriding devotion to his duty. "I'm your wife and love you but, just as deeply, I believe we must stay with my family here on the reservation." Yellowsnake was disappointed, though not surprised by her decision. He should have known better and perhaps he had known it all along, but had blocked it out of his mind.

The days raced by and found the three of them together day and night, with Maria working an occasional short day. She wanted their family to be together as much as possible before Yellowsnake departed. His thirty days of leave came to an end far too soon.

Saying goodbye to his beautiful Comanche wife and son was not easy, but Yellowsnake had no choice. He was saddened knowing she would not be joining him at Fort Benning, but he respected her deep-seated convictions. He would not impose his will upon her.

Yellowsnake said his good-byes to Hotona and his father, and was given the keys to the old pickup truck at Jimmy's insistence. "Here, take the old son of a bitch. I don't want it anymore. You can have it, and maybe it'll get you home from Benning, if you're lucky." Yellowsnake placed his duffel bag in the bed of the old truck, then paused for a moment and took in his surroundings: the dusty open land, the unrelentingly blue sky, the good people who loved him. He knew the place would always be the same and the people would keep loving him no matter where he went or what he did. Yellowsnake muscled the old cab door open and climbed in alone.

He gave them a final nod as he backed out of the drive and headed off to Fort Benning, already feeling lonely in the new life which awaited him.

Yellowsnake was still feeling saddened by Maria's decision as he traveled the long, monotonous road to his new duty assignment. His thoughts soon reverted to his more recent life in Vietnam. While he drove in a semi trance, his mind drifted, recalling the array of events which had occurred from the first day he arrived in the forbidding country. The gutsy little Montagnards, the vicious unrelenting VC attacks on American outpost camps and sadly, their own villages. He remembered the caravan of huge gray elephants he'd seen serving as supply trucks to pack in fuel and munitions for the VC and, above all, he remembered his trusted Colonel. Since he had returned home, he had, most disturbingly, often found himself disoriented in settings that should have been comfortable and familiar. Most men would feel comfortable, but not the jungle fighter!

Throughout his many dangerous and eventful treks through the jungle, one thing had always intrigued him. Whenever he was tracking his enemy or traveling a lonely uninhabited trail, it was commonplace to see an American fighter jet pass overhead or hear the whirl of helicopter blades off in the distance. Invariably, the same thought occurred each time the helicopters were near. *Those chopper pilots really have it made. They're a smooth bunch. They always seem to be in control, with nerves of steel and hand to eye coordination as precise as robots performing an endless task. If those guys can fly, then I'm damn well up to it. Those babies sure look like a lot of fun.*

Of course, being a chopper pilot meant they were properly commissioned army officers. They had been skillfully taught during their months of training, but what the hell, it wasn't anything he couldn't accomplish. Yellowsnake knew someday he would have to get a meaningful civilian job, and flying those birds looked like an exciting way to make a living. His momentary dream had eased his sadness, and had generated a new spark of hope for his days ahead.

He arrived at Benning hours later. The familiar sights, sounds and smells of the camp smothered him, welcoming him back to the world he had known more than a year earlier. The difference he immediately noticed was the vastly increased number of troops scurrying about the base. He presented his orders to the Sergeant manning the main gate and was issued a base permit for his old pickup truck.

He entered the brown brick building which housed the Battalion Headquarters command unit and introduced himself as "Yellowsnake", as he handed the friendly clerk his orders and personnel file. The surprised clerk, in turn, handed his orders and personnel file to the Captain sitting nearby. The Captain glanced at Yellowsnake's orders, then he entered the Battalion Commander's office directly behind him.

In a few minutes, Colonel Bradford stepped out of his office. "Come in, soldier, let's take a look at your orders." He was startled, and Yellowsnake wondered why he was suddenly being ushered into the Colonel's office. After all, he was only reporting in for his new duty.

He obediently entered Colonel Bradford's office and as he stood at neat attention in front of the desk, he was told to take a seat. While he curiously examined Yellowsnake's yellowed and tattered personnel file, the Colonel spoke in monotone, "It says here your name is Yellowsnake. Our soldiers are all known by their given names, but it appears you've been given the privilege of being known by a name which goes back to your Indian heritage."

"Yes sir, that's true," Yellowsnake confirmed.

The Colonel looked slightly bewildered, as he spoke. "I guess we won't have a problem with that. Besides, it sounds like you have some friends in pretty high places. A couple of weeks ago, I received a call from a Colonel Lincoln at the Pentagon in Washington, D.C. He gave me a run down on who you are and what role you played with him during your tour in Vietnam. Sounds like you had a hell of a time over there. Colonel Lincoln was telling me that in spite of all of the choices of duty available to you, you chose to be back here at Benning. That's surprising!"

Yellowsnake hesitated for only a moment before he replied. "Not really sir. This is where I would want to be if I wasn't in Vietnam."

The ring of the Commander's words left no mistake that he was still doubting Yellowsnake's wisdom. "Colonel Lincoln told me you would like to resume teaching survival and hand to hand combat to our men. With respect for the Colonel's rank, I'll certainly do everything I can to see you're given duty you're comfortable with. It looks like you did a fine job when you were here with the 11th Rangers a year or so ago, so I see no reason why you can't resume those same duties.

"You realize, of course, this is a rather strange situation. Remember, you're still officially a member of the 11th Rangers, but you're on special assignment here. However, I don't see why it should make any difference. A Ranger is a Ranger as far as I'm concerned."

Yellowsnake agreed as he listened to Colonel Bradford's accommodating words, and now realizing Colonel Lincoln hadn't forgotten him, he was feeling more at ease. Colonel

Bradford ended Yellowsnake's brief duty description, saying, "You've probably observed the number of troops that are swarming around here. As you can well imagine, this thing in Vietnam is really heating up. We're moving a lot of troops in and out, and it's damn important that we get them prepared for what's ahead of them in Nam. By the looks of your file, you mastered all the tricks of surviving while you were there. Hopefully, you can pass that information onto our boys. They're a green bunch, but they're mean and cocky as hell, and when they leave this training sector, they'll be headed to Nam."

Bradford cordially dismissed Yellowsnake, telling him to see the company Sergeant next for his barracks assignment. Then he concluded. "Your personnel file says you were married sometime back and have a child. Will your family be joining you here at the base?"

A shadow crossed Yellowsnake's face as he spoke. "No, sir. They'll be staying at the reservation. I couldn't persuade them to join me." After he received his room assignment in the instructors' barracks, the weary tracker unpacked his gear. He couldn't help overhearing the conversations taking place around him. With some sadness, he observed that the voices and mannerisms did not reflect those of the jungle fighters he had become so accustomed to. These men, unlike him, had never seen the jungle. They were a new breed of Ranger instructors who had never experienced war, and, as a result, had an entirely different attitude toward living and dying.

He soon was back in the thick of it, performing his day to day duties of training new troops in jungle fighting and survival. He continued to stress the need for them to avoid making costly mistakes, especially those which might end their lives. They needed it badly.

The instructors around him also noticed the difference in his style, and in particular, his depth of knowledge in the technique in survival and killing. This man, they observed, was teaching and speaking about the art of staying alive from firsthand experience.

It wasn't long before he was closely acquainted with the other instructors, giving them inside tips on how to stay alive in warfare. Since none of them had spent any time in Vietnam, they eagerly absorbed his knowledge, knowing it might someday save their lives.

The days turned into weeks and, just as quickly, the weeks turned into months of perpetual training. Like Colonel Bradford had said, the troops arriving at Fort Benning were indeed a different breed of soldier. They were mean and cocky and, almost without exception, seemed arrogant. The large number of troops now included a select unit of eager fighters who were assigned to Yellowsnake and a few of his fellow instructors. The elite group had been carefully selected as the cream of the crop of Special Force troops undergoing training.

If they were successful in completing their training, these select soldiers, known as Green Berets, would be sent to fight in Vietnam. They were, without a doubt, a feisty bunch.

They had been chosen for the Green Berets after being screened for their intellect, physical skills and endurance for the future action they would face in southeast Asia. They didn't hesitate to speak with a tone of superiority in their voice, but paid attention when Yellowsnake spoke. They listened closely to his words of wisdom when it came to fighting and outwitting Charlie. Stories had soon spread about his tour in Vietnam, and how he was awarded his clustered Purple Heart, Silver Star and the Distinguished Service Cross. They were valorous awards, and drew the attention of every Beret trainee in the unit.

Throughout his intense instruction, the blue eyed Comanche never hesitated to embarrass or intimidate the high spirited fighters. It was all too evident that they were a cocky bunch and acted like they knew it all. It wouldn't be long before they found they didn't know a fraction of what he was about to teach them.

His duty assignment was now focused on teaching the Green Beret troops the advanced techniques of jungle fighting, and especially how to avoid being killed by the devious moves and traps of the VC. When the well-trained and highly disciplined groups of egotistical warriors completed their training, they were ready for the real war ahead of them.

He would never forget one of the many eight week training sessions he was conducting during which a young Sergeant was placed among the Beret trainees for special training like all the others. An army regular, he was a loner and had no attachment to the Green Berets. The soldier was being trained and groomed for a top secret mission unrelated to the activities of the Berets.

Yellowsnake had not been given any details about the man's future assignment when he was requested to personally supervise and direct him during his hand to hand combat training. The soldier had to become not only as skilled, but more skilled than the other trainees. He had ahead of him a perilous mission, known only by the highest levels of army command.

The young Sergeant was a fast learner and quickly absorbed Yellowsnake's teaching and techniques. He was becoming extremely adept at handling a knife; he was good, but not quite as good as Yellowsnake. After all, the young Sergeant was not a Comanche.

It was a hot night following a grueling field session and the Beret trainees were descending upon the chow hall for evening mess. Yellowsnake spotted the quiet Sergeant walking toward his barracks for the night. Two Green Beret soldiers who were part of the regular training program abruptly stopped him. Yellowsnake approached the threesome, and could hear their voices becoming louder and louder.

It was obvious that the troublesome pair, for whatever reason, had chosen to confront the Sergeant. They knew he was assigned to participate in the Beret training program, but was not a member of their elite group. His intrusion into their eliteness had pissed them off, and their anger burned brightly.

As Yellowsnake got closer, he could hear the challenging words of the Berets being directed at the Sergeant. The Berets were pumping the Sergeant for information and taunting him. "It's none of your damn business, and who the hell do you guys think you are anyway?" the Sergeant had replied.

Yellowsnake heard the Berets angry threat. "Hey man, we're the real Green Berets. You know who the hell we are! And if you think you're as bad as us, just step aside Sarge, and you'll get your ass kicked."

Yellowsnake waited to see what the Sergeant's reaction would be. He was sure a fight would break out at any moment.

Instead, the Sergeant turned squarely and faced the Green Beret hotheads. He watched the Sergeant's face redden slowly, his ears absorbing their strong verbal attack while he stood unflinching, his fists clenched at his sides. Suddenly, the Sergeant, with the good sense Yellowsnake had hoped would prevail, turned and did an about face, walking slowly away from his antagonists. His contained anger infuriated them even more. They had been beaten, and the Sergeant had never lifted a finger.

The young Sergeant walked slowly toward Yellowsnake while still ignoring the jesting remarks of the belligerent trainees, then his eyes acknowledged Yellowsnake's presence. When he stopped momentarily, he spoke with fire in his voice. "I'll be glad when those assholes are shipped out of here and over to Vietnam where they belong. They think they're bad asses, but they'll be singing a different tune when they return from Nam. That is, if they return."

Yellowsnake just smiled and nodded in agreement. No words were necessary between the two men, for both possessed the strength of good judgment.

The wise soldier knew Yellowsnake was silently commending him for having made an intelligent decision in walking away from the instigators. Little did anyone know, Yellowsnake included, the outsider would soon be in Vietnam leading an extremely dangerous mission deep into the stronghold of the Viet Cong in North Vietnam. Word arrived months later that the Sergeant had successfully led a rescue mission into two prisoner of war camps to rescue crew members of downed aircraft. Many of the POW's he led out had long since been declared dead or missing in action. And like Yellowsnake, the heroic Sergeant would receive the Distinguished Service Cross for his actions. His wisdom in restraining himself that day on the base proved to be one of the traits which had kept him alive during his perilous mission. His discipline and courage, not his mouth, had kept him out of harm's way.

When he returned to his barracks that evening, Yellowsnake retold the story of the encounter between the Sergeant and the troublemakers, disgustedly telling them how the Green Berets thought they were real bad asses. His story caused an outburst of laughter from the other Rangers. The instructors knew that despite their eliteness, the Berets were inexperienced trainees just like everyone else. It soon became a private joke among them to refer to the trainees as the "bad asses". They were bad all right, but only in their sense of superiority. That trait would vanish after they arrived in Vietnam.

Two years roared past and 1964 was just around the corner. During those fleeting years, Yellowsnake returned whenever time permitted to see Maria and Nikoma on the reservation.

He wasn't much on writing letters, so his means of keeping his family informed was limited to what he passed on to them each time he returned. Whenever he was home, he asked Maria the same question. "Will you come back with me to Fort Benning?" And in each instance, he received the same answer. "No, I'm sorry, I can't leave the reservation. Nik and I must stay here."

He expected no sympathy when discussing the matter with his parents because he knew in his heart that this was Maria's unwavering decision. He, unfortunately, had chosen not to believe it when he was younger, and was now paying the price.

Yellowsnake was always loved and welcomed by Maria and Nikoma when he returned home, but that love and welcome always remained within the confines of the reservation. He dearly loved and admired his young Comanche son, and knew the boy's youth was destined to be spent there for the most part. He could only hope that someday Nik would be able to escape the reservation like he had years earlier.

The months of relentless training continued at a frantic pace, and with the year nearing it's end, Yellowsnake grew restless and anxious for a change of routine. He had heard nothing from Colonel Lincoln during his two years as an instructor and he wondered if the Colonel had forgotten him. The conversation which had occurred between them years earlier still lingered in his mind. "You take care of me and I'll take care of you." He still didn't have the answer to what the Colonel meant by his words. *The Colonel has probably forgotten all about me by now, and is buried in his work at the Pentagon.* Yellowsnake wondered if he would ever see his friend again.

Although Yellowsnake enjoyed his day to day duties, they had become routine and, unfortunately, dull. When he thought about Vietnam, his present duty assignment bore no resemblance to the daily uncertainties of jungle fighting. He had gained satisfaction, however, in knowing that the hundreds of Green Beret troops he had trained over the years had been taught all the skill and cunning that could be implanted in any one soldier's mind. If they didn't survive, it was not because they had been poorly trained.

With 1963 nearly concluded, Yellowsnake's enlistment in the United States Army was about to end. He had done his job, and done it well. He had performed everything that was asked of him from the day he had enlisted to the time he met Colonel Lincoln and agreed to their strange deal. He had, most importantly, fulfilled his commitment to training the Green Berets for their future warfare in Vietnam. There was nothing more he could do.

He was feeling a little remorseful as he packed his duffel bag for the final time. After saying goodbye to his friends and comrades, he was ready to leave the Army. He had received his discharge papers from the Captain with a mixture of pleasure and sadness. When Colonel Bradford overheard the Captain wishing him well upon leaving the Army, he stepped out of his office and offered his handshake. "Yellowsnake," he said, "I wish you the very best. You've done a good job as a soldier with this man's' outfit, and I'm sure you'll do well as a civilian."

Bradford's final words to the departing warrior rang piercingly clear. "By the way, did you ever hear anything more from your Colonel friend at the Pentagon?" Yellowsnake hesitated, then replied somewhat sadly, "No sir, I haven't heard from him in a long time."

With a mighty heave, he threw his frayed duffel bag in the back of the badly deteriorated pickup truck. Yellowsnake was seeing Fort Benning for his last time, and once again he was alone and entering into an ever changing world. He had been freed from the adventure and regimen provided by the Army, and now he had to reenter a world of greatly expanded horizons. For the first time in many years, he was without a destination.

He wasn't afraid, but at the same time he was unaccustomed to traveling through life without a clear view of his next objective.

Chapter 6

The Comanche Chopper

Yellowsnake was not yet accustomed to the idea that he was now a civilian as he poked along at a slow, steady speed in his weary old pickup truck along the familiar potholed highway. He struggled relentlessly to free himself of the imprinted mental habits which had gradually taken over his mind during his year in the jungle. He knew his thoughts would have to blend with those of the white man's world he was once again entering.

His tattered duffel bag bounced from side to side in the rusty bed of the truck. Tucked securely in his bag were his most valuable possessions; his much traveled Comanche knife, and the medals he had earned with bravery and blood. He was feeling apprehensive as he bounced along the washboard road leading to the reservation. The reservation was home to his wife and son, but sadly, he knew it could never again be a permanent resting place for his restless spirit.

Nevertheless, he was more than eager to see Maria and Nikoma, along with the rest of his family. His first stop was the general store. When he eased through the screen door, his presence immediately caught the eye of Maria. Her delight startled him. She left a customer standing at the counter and threw her arms around his neck, grasping him tightly. He held her snug to his body, feeling her long black hair brushing his face. Then, Yellowsnake was surprised by the light touch of a much smaller hand on his leg. It was Nikoma!

He had pushed his way through the small swinging gate and his short legs had brought him to Yellowsnake's starched khaki pant leg. Although Nikoma knew little of his Comanche father, his young mind told him the towering figure was a member of the family and an important part of his life.

While he held the squirming three year old in his arms and looked admiringly into his deep blue eyes, Yellowsnake waited patiently while Maria finished filling her customer's order. He reached deep into his pocket and retrieved a Swiss army knife which he often carried with him. He placed it in Nik's tiny hand, watching as the youngster's eyes grew wide, his pudgy little hands holding it as though he had been given a priceless treasure.

When his anxious wife returned, the three of them again held each other close and talked eagerly of returning to the small gray bungalow which had become a comfortable retreat during his visits from Fort Benning.

A while later, a more relaxed and happy Yellowsnake left Maria and Nikoma and climbing back in his truck, pointed it toward his parents' home. He, predictably, surprised his mother and father with his unceremonial, but welcome arrival. He was promptly herded by Hotona into her kitchen, and while he sat in his familiar chair at the table, he inhaled Hotona's baked goods, recounting the final weeks of his army enlistment.

Hotona listened to her son declare his eagerness to return to civilian life. She detected the tension in his voice, and read the uncertainty in his eyes. She could see that her Comanche son was no longer a boy, but a mature man looking into an uncertain future. She sensed things as only a mother can, becoming suddenly aware that her son may never again be content to stay within the boundaries of the reservation; and this troubled her. She knew the young man sitting before her was not only lost, but searching for an unmarked path.

He listened tolerantly as Jimmy asked about his plans. Yellowsnake confided that he had no idea at that moment. "I'll just have to look around and see what's available." An hour later, he was traveling the dusty road toward town to pick up his wife and son from the store.

He played toddler games so unfamiliar to a jungle warrior and, after placing Nikoma securely into bed later that evening, the joy of their long awaited reunion exploded in the passionate embrace they had both so eagerly awaited. The joy of their love was fighting valiantly to regain control of his hardened, feral mind. But feeling the pangs of withdrawal from the only life he had known the past four years, he knew the transition wouldn't be easy.

A few days later, Yellowsnake found himself sitting with

some of his old reservation acquaintances, listening to the sheltered events of their lives.

He was keeping a watchful eye on the fast approaching rain clouds as he and Edward Red Sky, his close boyhood friend, sat talking on the front step of Edward's porch. Edward considerately filled Yellowsnake in on a rare job possibility, hoping he could help his friend regain his bearings. Edward had heard there might be a couple of bronc rider jobs open at the Howard Riggs Ranch, just west of the reservation. Yellowsnake had passed by the ranch numerous times and knew the operation was centered around breaking, training, and selling top quality horses. As soon as Edward told him of the job, his mind raced. *I could do that job. It would come natural to me,* he concluded.

He had, as a teenager, worked with his uncles breaking horses on the reservation, and had gained a feel for their unexpected moves and tricks as few youngsters had. He was bigger than most of the other Indian boys and as such, was much stronger. He was able to handle the arduous task of roping horses, bringing them to a standstill, then handling the job of breaking them.

Early the next morning, Yellowsnake rode over to the Riggs Ranch. He sought out Curly Winston, the wiry, gray-haired foreman of the operation, telling him he'd like a job breaking horses. The skeptical foreman frowned. "Son, are you sure you even know how to break a horse?" Yellowsnake laughed loudly, as if challenged by the devil himself. "Sure, would you like me to show you how to do it?"

Curly pointed out a wild-eyed mustang, then tossed a rope to Yellowsnake. "Here, show me how it's done," he commanded. Once he had isolated the edgy mustang from the others waiting to be broken, Yellowsnake and the unpredictable steed circled each other warily inside the corral while two curious ranch hands looked on. They glanced at each other curiously, "What's he planning to do next?"

He inched gradually toward the mustang. Yellowsnake had planned his strategy and, within minutes, he had placed a lasso around the horse's neck. The frightened animal was furious at the coarse rope rubbing his smooth neck. The mustang bucked and jerked in protest, trying desperately to escape capture by the strange-looking conqueror. The hooves of the wild chestnut mustang finally ceased rearing up, and he appeared, for the moment, ready to tolerate Yellowsnake.

Yellowsnake edged closer and closer to the unpredictable stallion which, until now had been untamed, soothing the scared horse. Then, he whispered muted Comanche words which only the horse would understand. A few minutes later, he was standing alongside the calm stallion, his arm draped casually over the horse's neck. He had deservingly captured the amazement of the onlooking ranch hands and the dubious eye of Curly.

He and the steed stood for nearly ten minutes, gently moving around and sizing each other up. The longer they were in the corral, the more obvious it was that Yellowsnake had gained the horse's trust. He followed as Yellowsnake led him over to the unbelieving ranch boss who was waiting outside the corral gate. The surprised, keen eyed foreman had been swallowed up by the unmistakable expertise of the Comanche horseman.

When he reached Curly, Yellowsnake demonstrated with ease how to slip a bridle over the horse's head without so much as a whinny of protest. He motioned for the foreman to hand him a saddle and blanket. He edged the strange objects closer and closer to the mustang's face. Wisely, he gave the spooked animal an opportunity to become comfortable with the sight and smell of the blanket and saddle about to be placed on his back. By now, a curious crowd of ranch hands had gathered around the perimeter of the fence, watching in skeptical admiration.

When Yellowsnake was a curiously observant seven year old, he had been taught by the Elders and his uncles that the first thing a good horseman must do was gain the confidence and trust of his steed. This could only be accomplished by letting the horse know that you had no fear as a rider while, at the same time, eliminating the fears of the nervous animal.

Yellowsnake gently flipped the blanket over the sweaty animal's back, becoming more and more eager to test the will of the strong mustang. Sure handedly, he placed the well-worn saddle on the back of the stallion, cinching the belly strap securely. As he eased the jittery horse closer to the rail, he talked to his trusting mount in a calm and reassuring voice. The bronc watched him as he slipped on his gloves, readying himself to climb aboard the pent up tornado. In a flash he was astride the surprised horse.

The mustang had been caught off guard. The horse whinnied and reared his head back, signaling he was ready to test the will of his determined rider. The bronc would-be rider surehandedly grasped the saddle horn and clung tightly to avoid being thrown as the stallion snorted and arched his spine. The mustang's eyes were filled with anger, as it desperately attempted to dislodge the load from his back. However, the fierce fighter soon discovered he had met his match. Yellowsnake's long legs were wrapped around the great beast's torso, and he was determined to win the fight. For several minutes, the mustang did everything possible to jolt the rider from his back. Once the tiring bronc finally realized that his undaunted conqueror was a permanent fixture on his back, he settled down. He had lost the fight.

The stallion snorted loudly with flaring nostrils before his gallop slowed to a soft gait, and finally, a slow walk. Yellowsnake leaned forward and gently ran his hand across the tender ears and forehead of the now broken beauty, comforting him to a final level of trust so he could be dismounted.

Curly didn't bother to disguise his smile and the kinky haired foreman chirped, "When can you start?" Yellowsnake was now an employee of the Riggs Mustang Ranch and was beginning to feel at peace, at least for the moment.

Each encounter with the unpredictable mustangs proved to be a true challenge and more than just a test of wills between the wild spirited animals and their determined riders. Now that he was a bronc rider, he was feeling somewhat pleased at having once again found a new niche in life. But Yellowsnake's spirit was not entirely at peace. Even though he was slowly adjusting to his new life, he was still struggling with a deep-seated feeling within that told him he wasn't where he belonged.

Fire struck unexpectedly when, suddenly, someone out of the past appeared at his front door. When he answered the knock, Yellowsnake opened the door and couldn't hide his surprise when he looked into the weathered face of his cousin, Max, whom he hadn't seen in many, many years.

Max was years older than Yellowsnake and, though older, he and Yellowsnake shared one thing in common; Max had served in Korea during the fifties and had lived through many of the same harrowing experiences as his cousin. After the Korean war ended, Max too had reluctantly returned to the reservation. He had desperately, and for a time unsuccessfully, searched throughout the surrounding area for employment. Finding jobs on or around the reservation was a chronic problem for the men who stayed.

For the past six years, Max had worked at an aircraft parts warehouse located on the outskirts of tribal lands. A few weeks earlier, he had heard through relatives that Yellowsnake had developed a keen interest in learning to fly a helicopter. Because of his job, Max was always one of the first employees to learn who was ordering parts for aircraft, along with the aircraft's location. Just a few days earlier, he had heard that the reservation's Indian Agent had a used helicopter in his possession, and hoped to sell it after restoring it to a semi-workable condition.

Max had checked out the rumor and felt compelled to let Yellowsnake know about such an opportunity, knowing this would be a rare chance for him to learn to fly a chopper.

While the two reminisced and sipped on their cold beer, they talked at length about how the agent had come to own the helicopter. And more importantly, what it might cost Yellowsnake to buy it and learn how to operate it. Yellowsnake responded with undisguised eagerness, uncharacteristic of his normally taciturn nature.

Max offered to call the agent and arrange a meeting to check out the condition of the helicopter the following Sunday. "Damn, I'm ready to head over there right now but, if you can arrange it for Sunday, let's get an early start and see if we can make a deal."

Sunday morning arrived, and church bells filled the air as they headed toward the agent's house.

As they stepped out of Max's new high-powered pickup, Yellowsnake was introduced to the agent. Cousin Max had done some checking on the crafty salesman, and had learned he had a reputation for being a real wheeler dealer. The Indian Agent escorted the two out to the pole building behind his home. He opened it's large sliding door, revealing the dusty gem. Snugly secured to a flatbed trailer sat the sourful looking, paint peeled Bell 47 helicopter.

During his tour in Korea, Max had managed to negotiate his way out of an artillery unit and into a motor pool as a mechanic. Within a few short months, he again maneuvered himself into an even more desirable job as an aircraft engine mechanic. He had obtained the special skills, hoping it would help him to get a good job following the war.

Yellowsnake sat awkwardly behind the control panel in the pilot's seat as Max wiggled into the seat next to him. While able to mechanically understand the movement of its working parts, Yellowsnake had no idea how to navigate the strange machine. He whispered to Max, "If I buy this thing, how in the hell am I going to learn to fly it?"

"Don't you worry about that. I've got it covered," Max reassured. "If you've got enough money to buy it, I'll teach you how to fly the son of a bitch."

They carefully inspected the body of the long-neglected machine, then began their negotiation with the agent. Max listed the numerous repairs which would have to be undertaken in order to get the aging chopper into decent operating condition and, emphasized it's pathetic condition. Then resolutely, Max proceeded to tell the agent how little the helicopter was worth.

The agent had been asking forty-five hundred dollars for his unclaimed treasure, but by the end of Max's performance, he had been talked into accepting twenty-five hundred dollars in cash. The three of them shook hands, solidifying the deal.

During his years in the Army, Yellowsnake had managed to set aside a few dollars each payday and had accumulated enough money to buy, in his opinion, this magnificent piece of steel.

When the negotiations had ended, he reached into his pocket and pulled out a hundred dollar bill to serve as a deposit on the aircraft until it could be picked up a few days later.

Although Maria was not completely delighted with Yellowsnake's decision to purchase the old helicopter, she reluctantly consented. She had reasoned that maybe this was more important to him than she realized. And maybe it would help ease his restless spirit.

Friday was an anxious day, as Yellowsnake and Max returned to the agent's home and paid him the balance due for the flying machine. Within minutes, the two men had the flatbed trailer hooked up to Max's pickup, ready for their return trip across the reservation. A few hours later, the helicopter and trailer were parked behind the home of Hotona and Jimmy. The level field behind their house would serve nicely as a safe resting place and future test area for the chopper once it had been restored.

Max and Yellowsnake faithfully devoted all of their precious spare time to the wonder machine, diligently combing the helicopter inch by inch. No bolt, nut or screw was left uninspected. Their goal was to ensure the aging craft was in sound working condition before any attempt was made to get it into the air.

Although Max had a thorough working knowledge of helicopters from his previous experience, he had never actually flown one. This challenging new task belonged to Yellowsnake.

They spent weeks tinkering and fine-tuning the engine, testing its smoothness over and over while still on solid ground. They checked details such as proper alignment of the rotor blades and balancing the navigational board, until finally it was time. Time for Yellowsnake to fulfill an ambitious dream. "I still don't know how I'm going to learn to fly this thing," he repeated over and over to Max.

"Don't worry, cousin, I've got it covered." With a ring of confidence in his voice, Max explained how the feat would be accomplished. "I've picked up a basic operating manual. Here's what we'll do. You'll sit in the pilot seat and man the controls. I'm going to be reading from the manual and will walk you through this thing, step by step. We're going to learn to fly together!"

Though brave at heart, Yellowsnake felt a pang of uncertainty shoot through his gut. For some reason, he still didn't feel too confident about Max's method of self-teaching. However, at this moment of truth, he had no better option.

The day of reckoning had arrived. Yellowsnake had already carefully gone over the operating manual by himself, but reading is one thing and doing is quite another. Max put it simply, "It's time to fish or cut bait, Yellowsnake." It was time to rise to the challenge, so the reluctant warrior seated himself in the pilot's seat.

While he grasped the strange sticks located in front of him, and while placing his feet firmly on the pedals below him, he drew a deep breath. He was securely buckled into a ready position, listening intently as Max began reading, word for word, the flying instructions from the manual lying on his lap. The pilots carefully followed each pre-flight checklist procedure, then the time arrived to ignite the mighty engine.

Ever so slowly, the overhead rotor blade began to turn. When the whirling blade had reached it's proper speed, they knew it was time to lift off. Yellowsnake gripped the steering sticks tightly while inching them forward and backward, and side to side. He simultaneously maneuvered the awkward foot pedals, then Yellowsnake felt the craft began to wobble unsteadily, much like an infant learning to walk. Max hadn't even lifted his eyes to look out the window and was seemingly oblivious to the likelihood of crashing and losing his life. He maintained his focus, continuing his reading from the open manual.

The big bird slowly rose to a treacherous altitude of twenty feet, then it began to vibrate. It hovered in the air, moving back and forth in a tipping motion, then started to spin in a harrowing circular motion, heading downward toward the ground from which it had just departed.

The out of control craft descended to the ground and, most fortunately, landed safely on its aging skids. Max barely noticed the impact of the noisy machine. He looked up, then looked around. "What's going on?", he growled, acting irritated and surprised they were not yet airborne. Yellowsnake exploded with tension relieving, albeit somewhat hysterical, laughter. It was a couple of minutes before he gained enough composure to explain to a somewhat mystified Max what had just occurred.

When he finally regained his composure, the nervous pilot sat patiently as Max again repeated the simple instructions for initial flight procedures. The chopper had wisely been placed far enough from his parent's home so that if the erratic prize crashed unexpectedly, no one would be injured. No one, that is, except the two of them. It was time to give it another try, and Yellowsnake didn't dare reveal his crossed fingers to Max!

For the second time, he cautiously manipulated the steering sticks and gently maneuvered the foot pedals. The craft began to rise. It swept gently from left to right, then left again, and finally forward, while steadily rising to greater and greater heights. The ugly duckling was soon hovering fifty feet above the ground and, looking out the window, Yellowsnake felt like they were on the peak of Mount Everest peering down on the rest of the world.

Yellowsnake awkwardly moved the strange sticks with his hands, carefully lowering the aircraft back down toward the ground. They were approaching their landing site and hovering ten feet above, when suddenly he felt the chopper losing control. He, in fact, had lost control of the aircraft and in moments it hit the ground with a sudden jolt. It was the ugliest landing either of them had ever seen. By now, Max was beginning to wonder if this was such a good idea after all.

They scooted out through the small doors, noticing right away that the left skid had broken cleanly apart upon impact. It was time to end today's flying lesson. They were faced with major repair work before attempting a second venture into the sky.

It took a couple of days to settle their nerves and repair the broken skid, then it was time to try again. Each lift off was a new adventure, and each flight proved less and less eventful. Yellowsnake's confidence was steadily increasing, and he was feeling more and more in control of his awesome ship. And with each learning session, Max continued reading his instructions, word by word, from the tattered manual lying on his lap. Max had never doubted that they would make it to the ground in one piece, and the diligent instructor knew they were nearing the end of their pursuit of excellence. Yellowsnake was becoming an accomplished pilot, and had mastered his new challenge with the perseverance of a bulldog.

Three weeks later, they found themselves sweeping gracefully over the reservation, looking down upon a world they'd never seen from the air. It was a beautiful sight and Yellowsnake chuckled smugly, "If anyone in their right mind could see us buzzing around up here, they'd have us both thrown in the crazy house!" Max hooted his agreement. A moment later, war whoops filled the crisp blue morning air high over the reservation. Not to be denied, Yellowsnake was on his way to becoming an accomplished pilot.

Eventhough Yellowsnake had continued breaking mustangs at the Riggs Ranch, he took advantage of every available hour to fly his new plaything. He flew further and further above the reservation; little by little, he was ranging far outside it's boundaries. The happy flyer hungrily covered vast chunks of countryside, much of which he'd never seen. Each time he and Max were ready to lift off the ground for another flying session, the fearless pilot intoned confidently, "Load your bombs Max, we're shagging ass!"

He had amassed hundreds of hours, skillfully learning to fly the delicate bird which had become his love. Yellowsnake's new routine now gave him even greater pleasure. Each morning he faithfully reported to the Riggs mustang ranch to work the mustangs assigned to him; each evening, though tired and sore, he found the strength to indulge his desire to fly his helicopter further into new territories.

His uneasy spirit was resting for the moment, for he was enjoying his expanded life. Then, he received an unexpected call from Max. He called to ask Yellowsnake if he would be interested in taking a job at Fort Walter, working on helicopters in the base maintenance garage. Max emphasized that the job paid very well and he would, more importantly, receive the additional training he needed to properly maintain his helicopter.

Max also took the opportunity to remind Yellowsnake he was not yet certified to fly his helicopter. He had better think about taking his pilot's test. Once again, Yellowsnake didn't relish the decision he had to make. His life with his family was a happy one, yet his spirit was restless. Maria, as expected, wasn't thrilled with the idea of him leaving the reservation to take another job. But, she knew it would be fruitless to try to persuade him to do otherwise.

As much as he enjoyed breaking wild mustangs at the Riggs Ranch, Yellowsnake couldn't resist the allure of his new job opportunity. Max was right, he needed more on-the-job training in engine repair and maintenance. And, he certainly needed to get tested so he could fly his chopper lawfully. After he had bid Curly a grateful goodbye, he was ready to depart for Fort Walter. The friendly ramrod shook his hand and wished him well. "If you ever decide you want to come back to breaking these wild bastards, let me know and I'll have a job for you."

Yellowsnake didn't waste time and, three days later, he was being interviewed by the chief flight mechanic at the Fort Walter Maintenance Station. The chief listened to Yellowsnake's work history and chuckled at his amusing story of how he had become a self-taught, unlicensed mechanic. The good natured supervisor figured Yellowsnake needed a chance, so he hired him. He had completed his week of orientation and training, and was ready to mix in. His first assignment found him lubricating and maintaining the hydraulic systems of various helicopters located within the huge hanger. Since he was surrounded by highly skilled mechanics, he asked countless questions while he worked, all the while absorbing much of their expertise. Soon after his first helicopter flight to Fort Walter, he knew he would have to inform them that he was not a certified pilot. He listened, predictably, to a thorough scolding from his supervisor, then he was directed to see the base's flight instructor to get himself tested and properly certified.

He reluctantly met with the flight instructor a few days later, sheepishly telling him he was an accomplished pilot. He wanted to be licensed, but had never received professional instruction. The instructor nearly fell off his chair laughing before the determined Comanche exercised strong persuasion. Yellowsnake soon had the instructor agreeing to take a flight with him to check him out.

When they boarded the training helicopter, the instructor apprehensively took his place in the co-pilot's seat. With calculated precision, Yellowsnake displayed his cautious moves as he went through his preliminary flight procedures in preparation for lift off. He got a nervous nod of approval from the instructor and in moments, they were ready to lift into the air. With the smooth and gentle touch of a highly skilled professional, Yellowsnake soon had the aircraft high off the ground, flying effortlessly across the miles of airstrip lying below.

Not only did the flight instructor have his doubts about Yellowsnake flying the chopper, he thought it preposterous that someone could teach himself such a complicated task. It just couldn't be done. They had completed a soft smooth landing on the tarmac when the instructor, again laughing, finally admitted, "Yellowsnake, you're an exception to the rule." The proud pilot was breathing easier now, knowing he had passed the real acid test.

A few days later, the instructor told him he could soon make his solo flight, knowing Yellowsnake's success was imminent. Once he had completed his flight, he could fly legally. He had studied hard for a week, and after completing a written examination before his solo flight, Yellowsnake was issued the valuable license he had worked so hard to obtain. *Now I can fly this baby anywhere I'd like,* he trumpeted silently. His satisfaction had reached a new level.

The bonus here was, he could now step aboard his trusty Comanche chopper and fly home every weekend to see his family, saving many precious hours of travel time.

A few hours after he arrived home for the weekend, he was bloated with a sense of pride and wanted to visit Max to proudly announce his accomplishment. When Max saw the pocket size document, he laughed heartily. "Snake, I always knew you were a little crazy. Now you're a crazy licensed Comanche pilot. Watch out world, here comes Yellowsnake!"

The echo of Max's words was music to his ears. Yellowsnake was beaming with satisfaction, for he had fulfilled a seemingly impossible dream. Little did he know he had just, with perhaps a little guidance from his ancestral spirits, taken a big step towards his next engagement with destiny.

Chapter 7

The Company

Yellowsnake enjoyed his new job at Fort Walter even more than breaking horses at the Riggs Ranch, of which he still held fond memories. The crew chief soon recognized Yellowsnake's skills far exceeded those needed to lubricate and maintain hydraulic systems. After his keen eye observed Yellowsnake's remarkable grasp of details, the chief mechanic decided to give him an assignment which would test his learning curve.

State-of-the-art, heavy duty, helicopter gunships were secretly arriving at Fort Walter. The massive new gunships were equipped with powerful turbine engines which required testing by competent pilots. Since Yellowsnake was now certified, the chief gave the challenging and dangerous assignment to him. As the crew chief had expected, the flight-crazed warrior was delighted.

Although Fort Walter was primarily a training center for pilots learning to fly much smaller helicopters, the mighty gunships had been quietly delivered to the base from Fort Rucker to be checked out. The testing was being conducted within a secluded area on the base, well out of sight of most of the base personnel. Once they had been tested, they would be returned just as quietly to Fort Rucker, with Vietnam their ultimate destination.

Yellowsnake had undergone three weeks of special training at Fort Rucker, focusing on the mechanical intricacies of turbine engines, and now he was ready to carry out his new assignment. After each one of the beefy new choppers had been thoroughly inspected and ground tested by the mechanics, it was Yellowsnake's job to test them airborne. If they met safety and performance criteria, they were deemed suitable for use in Vietnam. Testing the massive gunships made him feel a bond with the courageous helicopter pilots he had known in Vietnam, along with the new fighters who would soon be flying them into battle zones.

Yellowsnake treated each aircraft with the same caution and respect given an unbroken mustang. He knew that it was never certain what one of the turbine engines might do. They seemed to have a mind of their own, much like a wild horse. As soon as he sensed one of the costly birds was beginning to act erratically, Yellowsnake smoothly lowered it back to the ground. His keen eyes diligently studied the highly trained mechanics as they adjusted and fine-tuned the delicate turbines. And, as the chief mechanic had anticipated, Yellowsnake had acquired a sound working knowledge of turbine engines, inside and out.

The knowledge he had gained had made him totally confident in his ability to maintain and repair his own helicopter, no matter what the problem. In fact, Yellowsnake was so confident, he believed he could build an entire helicopter from the ground up.

With the days growing shorter and colder, 1965 drew to an end. Yellowsnake was feeling a sense of fulfillment in his new job, content in his day to day tasks. At Fort Walter, there was always a steady flow of air traffic in and out. Many times, high-ranking military officers, often accompanied by upper level government officials, arrived at the base unannounced.

On Friday morning, after having received his handsome paycheck, Yellowsnake was ready to begin his daily duties. He glimpsed out the door of the huge hangar, watching as a sleek, white Lear jet approached, preparing to make a clean landing on a nearby runway.

"Now that's a gorgeous piece of machinery. I think that'll be next on my list," said Yellowsnake to no one in particular. He admired it's smooth, graceful movement as the sleek aircraft slowly taxied towards the open door of his hangar. He chuckled. " I wonder if the pilot is lost and needs directions?"

Yellowsnake watched the passenger door open and a step ramp lower to the ground. With a look of mild shock on his face, he squinted at the familiar figure descending the ramp. "I'll be damned," he muttered in disbelief. "Is that you, Colonel

Lincoln?" Sure enough, approaching him was Colonel John Lincoln.

He was wearing dark sunglasses and sporting a trim, expensively tailored suit. The Colonel walked directly toward Yellowsnake, and with a broad grin on his face he gripped his war buddy's hand firmly. "And how's my old warrior friend?" Yellowsnake was nearly speechless.

He was grasping for words, as he shook the Colonel's hand. "I never thought I'd see you again."

Colonel Lincoln's laugh was familiar as he replied. "There's no way you're going to get rid of me, son! I knew I'd be seeing you sooner or later. And besides, I still have my end of our deal to keep. Have you forgotten?"

Revealing his naked uncertainty, Yellowsnake mumbled, "I'm not sure I ever understood our deal, Colonel. Maybe now you can tell me."

"I'm not here to try to fulfill my end of our deal entirely," the handsome Colonel replied, "but what I've got to say to you might be a start toward showing my appreciation for what you did for me in Nam. Then again, you might think I've lost my marbles when you hear what I'm about to lay on you."

The two of them walked slowly toward the lunch room inside the giant aircraft hangar. The Colonel disclosed to Yellowsnake that he had resigned from the Army a year earlier and was now an official with the Central Intelligence Agency, commonly known as the CIA. With an astounded look on his face, Yellowsnake's jaw dropped. "Sir, I never had any idea that's where you'd end up after the army." Although John Lincoln was now a civilian, he would always be the Colonel in Yellowsnake's mind.

The Colonel confided that he had known for years that he would be assigned an important mid-level position with the CIA once he had resigned from the Army. They seated themselves at a long table, away from the other employees in the hangar. Colonel Lincoln began laying out the mysterious reason he was there.

"Soon after you arrived at Fort Benning, I began keeping tabs on you from my Pentagon office, and have followed your progress from my CIA office. Before I left Langley, I took the liberty of calling your crew chief's superiors to let them know I was coming for a special reason. They're fully aware of my presence. Snake, you're not going to believe what I'm about to tell you, but it's true. As you know, the war we knew in Vietnam has changed dramatically. Now, it's a big, festering, unpopular war deeply dividing many people in our country. The movements and actions of our troops in Vietnam have increased dramatically and, now, there are no longer any boundaries defining the war as we knew it. Now, we've got men in Laos, Cambodia, Vietnam and anywhere else they're needed. Although we won't admit it, we have hundreds of agents operating throughout southeast Asia." Yellowsnake listened intently.

The Colonel rubbed his finger on the sticky table as he spoke, explaining in great detail how he would be returning to Vietnam to direct covert missions of agents throughout the area. Yellowsnake was flabbergasted and his ears were burning with the Colonel's words.

"This new job of mine has taken me back to that hell-hole jungle and, frankly, if I'm going back," the Colonel declared, "I want you with me. I know you have a wife and son, and undoubtedly you're leading a happy life now. But if you're willing to put the good life aside, I'll take you back to the jungle with me and we'll go after Charlie's ass with a new set of rules to play by.

This will be an entirely new ball game, and I'll be totally honest with you. It'll probably be even more dangerous than when we were there four or five years ago. And unfortunately, this isn't just a one year tour of duty. I have no idea how long we might be gone if you decide to join me. The CIA doesn't work with time limits. They work until the mission is finished."

He was stunned by the bombshell proposal. Yellowsnake didn't know what to say. He was experiencing a new high, just as intense as the moment he had learned he was a daddy.

"I can't tell you exactly what your duties would be until we get there. But I can tell you, they'll be damned dangerous and very similar to what you were doing before," the Colonel warned. "Also, your new employer will be in a position to pay you a hell of a lot more money than you're earning now. And, if you choose to join me, you'll no doubt earn every penny of it."

He drew a deep breath. Yellowsnake was again facing an important decision which would have a profound affect on not only his life, but his wife and son's future as well. How could he possibly go home and tell Maria he was now considering returning to Vietnam? He had already survived its madness once. Could he really go back for a second round? The Colonel knew Yellowsnake was struggling with himself and the startling proposition. Then he added, "And don't forget, along with your new paycheck, we will provide your family with a home anywhere in the United States you might choose. The Company realizes your family will be making a great sacrifice if they agree to let you come with me."

The Colonel's jargon caught Yellowsnake's attention. "What do you mean 'The Company?'"

The Colonel just smiled. "The Agency doesn't refer to itself as the CIA, but rather 'The Company'. If you come to work for me, the Company will never admit you are an employee of the Central Intelligence Agency. You will be a nonexistent employee and will be paid by a bogus corporation. The Company will never even acknowledge you exist."

The rush of adrenaline made his body tremble like a volcano moments before it's eruption. His sleeping warrior spirit was beginning to stir again. From the moment the Colonel's words reached his ears, Yellowsnake had made his decision. Now, most dreadfully, he must break the news to Maria and his family. He knew full well the consequences of his move and the impact his decision would have on his family. Nevertheless, he had chosen to accept the new adventure. He had placed his faith in the brave commander years earlier, and knew it would be best to leave the details of his new job in the Colonel's hands.

Yellowsnake looked into the intense, brown eyes of his long-absent leader. "I don't relish telling my family tonight that I have a new job. However, I'll do what must be done." He was handed a calling card with the Colonel's office address, telephone number and a handwritten number on the back of the card. Yellowsnake promised to call him at ten o'clock the following morning with his final decision.

The remainder of Yellowsnake's work day seemed an eternity. The only thoughts in his mind were of the new battles and life-threatening terror which probably lay ahead of him.

That evening, with Nik climbing on his back, Yellowsnake finally announced to Maria that Colonel Lincoln had returned, and of the Colonel's startling request that he join up with him for a new job back in Southeast Asia. Maria shed no tears, although she was obviously distressed. Her heart had warned her that sooner or later something like this would happen. She had, long ago, prepared herself for this moment. Without angry reprisal, she attempted to persuade him in a firm, yet gentle manner to reconsider his decision. She knew nothing of the Central Intelligence Agency, and cared little for things outside the reservation which might disrupt life as she knew it.

Throughout their lengthy conversation, Yellowsnake was cautious not to tell Maria exactly what his new job would entail. He felt it would be best to share with her his perception of the job offer in only the broadest sense, knowing the details would surely frighten her.

He told her he would be paid handsomely for his job skills, and the Company would provide her and Nikoma with a comfortable home anywhere in the United States. He feared her response. He avoided eye contact when he suggested that a good place to live might be somewhere between Los Angeles and San Francisco. He had tried to maintain a positive tone of voice, hoping she would become excited by the prospect of sharing the unexpected opportunity in new surroundings outside the reservation. "The Company will fly me home on a regular basis, and I'll be able to see you nearly as often as when I was at Fort Benning."

Without hesitation, she spoke with the absolute resolve he feared. "Yellowsnake, you know I love you, but Nikoma and I cannot leave the reservation. This is where we belong." He was disheartened, knowing this might be the final time he would ask her to join him to live outside the reservation.

Yellowsnake called the Colonel at ten o'clock with his

promised decision. As he spoke in a tone reflecting both distress and anxiety, he told the Colonel he'd join him. He also confided that he would probably pay a high price for leaving his family. Despite the high stakes, Yellowsnake was committed to the Colonel, and his country's needs.

Lincoln acknowledged that Yellowsnake might indeed pay a painful price for his decision. His relationship with his family could end up destroyed or severely damaged by his high risk, long term absence. Their deal had been cemented when the Colonel informed Yellowsnake that in a week's time, a Company jet would arrive to pick him up and fly him back to Langley to meet some of the hierarchy within the CIA. He had told them a great deal about Yellowsnake's accomplishments and his desire to have him at his side if he was going back to the war zone. The Colonel's bosses were eager to meet him.

A week later he said his final good-byes, thanking the crew chief for affording him the opportunity to work at Fort Walter. Although the chief was aware of the Colonel's intentions well before his arrival, he regretted seeing Yellowsnake leave, for he had proven to be a fine man and an exceptional worker.

The sleek white jet arrived to pick up it's new Company employee for transport to headquarters. When he touched down at Langley hours later, the excited Company rookie was escorted by limousine to CIA headquarters. Inside his soft, blue duffel bag he had stashed his Comanche knife and badly worn headband. These few belongings were all he needed if he had to leave quick. In the business of war, you never knew when you'd have to go. The medals he had earned years earlier would remain tucked away in his closet for posterity.

Yellowsnake clumsily dropped his bag next to a richly hewn door inside CIA headquarters, and was ushered into a large, tastefully appointed office. Four authoritative looking people along with Colonel Lincoln stood to greet him. He was introduced to each in turn, then directed to a seat. The highest ranking man present was an Assistant Deputy Director. After they gathered around the massive mahogany table and were seated in soft chairs, sipping coffee, the Assistant spoke first.

"Mr. Lincoln has specifically requested that you be a part of his team returning to southeast Asia. Of course, we want to see he is provided with people he has high confidence in. You seem to be at the top of his list. You understand, of course, this job is an assignment which will never be acknowledged as having existed. I'm sure the Colonel has explained that due to the sensitive nature of our operations in the war zone, we're careful not to reveal to anyone, public or private, that an individual is employed by the Company. This means that no one in this office will ever admit to knowing you or that you even exist. Do you understand what I'm saying?" The Assistant Director's words of warning rang clearly in his ears, and his declaration of denial was unmistakable.

"Yellowsnake," continued the Assistant, "your starting salary will be fifty eight thousand dollars a year and, as soon as you've decided where your family wants to live, we'll see that they are provided with adequate quarters."

"It won't be necessary to provide my family with housing, sir. My wife and son will be remaining on the reservation," replied Yellowsnake.

The Assistant dominated their conversation. "Since you, for all practical purposes, are a phantom operative in our southeast Asia activities, your only contact will be with Mr. Lincoln. And, other than that, the only communication you'll receive will come from the Blue Ridge Corporation in Utah. That will be the company paying your salary and expense account allowance."

Throughout the conversation, Yellowsnake's concerns began to mount. *These dudes are as slippery as a bunch of greased pigs. I don't think I'd trust a single one of them except the Colonel.*

The cautious warrior and his leader walked down the plushly carpeted hallway after the meeting. Yellowsnake asked the Colonel what he should do next. The Colonel answered, "Nothing. It's all taken care of."

"Well, don't I have to sign some papers and get on the records?", asked Yellowsnake incredulously.

"No, there's nothing more for you to do." The Colonel knew the Company jet was awaiting Yellowsnake, and he urged him to hurry. "Grab your bag and go home. Take care of your family matters because we'll probably be gone a long time. Above all, if you have any afterthoughts or don't think you can go through with this, please call me. I'll understand."

Now bound by the ties of his irreversible commitment, Yellowsnake gripped the Colonel's hand with a final handshake. "This is something I have to do. I'll be ready to leave when you are. By the way, where are we headed?"

The Colonel cut to the quick with his words. "We'll be heading back into familiar territory. Our next stop will be Danang."

Maria knew from the earliest moments of his announcement that Yellowsnake's decision was just as irreversible as her choice to remain on the reservation. They both were being forced to live by their firm convictions. In the waning moments before his departure, she told him her love for him would not vanish just because he was gone. Yellowsnake, in like manner, knew he couldn't put her out of his mind, not to mention his steadfast love for Nikoma. Both of them would remain in his heart.

For the moment, he had settled all of his affairs with mankind. Few words were needed to gain Hotona and Jimmy's understanding of his situation. He was leaving with their hopes and prayers on his side.

Ten days later, with his tattered army duffel bag in hand, Yellowsnake was ready to depart. His necessities, including his fearsome knife which had seen so many lives vanish before it, along with his tattered headband were tucked neatly inside. Now aboard a jet bound for Danang, Yellowsnake and the Colonel were heading toward a new adventure.

Suddenly he felt a thud, as the wheels of the aircraft touched down on the massive airstrip. He was back in familiar country, and faded memories of the past were returning.

A Company car was awaiting their arrival, and whisked them away to an isolated, nondescript office complex in Danang. "This," the Colonel proclaimed, "is my new luxury suite of offices." Though poorly decorated, it was well-equipped with electronic equipment, most of which Yellowsnake did not recognize. The drab looking building would serve as the Colonel's headquarters from which all of the operative activities within the area would be directed.

The Colonel seated himself behind his desk with sweat trickling down his furrowed brow. He was trying to decide how to best utilize Yellowsnake's skills in their new arena of battle. He studied the situation for a few minutes, then Lincoln reached his decision.

"Snake, I know you got along well with the Montagnards, and they certainly had a deep respect for you. The way things are going now, you're more than capable of leading a large group of Montagnard fighters to achieve what we need. What I'd like to do is send you back to the compound where we lived years ago. Inside the compound, I'm going to set up an area which will house you and two hundred of the Montagnard soldiers. Your group will have their own facilities, including all of the things you'll need for comfort, but you'll be separate from the other troops for security purposes. The only communication between your group and this office will be between you and me. I'll have the necessary communication equipment sent over to your area so you and I can talk on a daily basis."

During their closely guarded discussion within the walls of the Colonel's office, the Colonel remarked, "I had forgotten, but your records indicate you've become a certified helicopter pilot. I'm happy to hear that. Do you feel you're capable of flying one of our rescue or gunship choppers if you had to?"

"Hell yes," responded Yellowsnake without hesitation. "I can fly anything that can get off the ground. Colonel, I love those birds, and someday I'm going to learn to fly that Lear jet that took me over to Langley. As a matter of fact, I guarantee that before we're through, there won't be anything I can't fly." Not for a moment did the Colonel doubt Yellowsnake's words.

The secluded area within the familiar confines of the former English compound had been set up and soon Yellowsnake and his two hundred Montagnards had become a community within the city. The Montagnards had been carefully screened weeks earlier. They were selected for their willingness to remain silent about their dirty work, along with their ability to fight in the jungle without questioning their objective. Once they were deemed worthy of serving in the exclusive group of fighters, each Montagnard would be paid a bonus for participating in the perilous missions ahead of them.

Yellowsnake's observant eyes flashed as he looked around, and it seemed that he had left the compound only yesterday. The lush, menacing jungle surrounding him had not changed a bit.

Within days, he received his first assignment from John Lincoln in Danang, and not surprising, the mission was a real hum-dinger. Yellowsnake and ninety of his Montagnards would be choppered into a landing zone near the North Vietnamese border. From there, he and his fearless troops would have to cross the border into enemy territory on a trek of great peril.

Their mission was to locate a newly constructed airfield housing a number of Russian-built helicopters and a large supply of air-to-ground missiles. Once they had reached their target, they were to destroy as many of the helicopters as possible and blow up the supply of deadly missiles. *Shit,* Yellowsnake mused to himself, *things have really changed! Now this is going to be a real mission."*

Twenty-four hours later, he and his band of loyal Montagnards were flying through the silent darkness of night toward the dangerously remote landing zone. His pulse quickened. *Son of a bitch*, he thought to himself. *We'll be in North Vietnam and our asses will be history if we get caught. That's Charlie's turf.*

The group of hearty fighters were heavily armed with mortars and ground-to-ground missiles as they departed their helicopters. With Yellowsnake in his customary point position, they began their march through the unfamiliar jungle toward the North Vietnamese border. Soon they were well into the heart of enemy country, controlled solely by the North Vietnamese Army. They arrived at their target three hours later, still under the cover of darkness. He gathered about him the Montagnard group leaders who were able to speak enough English to communicate about their target. He directed them to spread out quietly around the small landing strip and helicopter storage area. They would wait until dawn to begin their attack.

As the sky grew lighter, the Comanche leader and his brave warriors were in position to mount their attack on the North Vietnamese airfield. Just as the Colonel had predicted, there were sixteen helicopters covered in a shroud of camouflage netting, ready to fly at a moment's notice. His scanning eyes spotted what appeared to be a well-guarded supply of air to ground rockets.

On Yellowsnake's command, the attack group opened fire with their firepower and missiles directed foremost at the helicopters sitting helplessly on the ground. Likewise, their armament was directed at the weapons storage pile nearly a hundred yards away. The entire North Vietnamese compound was within moments, engulfed in mayhem. Everything was ablaze from the exploding force of the deadly supply of missiles. The early morning sky was illuminated with an eerie glow. Mixed among the explosions and erupting devastation were North Vietnamese soldiers running for cover while blindly firing into the undergrowth.

When the Montagnards were given the order to open fire on the badly disorganized enemy soldiers, they directed their rifle fire at any silhouette they could see running through the smoke and flames. Soon, the blazing area was in ruins and absent of enemy movement other than wounded bodies scattered about.

Yellowsnake was not about to linger once their job was done. He promptly regrouped his Montagnard fighters and headed them swiftly back along the trail toward the landing zone. His blood was running wild and, until now, he hadn't realized how much he missed the jungle and the hunt.

He and his fighters raced for over two hours toward the chopper pick-up zone, hoping to escape an enemy ambush. Their luck held out as the Montagnards followed his lead, finally reaching the LZ and, like the wind, they vanished into the sky. When he returned to the seclusion of his new home within the compound, he radioed the Colonel to report their successful outcome. Not hiding his delight, the Colonel chuckled. "Well, Comanche, you haven't lost your touch, have you?"

The days and months to follow brought results which were much the same, as Yellowsnake received his rigorous assignments and carried them out with the same skill and efficiency as a highly-trained, seasoned Army officer. More importantly, the many missions which he led resulted in very few fatalities or injuries to his fighters. They were indeed a spirited group, and the dedicated fighters didn't give a damn about boundaries. Boundaries were only lines drawn on maps and, now, they and the enemy would fight on equal terms, where and when they chose.

The compound, which he had years earlier called home, had been greatly expanded to accommodate increased numbers of troops along with their attack and rescue helicopters. With the assistance of Colonel Lincoln's persuasion and influence on the Ranger Commander who now directed the compound's activities, Yellowsnake received permission to fly the gunships and test their massive fire power. He soon learned that he hadn't lost his touch at navigating the delicate beauties, and in hours had refamiliarized himself with the deadly aircraft should a sudden call arise.

Yellowsnake soared high above the jungle in a safe zone and looked down upon the familiar green canopy below, feeling totally at ease. At hand were two of the things he loved most - the jungle and his helicopter. He had always been in control of his destiny while on the ground, and now he felt in command as the swift bird of destruction swept across the treetops, seeking a fantasy target far below.

As part of his promise, the Colonel arranged for Yellowsnake to be flown back to the United States every few weeks to visit his family. However, returning to the reservation was not the same as it once was. Although he was always anxious to see his family, things were no longer the same. Maria was unwavering, and wouldn't consider leaving the reservation.

As time went on, his visits home became less frequent, and more often during his off-duty hours, he visited Danang to see his friendly comrade, John Lincoln. When he visited Danang, he made it a point to stop off for a few drinks at his favorite watering hole, a dingy stopover called "Pete's Place." By now, Danang was heavily fortified with Green Beret troops who, unfortunately, were still a frightfully mouthy bunch. Like

Yellowsnake, they too enjoyed bar hopping at Pete's, usually guzzling beer and bragging about who was the best soldier in the group.

Late one evening in 1968, he was accompanied by Brick Wilson, a friend who had been a fellow Ranger instructor years earlier, and was now a Company operative like himself. Yellowsnake and Brick decided to stop by Pete's for a quick beer. Standing elbow to elbow at the bar, he and Brick quietly observed the ever-bloated Green Berets loudly boasting about their accomplishments and toughness. The twosome shook their heads and exchanged glances of disbelief as they watched a fearsome Beret pull a small green frog from his shirt pocket. They wondered, what in the hell did he plan to do with the squirming creature?

With the entire world of Pete's Place as his audience, the Beret popped the frog into his mouth and, with a nauseated look of stupid regret on his face, began chewing it up. He held the frog in his mouth, unable to swallow. The show off was rapidly becoming ill. As could be predicted, a spew of vomit shot forth from his mouth, along with the frog carcass. Brick had been watching the action, and much to Yellowsnake's amazement, he sat his mug of beer down on the bar counter and walked over to the pool of slimy vomit covering the bar table. With the sureness of a conquering opponent, he picked up the badly mangled frog, dipped it in a glass of beer and popped it into his mouth. And while tilting his head back, he swallowed it whole.

Brick's eyes revealed the pleasure of humiliating the onlooking Berets. He had been watching every move the Beret was making, and was sure he knew what the braggart was up to. He wouldn't let the opportunity slide. Brick maintained a stone cold look on his face, silently inviting a challenge from the blowhards while watching the anger build on the face of the astonished soldier.

"Troops," he declared, "that's the way Rangers get the job done. We never walk away from an unfinished mission. Some of our missions aren't for shit, but we never walk away." He was sporting a triumphant look on his face as he returned to his empty slot at the crowded bar, and in one swift motion, he gulped the remainder of his still cold mug of beer. His eyes were jumping with deep satisfaction when he looked at Yellowsnake, and Yellowsnake couldn't wait to hear about the feat.

He whispered to the brash challenger, who leaned swaggardly on his elbow at the bar. "Holy shit! Aren't you going to puke?"

"Hell no! The secret is to not let it touch your palate before it slides down your throat," Brick concluded. He beamed with the smugness of a triumphant hero. "It didn't bother me a bit. Besides, those Berets give me a royal pain in the ass."

Unlike Yellowsnake, Brick's duties with the Company had kept him confined behind a desk in Danang. He had graduated with a Master's Degree in Accounting, and was responsible for tracking the cash flow needs of South Vietnam's Army. The Generals badly needed cash to pay their soldiers and keep them in the fight against the VC and North Vietnamese army. As distasteful as it was, Wilson sometimes had to authorize flights of illegal drugs out of Vietnam into the waiting hands of notorious drug dealers. They were always eager to receive another shipment and, as such, were willing to pay large sums of cash. It was a dirty job, but like Brick said, "It comes with the territory." Brick had hardened his conscience to the unsavory task, mostly in knowing that his orders were handed down by his bosses at Langley.

It was only moments before the admiring Green Berets had ordered up six beers for Yellowsnake and his strong-willed companion. The final and prophetic words from Brick's narrow lips echoed loud and clear. "Rangers are Rangers, Berets are Berets, and the two will never meet." How true it was. Each was a different breed of animal.

During the exciting moments of the frog encounter, Yellowsnake had momentarily set aside a lingering urge which had become a festering need within him. He had intended to bring the matter up to Brick earlier, but was suddenly sidetracked by Brick's unexpected showmanship. Yellowsnake was iron willed, but now something had to give. He hadn't had a piece of ass in what seemed an eternity, and looking around the noisy bar didn't help matters. There were lots of good looking girls in Pete's Place, and most of them were for hire.

He waited patiently for Brick to wipe the beer foam off his lips, then Yellowsnake posed the proposition. "I don't know about you Brick, but I haven't been laid in weeks. Do you think you can handle a little poontang tonight?"

Brick choked on his swallow of beer. He grinned, as his squinty eyes began to dance. "Hell yes! I think this place is ripe pickins' tonight!" Indeed, the pickings were good. Yellowsnake looked over the herd, then spotted the mare he was looking for. His mission for tonight? Fulfill the need! In moments, he had caught the tallish beauty's attention and had brought her to his side at the bar. Brick was more concise in his selection, but succeeded in finalizing his choice within ten minutes.

Yellowsnake was in a hurry, and got to the point before the young Vietnamese lady had taken the third sip from her drink. Fortunately, neither Yellowsnake or his friend were in an arguing mood. He had set the price, and she had accepted. As he bid his farewell to Brick and his shapely companion, Yellowsnake could feel all of his vital joints hardening. It was time to go. The small two room apartment looked worse than some of the war torn tents he had slept in. It didn't matter though, because now, the night was his and she was his.

He sipped on a beer as he watched her carefully remove her dress. She sat on the edge of her sagging bed, finishing her tall cocktail. In minutes, and with little fanfare, the two passionate bodies were fully synchronized. The unbearable heat didn't help matters. Their bodies were like two slippery eels as they fought to overcome the sweat pouring off their skin. An hour later, he was nearly dead from exhaustion. He had completed his mission and had performed it well. He lay motionless on his back, staring at the revolving ceiling fan above. His eyes were closed as he heard the roar of a fighter jet passing overhead. The war was still out there, but for a brief moment, he had been successful in casting it aside.

The recent months had found Yellowsnake's daring assignments with his loyal Montagnards taking them many miles from camp for weeks at a time. They moved about like an invisible deadly vapor, living on whatever the jungle provided them. Their job was to locate hidden encampments of the Viet Cong and North Vietnamese Army. The strongholds then became targets of massive air strikes by the ever present and heavily armed U.S. fighter jets and attack helicopters. His covert assignments were proving to be much easier than earlier years because now, there were no rules and no boundaries. If he and his fighters didn't destroy a site, they simply reported its location and size, knowing their biggest danger would be their return trip to a helicopter pick-up zone. Nevertheless, they always traveled in numbers adequate to fight off an unexpected attack. Unlike his army tour in Vietnam, there was now an unpredictably large number of VC throughout the jungle. Since they had become so skilled in traveling like shadowy ghosts through the undergrowth, Yellowsnake and his Montagnards were usually able to avoid major casualties. They had acquired the knack of slyly positioning themselves to take out the enemy before they themselves were attacked by surprise. But as his war years began to mount, so did the odds against his survival. He had to make every effort to keep the odds stacked in favor of him and his loyal comrades. That was they only way they could win the game of life and death!

Chapter 8

Running Against the Odds

In early 1969 Yellowsnake received an exciting, though dangerous request from John Lincoln. As the war escalated, an increasing number of helicopter and jet fighter pilots were being shot down over enemy territory. Many of them were stranded along the Mekong River in Laos and Cambodia, placing them in grave danger once they hit the ground. Now, the Colonel was asking Yellowsnake to employ his talents as a helicopter pilot to make rescue flights deep into the heart of enemy territory. He accepted the assignment, agreeing to give it his best effort in an attempt to carry out his leader's perilous request.

Yellowsnake assigned a trusted assistant to lead the Montagnards should they be called upon to perform a mission during his absence from the compound. It took him less than a week to refamiliarize himself and sharpen his handling skills with the heavily armed Army helicopters. Then, he was given his first task.

A chopper carrying not only pilots, but Army troops as well had been shot down near the Mekong River. His mission was to rescue the pilots and their companions. The Army didn't want it's rescue pilots to be shot down or apprehended on the wrong side of the river. The area was off limits to them. Since the urgent mission was not being flown by an Army pilot, the formalities of proper flight procedures were dispensed with. Yellowsnake sought out one of his most skilled Montagnard gunmen and asked him to accompany him as co-pilot of the armed rescue helicopter.

His chopper was equipped with automatic rifles, a 50 caliber machine gun and several rockets, and was declared air ready. Soon, the two were high above, headed for the zone at which the downed helicopter and its crew had been reported lost. It seemed like only minutes had passed before the well-armed fortress arrived at the designated rescue area.

They swept in with reckless abandon toward the small clearing. Then, they could see the downed helicopter still smoking with American soldiers crouched close to its hull. While dropping down and keeping a sharp eye peeled for artillery and snipers, Yellowsnake's keen vision spotted enemy movement in the jungle below. The VC were rapidly approaching the demolished helicopter and were not more than a few hundred yards from where the defenseless troops were standing by. He unleashed his rockets toward the surprised attackers, sending them scurrying for cover.

Then, he dropped the mighty ship down as fast as possible without crashing into the ground. Once he had touched down, he kept his automatic rifle in a ready position, then waited for the frantic troops to scramble aboard the aircraft for retreat to safety. The unorthodox looking pilot wasted no time as the airmen and their companions crawled into the rescue ship, soon realizing it was being flown by the long-haired, headband adorned rescuer. The terror filled group was airborne in seconds, hoping to reach the safety of the compound. The incident caused Yellowsnake to reflect. *I may not be so lucky next time.* The enemy's rockets had escaped his chopper when he descended to the ground. He had gained a new awareness that one unlucky hit could send him home in a body bag.

They had no sooner lifted off the ground and risen a few hundred feet when suddenly they were greeted with heavy machine gunfire. Aside from a few bullet holes which had damaged the chopper's fuselage, and much to the confident rescue pilot's relief, they had nervously escaped being shot down by some recklessly aimed missile headed their way. The rescuer and the rescued were breathing easier once they had the compound in sight. It was his first air rescue mission, but not his last.

With the arrival of 1970, Yellowsnake found himself still leading his faithful troop of Montagnards on missions which carried them not only into North Vietnam, but also Laos, Cambodia and Thailand. The Colonel was right. It was a whole new ballgame. There were no longer any boundaries within which they had to fight the war. His duties had indeed become varied, for now he could regularly be seen leading a dangerous trek to some remote site in Laos, then responding to an urgent call to rescue a downed pilot. To his delight, he found himself being asked by his boss to pilot fully the armed gunships when the need arose.

He loved the power he possessed when he sat behind the controls of the massive warships. They were equipped with every imaginable weapon, and could devastate any enemy force, regardless of it's size.

Because they were so extensively equipped with air-to-ground missiles and intimidating gun power, the awesome gunships scared the hell out of the VC. His gunship prowess enabled him to display his array of bullets and missiles to the enemy. He loved sweeping in fast and low as he released his deadly rockets on what seemed like scrambling ants on the ground below. He loved, for special effect, to treat his co-pilot accomplices to war whoops and screams while he squeezed the trigger, spraying machine gun shells over the countryside. The VC might hit his chopper with a few rounds, but they would pay a dear price before the encounter ended.

In spite of the many years he spent in the jungle performing countless tasks for the Company, Yellowsnake had consistently exercised extreme caution, and had returned with nothing more than minor injuries.

Yellowsnake's cunning had pissed off the VC big time, and because of his increasing notoriety, he had become a marked man. When he led his troops on search and destroy missions, he was frequently on his field radio, squawking to chopper pilots or other attack groups in the area. His call name was, naturally, "Yellowsnake" when he communicated with his jungle comrades. As the years passed, the mere mention of 'Yellowsnake' caused excitement in his foes–it had become a targeted name. Many months later, he learned that a bounty had been placed on him. He had lost count of how many VC and North Vietnamese soldiers he had killed over the years, and was not surprised when he learned there was a price on his head.

By 1972, most of Yellowsnake's conflict was confined to dangerous rescue missions deep inside enemy territory. He had become highly adept at skimming his way across the treetops and dropping into impenetrable areas scarcely large enough to rescue the desperate soldiers waiting for him.

He'd become dangerously daring during his rescue pursuits, placing the downed Americans' lives above his own safety. During an intensely dangerous seven month period, Yellowsnake had found himself being plucked out of the jungle by other rescue helicopters not once, but three times. Each time, his own ship had been damaged by heavy gunfire as he neared the ground. But within a blink of the eye, he was always able to vanish like a chameleon into the dense undergrowth until another rescue ship arrived. The VC might get his chopper, but they weren't going to capture him!

Though he was skillful at hiding and leaving no evidence of his whereabouts, he still carried an uneasy feeling that his luck was running out. Having been downed three times told him he shouldn't even be alive, but here he was. He was never fearful of flying close to the treetops, because it kept him closer to the ground. The tactic had put him in greater danger than normal, but offered the safety of a quick landing if his chopper got hit. Taking the risk had enabled him to avoid being hit at higher altitudes.

During a monsoon-soaked day late in 1972, Yellowsnake received an urgent call from John Lincoln. Less than an hour earlier, it had been reported that an American fighter pilot was downed inside Laos, very close to the shore of the Mekong River. His task was to locate the downed fighter jet and rescue its defenseless pilot if he was still alive.

Yellowsnake always had his gear packed and his killing knife was always on his belt, so he could leave on a moment's notice. His mind raced as he adjusted his discolored headband and ran his fingers through his mane which now reached his shoulders. He knew it would be a hairy one when he decided he would go it alone. He watched impatiently as the torrents of side-swept rain beat unmercifully on the jungle canopy. There was a lonely, scared pilot out there awaiting his help. *No problem*, he reassured himself. *I'll get in and get out before anyone even sees me.* His gut, however, was giving him an uneasy warning. *Be careful!*

He checked to see that his radio was operating properly and made sure everything was ready. It was now or never if he was going to carry out the rescue plan. When he reached the dangerous area along the murky Mekong River, he peered through the relentless rain and spotted the site where the fighter pilot had been reported down. His eyes slowly scanned the rain-whipped, low visibility area. Soon, he sighted the wrecked aircraft. The smoldering body was no more than a crumpled heap of metal, cushioned by the boughs of thick tree cover below.

Yellowsnake deftly dropped his chopper to within seventy five feet of the aircraft's remains, then he saw the pilot lying face up on the ground. He knew the bloodied flyer was dead. He had survived the impact, but hadn't been able to escape the unseen killers lying in wait for the arrival of a rescue team. They had waited until Yellowsnake's chopper was in sight and, only then, did they execute the pilot. Now, they would take great delight in killing the rescuer, a rescuer who could now do nothing more than retrieve the dead pilot's body.

The rotor blades were whirling slowly when the sniper force lying well-hidden only yards away, opened full fire on his rescue chopper. His engine began belching smoke, and he knew he was in big trouble. He slung the fully loaded backpack onto his back, grabbed his rifle and all the ammo clips he could carry. It was a familiar mishap, and he was again being forced to run for his life. This time, however, escape would not come so easily.

There was only one of him against a horde of Viet Cong, now accompanied by Pathet Lao sympathizers scattered throughout the area. He lunged forward into a full run. With rain and sweat drenching his body and saturating his clothes, he ran until he could flee no further. He stopped momentarily, gulped a drink of water and listened for oncoming footsteps. The footsteps never seemed to end, causing him to continue his run. The trails in the area were unfamiliar to him, but he kept running with an ever wary eye on the ground for land mines and booby traps skillfully placed ahead of him.

He changed course repeatedly, trying to stay well ahead of

his pursuers. But they were a persistent bunch and seemed to never tire. Eventhough they were out of sight behind him, he could still hear them on his trail. Yellowsnake was totally exhausted when nightfall finally arrived. He needed some relief from his long day of running through the unfamiliar tangle of underbrush. His tired eyes spotted a shelter in an ancient tree fortress, then he fastened himself high up in the branches, hoping he'd get some badly needed rest. It was critical for him to regain enough energy to resume his flight the next morning. He knew his pack contained only a meager supply of rations, so he ate a small can of food to keep his strength up through the night.

Before dawn, he left his hiding spot and was on his way, hoping to lose his attackers. But no matter how hard he ran, sooner or later he could hear their chatter not too far behind. They refused to give up. He traveled far to the west, then backtracked east, hoping to shake them off his trail, but nothing seemed to work. He stopped when he could, refilling his canteen with fresh water, and kept moving. He was exhausted, but he knew if he stopped and was caught by the killers, they would skin him alive and take great delight in watching him suffer.

Finally, he stopped to radio the compound about his deteriorating dilemma. He transmitted an urgent mayday message. It was received by one of the Montagnard assistants who, in turn, relayed the message to the Colonel. Yellowsnake was in serious trouble somewhere in the vast swampy area along the enemy-infested Mekong River. There wasn't time to stay there until a plan was worked out. He heard footsteps getting nearer and nearer to his spot. He had to run.

With his mind in a trance-like state, Yellowsnake continued to run endlessly day after day. Eight days had passed, and he was still on the run. He couldn't figure out how they could persistently stay on his trail no matter which direction he turned. Little did he know, his pursuing attackers were radioing other troops in the vicinity advising them of his direction and warning them he was headed their way. And, like hyenas in pursuit of a wounded antelope, they knew they were chasing Yellowsnake, a wanted man with a hefty bounty on his head.

He had, predictably, run out of food and sought anything

edible in order to stay alive. His diet consisted of rodents, insects, watercress and anything else he could get his hands on. He had carried all of his weapons and ammunition throughout the chase, but they were becoming a cumbersome burden as his strength steadily diminished.

His ninth night of darkness had set in, and Yellowsnake was nearing total exhaustion. He didn't know how much longer he could keep running, so he again radioed the compound, frantically asking if anything could be done to help him out. He needed a plan, and he needed help. Because he had covered such a vast radius, his rescuers and concerned commander had no way of knowing where he was at any given moment. Yellowsnake's radio squawked his transmission, then a senior Ranger instructor at the compound got on the radio with a reply. "Yellowsnake, we have a priority request from your boss in Danang. He doesn't know where you're located, but can you tell me if you're able to make it to the Mekong River? How far away from it are you?"

The weary runner had no idea how far he was from the river because of the distance he had traveled inland through the dense undergrowth of the jungle, but estimated he was at least twenty miles from the river. He told the listening Ranger, "If I can reach the river, I should be able to get my bearings."

The Ranger sensed the urgency in Yellowsnake's voice and made his decision. "Try to get to Checkpoint BETA on your map. It's located near the edge of the river, and we'll try to get a Navy SEAL rescue team to take you out by boat." When he heard the message, Yellowsnake felt slightly relieved, but apprehensive. *Son of a bitch! I don't even know whether I can make it that far or not. I'm only guessing that's how far I am from the river. I could be forty miles away.* Although the situation seemed desperate, he knew he had no other choice. He had to garner up the strength to make it to the river.

Before sunrise, he was again on his way, this time without food in his stomach and only half a canteen of water on his belt. The grueling trek had taken it's toll on his body, and by now he had become thoroughly bloodied by the countless scratches and gouges he'd received while running through the underbrush. He had stripped down to his camouflage undershirt, which was badly torn and saturated with dirt and blood. His feet and toes were badly infected because he hadn't changed his wet socks or boots in many days.

He headed due east towards the Mekong. He didn't have a choice. His only means of survival would be to connect with the Navy rescue team, provided he was even able to locate the designated check point.

He was traveling through totally unfamiliar territory, now relying solely on his natural instincts to reach the river. His legs told him he had reached a point of terminal exhaustion, and he could run no further. The sun had dropped below the trees, blanketing the forest in somber darkness. He had to conserve his remaining energy while he rested high aloft in a treetop. He estimated that he had covered maybe fifteen miles that day. Now, his hunger had become severe, and he was getting weaker and more dehydrated with each hour. Although he was a strong Comanche warrior, he was still only a man and needed food and water to survive.

He silently dismounted the tree in which he had spent the night, then lowered himself to the ground well before daylight and though he was hungry, a little luck had come his way. The VC and Pathet Lao pursuers had, most strangely, given up their futile chase a day earlier. They had apparently become not only frustrated, but just as tired as him, and had chosen to give up the chase. Now, his only priority was to keep moving and stay alive. He glanced warily at the large brown snake wrapped around a nearby tree limb, still resting from it's feast the night before. He approached the unsuspecting snake and, with two mighty whacks, cut a large chunk of flesh from the reptile's body. He feverishly stripped away the smooth skin, then retrieved a can of cooking sterno from his pack. He seared the soft flesh, then devoured the meat to keep himself alive. It wasn't exactly a fried chicken dinner, but it served its purpose.

His burdensome pack was strapped on as he wearily resumed his run, not knowing if this was his last day. His strength had diminished to a point where he was rapidly losing his endurance. At four o'clock in the afternoon, the most welcome sight of his life appeared before him. On the horizon, only a few hundred yards away, lay the muddied waters of the Mekong River.

He was overjoyed at having reached the river. Yellowsnake knew he must now figure out his exact location. He stopped to retrieve a badly worn map from his backpack and opened it up so he could scan the designated check points. It took everything in him to force his hazy mind to focus and function. His sense of utter desperation nearly brought him to his knees when he realized he was four miles away from Checkpoint BETA. Now, he had serious doubts as to whether or not he could make it to the rendezvous point. However, the thought of losing his life at this perilous point scared the hell out of him.

He collected the shreds of his remaining strength, then made a final run for his life along the river. He headed downstream, staying far enough away from the river's edge to prevent being spotted by enemy troops who might still be roaming the shoreline in gunboats. Meanwhile, he had no way of knowing what lay ahead of him. For all he knew, he could run into a hundred more pursuers who'd be happy to bring his precious life to an end.

His mind and it's imagination was running wild, and he had become deliriously convinced that he had been guided by the watchful eye of his ancestral spirits. Lady Luck had been on his side, for he finally arrived at Checkpoint BETA shortly before six o'clock. There was no boat in sight, and no Americans to greet him. He had been told the SEAL rescue unit would try to pick him up at dark that night, if they themselves hadn't been discovered and destroyed. The next few hours would be the longest of his life as he waited for a rescue team which he wasn't certain would even appear. A few minutes past eight, he heard muffled sounds which would prove either welcome or horrifying to his ears. It was the sound of an oncoming gunboat. He held his breath, and watched intensely for the motor craft to round the curve directly ahead of him. He sighed with deep relief, for it was an American gunboat, heavily armed and manned by five Navy SEALS. It was the most welcome sight of his life. If it had been the enemy, death would have come in only a matter of minutes.

He clumsily pulled out his flashlight and signaled to the oncoming craft and, in moments, they had beached the boat. As they neared him, they saw that Yellowsnake was in bad shape, weak and nearly unable to walk. The husky SEALs leaped out of the bow of the craft, and while hoisting him by the arms and waist, they thrust him inside the gunboat. The rescue team had accomplished their mission, and once his feet hit the boat deck, they wasted no time in getting out. His Navy rescuers possessed the same skills and precision as the Army Rangers, and in seconds the highly trained SEAL unit had retreated from the river shore. Their boat traveled at top speed until they reached another checkpoint where they could drop Yellowsnake off to his Montagnards.

During the menacing trip which was shielded by darkness, Yellowsnake sat leaning against the steel reinforced bulkhead of the high powered rescue boat. His weary mind was still engulfed by his haunting question. *Has Shahana's spirit been with me during all of the dangerous days I've spent in this jungle death trap?* The mysterious old Yaqui Medicine Woman had accurately forecast the many perilous days of his recent life. *How could she know?* He could remember her words clearly. *You will have many perilous days ahead of you, but when you need me, I will be there.* Fate had been kind to him, and his conviction was firm. She must have been watching his every move through all of the dangerous moments during which his life was at stake.

The husky rescuers wasted no time in helping the exhausted warrior off the idling rescue boat. One of the SEALS nudged him, giving him a confident thumbs up. "Hey Indian, I'm Cherokee Meredith. Maybe someday we can smoke the pipe along with a cold brew." Yellowsnake managed a weak smile, knowing what his brave fellow Indian rescuer meant.

Hours later, he was safely back in the hands of his Montagnards and, with specific instructions from John Lincoln, he was escorted by his family back to the safety of the compound. His treacherous experience had, without question, been his most perilous mission. He had come dangerously close to losing his life several times, and only his wit and the help of the spirits had gotten him through.

He had survived eleven days in the jungle running from bloodthirsty VC and Pathet Lao pursuers, and knew he deserved to be dead. Yet he was alive and standing. When he and his band of escorts reached the compound, he was shuttled to the sick bay area. The doctor treated the multitude of wounds he'd suffered along the trail and, until now, had ignored. Everything on his lean frame ached from head to toe. None of his body parts had escaped the trauma of his brutal experience.

Within minutes after eating as much as his shrunken stomach would hold, he fell asleep, not caring if he ever woke up. He hurt all over, and both his body and mind were screaming for rest.

The next day, he was called into the Communications Center to hear his commander's message. "Son, you just added a lot of gray hair to my head! Needless to say, I was deeply concerned for your safety. I know you can't give me the details right now, but you must have had one bitch of a time out there. Thankfully, you're back in one piece. Get all the rest you need and build your strength back up. When you're feeling better, come into Danang and give me the details. After this episode, I'm going to see that your assignments ease up. I've pushed you to the brink of disaster with these nasty jobs and, from here on out, I'll keep you closer to home."

His ears barely absorbed the Colonel's comforting words. Yellowsnake returned to the peace of his cot, sleeping for nearly two days. It would take many days before the exhausted operative had fully renewed his strength.

Lincoln, meanwhile, had been informed of the bounty which had been placed on his dedicated fighter's head. He knew it would be extremely dangerous for him to venture too far from the compound, and he quietly feared for Yellowsnake's life.

Several days had passed before he felt his energy return, and Yellowsnake was eager to depart for Danang to see his leader. While they enjoyed breakfast and lunch civilian style, the government agents talked about Yellowsnake's hazardous rescue, both marveling at how he had managed to avoid capture for eleven days before his rendezvous with the Navy SEALS. Colonel Lincoln spoke modestly of his own assignments within Danang. His well chosen words reflected less and less optimism about the direction of the war, and it's probable outcome. He disclosed that all of the reports coming in from various battles throughout the region indicated South Vietnam was indeed losing the war. "It may not be long before all American troops and civilians are evacuated from Vietnam," he concluded.

Yellowsnake's boss was letter perfect when it came to making predictions, and his words soon became reality. Not surprisingly, in 1973, President Nixon announced that all American troops were being withdrawn and brought home. Although the American forces were being pulled out of Vietnam, the covert operatives, unfortunately, would be some of the last personnel to leave the country, some nearly two years later.

Following Yellowsnake's grueling eleven day encounter with his pursuers, his tasks for the next year were carefully selected so not to jeopardize his life and had, as the Colonel had insisted, kept him closer to the compound. The Colonel had decided it would be best to keep him out of rescue missions and gunship fights. His feet remained on ground where he had a greater chance for survival. His safe haven duty had caused him to return to his job of leading his Montagnard fighters on high impact search and destroy missions, but never too distant from the compound.

Even though many months had passed after the withdrawal of the American troops, the Colonel and Yellowsnake found themselves still in the war torn country, both being pushed closer and closer to fleeing for their lives.

For many long treacherous months following the final withdrawal of American troops, Yellowsnake found himself spending much of his time moving around, keeping out of sight of the Viet Cong, North Vietnamese soldiers and most recently, the Pathet Lao sympathizers. His compound had finally been overrun by the onslaught of North Vietnamese soldiers, and had sent him running for his life. Despite the fact that stealth was Yellowsnake's strong suit, his luck was running out. Then,

Lincoln wisely ordered him to join his highly secret command post, which was now located many miles south of Danang. Yellowsnake dutifully acknowledged his leader's order, and given the situation, he wasn't about to protest.

In early 1975 the Colonel, after talking to command headquarters, proclaimed with a ring of finality, "We're getting the hell out of Vietnam and won't be returning." As he had predicted, the enemy was forcing them to move out and seek the shelter of Saigon. And, with a little luck, they too would be removed from the battle zone, along with the few remaining Americans in the country.

The urgency of the final moments had forced Yellowsnake and Colonel Lincoln to jump aboard the Colonel's waiting helicopter, headed for Saigon. Lincoln possessed a clear view of the situation in Vietnam, and wisely directed Yellowsnake to lay low and buy time in Saigon. He wanted Yellowsnake to try to help the remaining civilians get safely aboard evacuation helicopters. There wasn't much time left to get them out of the country before the oncoming North Vietnamese Army assaulted Saigon. Yellowsnake was comforted in knowing the Colonel had never made an incorrect call during all the years he'd known him, and this was no time to question his judgment. He would carry out his leader's request.

In the final hours of the war, Saigon was in shambles and adrift in pure madness as everyone sought to escape the oncoming rush of the North Vietnamese army. Yellowsnake remained at the Colonel's side inside the U.S. Embassy while they watched the handful of remaining Americans scramble aboard the awaiting evacuation helicopters. They were quickly filled to capacity each time they landed on the Embassy grounds. The war had been lost, and now his and the Colonel's final task was to escape the clutches of an enemy who energetically sought to destroy them.

Early in the final hours of their long and hazardous life in Vietnam, the Colonel summoned Yellowsnake. "I've been ordered to board the Company plane for shuttle back to Langley. Within two hours, you'll be aboard one of the last choppers leaving this mess. You'll be taken to an awaiting aircraft carrier and, from there, to Bangkok for evac back to the states. When you get your feet safely back on American soil, call me at Langley. Help all of the remaining civilians you can and, when you get back, we'll find out what kind of fun the Company has in store for us. If you're willing to stay with me, we'll find another hot spot."

Yellowsnake smiled. "Don't worry! I'll be around as long as you want me." An hour later, the anxious warrior was indeed aboard the third to last chopper departing from the U.S. Embassy. He was headed in a direction which would ultimately lead to the safety and sanity of life in the United States. His thoughts were of the chapter in his life which was coming to an end. *This stop over has been one hell of a jaunt. I think I've witnessed all of the vicious brutality this ravaged country has to offer, and I hope I'm seeing it for the last time.*

The Gods of War had favored him once more, allowing him to survive the insanity offered by the many years he had endured in the unforgiving jungle. His rejuvenated mind had cast out any lingering doubts about wanting to stay a moment longer, and the eager warrior was ready for his long overdue return to a new and safer life, never to look back.

Chapter 9

Transition

When he felt the wheels of the mighty military transport aircraft lift off the airstrip in Bangkok, Yellowsnake looked out the window to capture a last, and hopefully final, glimpse of southeast Asia. He had spent nearly a third of his life in the jungle below and knew his life was about to take a new turn under the watchful guidance of his boss, John Lincoln. Yellowsnake's fervent hope was that the brutality and ugliness of the jungle, which had become so much a part of him, would not tarnish those near and dear to him back home.

Soon after the huge jet touched down in El Paso, he retrieved the Colonel's calling card from his pocket and found a nearby telephone to let him know he was back on safe ground. When the call went through, Yellowsnake was warmly greeted by his CIA counterpart and friend. Colonel Lincoln knew he faced a period of adjustment and told Yellowsnake to go home and see his family. The returning warrior must try to get his mind in tune with life on American soil. Once he had become settled in, and at his leisure, he was to contact the Colonel's office at Langley. If an emergency assignment arose, the Colonel would send a Company jet to pick up Yellowsnake. He smiled to himself as he rented a civilian car for his trip. Jeeps had been his only transportation for so long.

He maintained his usual element of surprise, driving slowly toward the reservation with a feeling of great uncertainty. During his final and most recent years in the jungle, he had become more and more aware of the distance that had developed between himself and Maria. To make matters worse, there was no doubt in his mind as to Maria and her future life. It had become painfully clear that she would never leave the reservation.

Though his arrival back at the reservation was warmly received by Maria, Nikoma, and his family, he knew that by now his fortunes had carried him much too far afield. He could never be at peace with himself living on the small and confining reservation which had been his childhood home.

Although his CIA entry level salary had been fifty-eight thousand dollars, by 1974 his income had escalated to slightly over seventy-two thousand dollars a year. During this time, he had faithfully sent Maria half his income and the other half had been placed in the dependable hands of his mother. Through the years, he had never bothered to ask Hotona about the value of his accumulated savings, for at the time, it didn't make any difference to him. In the jungle, his only necessities were food, water and cigarettes; his expense allowance provided by the Company was more than adequate to cover those needs. His salary, in its entirety, went to his family.

His reunion with his family brought a warm feeling to his uneasy gut. Maria and his excited son welcomed him with love and acceptance back into their sheltered lives. He was back in their world and they had little knowledge of the perilous world from which he had just returned.

An element of discontentment lingered inside him as he settled himself back into the mundane routine of life on the reservation. Though comfortably reunited with Maria and Nik, deep in his heart dwelled a problem which had to be dealt with. He knew the quandary was his, and his alone. He had to decide how to deal with the situation which had come to trouble him more and more. Just as resolutely as Maria had declared she and Nikoma could never leave the reservation, Yellowsnake knew that he, with equal conviction, could no longer dedicate himself to reservation life.

After a lot of soul searching, he decided to confront Maria and deal with the situation head on. He would ask her one final time to leave the reservation and relocate with him so that together they might pursue a mutual happiness. He hoped they might find peace in a new environment. As expected, Maria brought finality to the issue of moving away from the reservation. Her answer was no.

During the years in which he had sent his CIA salary to Maria and Hotona, he was fully aware that Maria had accumulated a sizable sum of money which would be more than adequate to support her and their son Nikoma. Those same long years of his absence had seen her continue working for her father at the general store. She had added even more to the growing nest egg while living comfortably on the money she earned.

After reassuring himself that all financial considerations were taken care of, he kindly, but firmly, informed her he could no longer live within the boundaries of the reservation and make it a part of his future life.

Maria was saddened. But without tears, she accepted his decision without challenge. She had known, perhaps all long, that the warrior's spirit would not be content living the simple life which she so greatly enjoyed. She reluctantly agreed to accept his decision provided he would not attempt to remove Nikoma from the reservation. That would surely break her heart, and they both knew it.

They ended their conversation that evening with an agreement for divorce. It was against Maria's religion to divorce, but she consented to having Yellowsnake take care of the legal details. However, she would never be able to marry again in her church. Neither Yellowsnake or Maria got much sleep that night.

From the moment of his return from Vietnam, he could clearly see that Nikoma had become deeply entrenched in the daily routine of life on the reservation. From infancy, Nikoma had become accustomed to a structured life centered around Indian custom and tradition. Deep in his gut Yellowsnake also harbored a fear that the violence and bloodshed he had encountered throughout the years would in some way become embedded in his innocent and loving son, and this he would not permit.

Although Hotona and Jimmy understood his situation, they knew better than anyone else that his restless spirit had not yet found it's home. They were saddened, knowing he was leaving the reservation for good, and would probably never return for more than a brief visit.

With his farewell bid to his parents, Yellowsnake's life on the reservation had reached it's end.   Earlier, Hotona had retrieved from her hidden strongbox a list of Yellowsnake's accumulated investments and their values. She placed it in his hands with a confident gesture. He opened the carefully folded sheets which revealed a startling summary of his assets. He now realized with surprise that the money he'd sent home over the years had now grown to over three hundred thousand dollars. Since he had lived on the reservation all of his childhood years, he had witnessed the many disservices and inequities endured by the Indians. He had placed sole trust in Hotona to manage the investment and proper placement of his money.

Before leaving, he spoke privately with his saddened mother. "Someday I will call and ask you to gather up those funds for me because you know I've never trusted the white man's honesty, especially when it comes to handling Indian's money." She acknowledged his request by kissing him warmly on his cheek, wrapping her short, chunky arms around his waist. She hugged him for what she feared might be the final time.

He was disappointed and saddened when he said his last sad goodbye to Maria. With love in his heart, he spared Nikoma the unpleasantness of knowing how long he might be absent from his life.   He promised his growing Comanche son that even though he was still working for the Company, he would return to visit him whenever he could. In his own way, Nikoma seemed to understand. Yellowsnake had reached a point of no return, and his final task before leaving was to notify Colonel John of the events which had occurred since his return from Vietnam. Yellowsnake reached him at the private phone number scrawled on the back of the card. John Lincoln, a man of perception, recognized the pain and distress in Yellowsnake's voice. After asking what the problem was, he learned that Yellowsnake had made what might prove to be the most monumental decision of his life.

There was unmistakable concern in the Colonel's voice when he questioned Yellowsnake's decision to leave the reservation and, more importantly, his family. Had the Colonel caused his turmoil when he invited Yellowsnake join him in his treacherous job with the CIA? If so, he truly regretted ever having allowed him to join the madness which they had experienced. Yellowsnake was quick to remove John Lincoln from potential blame at the very onset. He reassured Lincoln that nothing which had occurred during their torrid years of jungle fighting had motivated his decision. The decision had been reached by a warrior whose spirit still searched for a permanent home. Until that restless spirit found a resting place, he must continue to follow his spirits' call.

Colonel Lincoln regretted hearing Yellowsnake's disconcerting words and sensing the air had been cleared concerning the upheaval in his life, informed Yellowsnake that the past couple of weeks had drawn him into a series of events developing in Central America. However, at the present time, neither he nor Yellowsnake had been given a specific assignment. It would be some months before the peculiar situation in Central America would peak. The officials at Company headquarters had agreed with the Colonel that in the meantime Yellowsnake should continue his leave until a new assignment materialized.

Yellowsnake would continue to receive his handsome salary and, until such time as he was contacted by Colonel Lincoln, he was free to do whatever he pleased. "Go on out into the world and have yourself a good time! You've earned it son!" encouraged the Colonel. "You have some hellacious years of war tucked under your belt, and deserve a few months off. Just let me know where you're located so we can stay in touch. As you've learned by now, we'll have to be ready to move at the drop of a hat."

Yellowsnake was beginning to feel more comfortable with his decision, in spite of the sadness he'd endured with his family. "I think I'll head towards Arizona. It's warm and dry there, and I've had enough of the wet climate. It sounds like a good place to rest and, besides that, it'll give me a chance to fly my helicopter." Deep in his heart, Yellowsnake didn't really know where his escape route would take him. His spirit was telling him to seek the solitude of the mountains.

The Colonel's final parting words were blunt. "Don't you dare crash that son of a bitch! You know we've got a lot of work ahead of us. Now have a good time."

He hadn't flown his Bell 47 Comanche chopper in many years. It had been stored in the shed behind his parent's house and was covered with dust, pigeon droppings and other debris. Once his plan was formed, Yellowsnake had it ready to fly within two days. Within hours, he was seated in his magnificent machine, headed upward and onward, toward the great, unknown barrens of Arizona. As the smooth air currents carried him over the mysterious, forbidding mountains of New Mexico, Yellowsnake warmly recalled the stories Shahana had shared with him about the Peraltas. The Peraltas were an adventurous family of Mexican explorers who had ventured through her Yaqui village many years earlier in their quest to discover gold in the mountains of New Mexico and Arizona.

His eyes looked downward. *Damn! That country down there could gobble you up as quickly as the jungles of Vietnam. Those mountains sure look wicked!* reflected Yellowsnake with admiration. He passed over the snow covered peaks of New Mexico and approached the vast desert lying before him, feeling the refreshing warmth of the dry desert air hitting his face. *Hell, I don't know anything about Arizona, let alone where I am at this moment, but I think I'll set my bird down around Apache Junction. After all, that's a good Indian name.*

Yellowsnake spotted what appeared to be a tiny airfield outside Apache Junction, then smoothly planted his ageless treasure on firm ground. He had no idea where his next move would take him. During his first few seconds of looking around, he immediately loved what he saw. In the near distance stood the foreboding and mysterious Superstition Mountains. Not far beyond them lay the scraggly peaks and rugged canyons which had been home to thousands of tormented Indians who had dwelt there during hundreds of years past. He sensed he could find peace and tranquility within the silent peaks of the mountains.

They offered a perfect fortress for someone seeking an escape from the harsh realities of life.

His short return visit to the reservation had revealed a new ugliness which lingered in his mind. He'd witnessed with disgust the longhaired hippies and war protesters displaying their disapproval of issues and traditions. The world had changed, and he wasn't at all certain he could fit into it anymore, much less learn to like it.

Yellowsnake now had plenty of time to ponder his future and face himself. He was a decent mechanic with both aircraft and automobiles, and knew he was certainly capable of going back to breaking mustangs if the need arose. He knew his most valuable tool at hand was his helicopter. Without knowing how many months might pass before he received an urgent call from John Lincoln to get back in the saddle, he wondered what he could do to earn a few dollars and keep himself busy.

He wasn't interested in seeking another woman to fill the needs in his life. Maria was still a part of him. And, he wasn't about to spend his idle hours slopping up beer and whiskey in some dingy saloon. He felt a need to do something exciting and productive with his time until he received a call from the Colonel.

Then, his memory reminded him that he had a friend in Arizona whom he had nearly forgotten about. It was his frog gulping friend Brick Wilson who, like himself, had been sent home after the Vietnam war. Brick was living somewhere outside Mesa. It should be easy to track him down. After all, Yellowsnake was a tracker! He stretched out on the soft bed in his cool motel room and retrieved a local phone book from the nightstand. Within seconds, he had flipped to Brick's phone number and address.

His heart felt lighter as soon as he heard Brick's familiar voice. Brick was a man of few words but, in like fashion, was one of the few white men Yellowsnake knew he could trust outside of the Colonel.

They happily reminisced and exchanged pleasantries, and then got around to talking about the events of the day. Yellowsnake told Brick that he'd left the reservation under less than ideal conditions, and thought it would be nice to spend some time in Arizona. He was in a limbo period, and until such time as he received his next assignment from John Lincoln, he needed some excitement and wanted to put a little extra money in his pocket.

Brick, having served the Company in Vietnam, was now working in the United States in an arrangement similar to Yellowsnake's. Only a few days earlier, he had received his next assignment. Brick understood Yellowsnake's need for action, and was quick to offer a solution.

"Why don't you take a trip into Phoenix and look up Ted Masters? Hang on a minute and I'll get you his phone number. Ted is in the business of buying gold and silver from some of the local miners and might have something right up your alley. I heard he was looking for someone to fly supplies in to some miners in the Superstition Mountains."

Brick knew Yellowsnake's eyes would light up with delight at hearing that there might be a worthwhile job for him and his faithful chopper. As fellow operatives, it went without saying that they would always do whatever they could to help each other. The two of them knew the stresses and strains they'd each encountered over the years, and had developed a mutual respect for each others' accomplishments. "Brick," said Yellowsnake in a thankful voice, "I really appreciate the tip, and I'll let you know how it turns out. Take care of yourself on your next assignment and I'll talk to you as soon as I can."

Yellowsnake had no idea where the suggestion would lead, but knew it sounded exciting and would give him a chance to use his helicopter. The opportunity might offer challenging conditions which he was unaccustomed to, carrying him deep into the mountains and exploring new territories. He knew he was capable of flying his dependable machine into rough terrain which neither man nor horse could reach safely. His chopper could be there in minutes, and find ways to reach areas which were deemed impassable simply by maneuvering in and landing on any flat area available. His dependable tool had many advantages over four legged horses, two legged men, and four wheel drives.

Since he and his helicopter had very few needs and the only possessions he carried were his clothes, his .357 magnum revolver and his Comanche knife, he was more than comfortable living in the tiny kitchenette unit outside of Apache Junction. It would serve nicely as his headquarters until he found out what the fortunes of war had in store for him down the road.

Chapter 10

Dynamite, Frostbite and Dictators

The pudgy little man sat tucked neatly behind his desk in his small office on the outskirts of Phoenix. Ted Masters looked up and smiled as the tall figure entered the room. Masters was a short, rotund, affable man. Yellowsnake, who had called ahead, leaned over and shook his hand firmly. "You and I have a mutual friend in Brick Wilson," he explained. Ted's face lit up at the mention of his friend's name. In Ted's mind, Brick was also a man of his word. Yellowsnake wasted no time getting right to the point. "Brick told me you might have a job for me and my chopper hauling supplies up to miners holed up in the Superstitions."

"Yeah, as a matter of fact, a guy I know called just the other day wanting a delivery to his camp up there but, at this point, I'm not sure what it is he wants. If you're interested in the job, I'll give you his camp coordinates and you can fly up there to get more specifics on what exactly he needs. The fellow I've spoken with is called "Crazy Jake". Whenever I see him, he has usually come in from the mountains by horseback and, when he reaches the foothills, has access to a car to get him here. Apparently, he has a girlfriend with him and, from what I hear, the two of them are doing some serious digging up there."

"Wait a minute! You said his name is Crazy Jake? By any chance, is his real name Jake Bennett?", Yellowsnake queried.

Ted scratched the wiry red hair covering his head. "Yup, I think it is. He's sort of a weird guy who doesn't say a hell of a lot. I've never seen his girlfriend, so I can only go by what I've been told by others."

Yellowsnake couldn't believe his ears. "Well, I'll be damned! If it's the same Crazy Jake I think it is, he's someone I've spent time with in Vietnam."

At the mention of Vietnam, Ted recollected Jake's background. "As a matter of fact, I think this guy worked with the government somewhere overseas–it may have been Vietnam." Yellowsnake didn't have to hear anymore. He was convinced that this had to be the same Jake Bennett he had known in Vietnam, another operative for the Company. Yellowsnake had met Bennett only casually and knew he was an expert in his own right. His specialty was handling highly sensitive explosives while operating throughout Southeast Asia. What's more, Yellowsnake had sensed early in his first meeting with Crazy Jake that he was not a person with whom you could place all of your trust. He was a cagey character, and not one to be relied upon to keep his word.

They scanned the map laying on Ted Master's desk and after having the coordinates pointed out to him, Yellowsnake concluded it would be an easy trip into the Superstition Mountains. He thanked Ted, then later seated himself in his helicopter, ready to depart into the great unknown. He was headed for LeBarge Canyon, located deep in the Superstition's.

In less than twenty minutes, he found himself hovering over the checkpoint Ted had indicated on the map. His eyes combed the ground below, then he spotted an olive drab tent with cookware scattered in disarray around it's entrance. While circling downward toward the campsite, he got a glimpse of two people sauntering along with their horses and burros. His helicopter gently touched down on the rocky terrain, then Yellowsnake stepped out from the protection of his trustworthy machine. He felt his hip to be certain his .357 magnum was strapped securely to his side. Yellowsnake had learned long ago to keep his pistol and knife within easy reach when venturing into the unknown.

Once he was within spitting range, Crazy Jake peered out from under the badly worn brim of his hat and was momentarily dumbfounded when he recognized the tall, lean figure hovering before him. "Holy hell, is that you Snake?"

"Bigger than life! And what the hell are you doing out here Jake?", a leery Yellowsnake asked. After introducing his female companion as Brenda, his mining partner, Jake continued. "I'm out here because I've known all along that there's treasure buried out here. And what's more, I think I've finally figured out where the Lost Dutchman Mine is!"

Poor Jake! thought Yellowsnake. *He's obviously gone over the deep end since returning from Nam.* This was not the same Crazy Jake that Yellowsnake had known in Vietnam.

Jake ordered Brenda to unload the burros and get some food cooking, then continued. "I've been holed up in the mountains for several months and, from time to time, I need to get my supplies restocked. Believe me, hauling it back by myself is a real pain in the ass." After I met Ted Masters, I asked him to find someone who was interested in flying supplies into me. "And what's your reason for being here?"

Yellowsnake had a quick answer. "Well, I guess I'm the guy who's going to be dropping off your supplies. Ted told me there was a miner in the Superstition's who needed to have supplies flown in and, frankly, I don't have a hell of a lot else to do right now." Without elaborating, Yellowsnake told Jake he was still working for the Company, but was between assignments and had no idea when and where he would be off to next. In the meantime, he wanted to do something to keep him and his chopper busy and put some gas money in his pocket.

Crazy Jake was a man of few words, explaining that he had retired from the Company and, since then, had spent every waking hour in the mountains searching for gold. "Snake, there are a bunch of supplies I want, but what I really need more than anything else is something you are real familiar with. I need some C-4 explosives."

Most operatives, including Yellowsnake, knew how to get hold of the C-4 and the other supplies needed by Jake and Brenda. He had some reservations about the request, but agreed to fly in their goods within a few days.

Jake was more than delighted, and agreed to pay him two hundred dollars for each visit in and out of Le Barge Canyon. His hand never strayed far from the revolver strapped on his hip, as Yellowsnake politely bid the couple goodbye, promising to return in a few days.

Three days later, he found himself back in the air, on course for Le Barge Canyon, hauling a hundred pounds of C-4 explosives, along with a lengthy list of food, supplies and sundry items. When he reached the remote and fairly well-hidden camp, Yellowsnake was paid without hesitation for his prompt delivery. Then with a tone of urgency in his voice, Jake abruptly bid Yellowsnake "adios", declaring he and Brenda had to get back up to their secret site. He told Yellowsnake he would contact Ted Masters when they once again were in need of supplies and equipment.

With two crisp one hundred dollar bills in his pocket, Yellowsnake lifted smoothly and effortlessly off the ground, pausing to hover over the vast and mysterious mountains below him. He admired it's beauty, as well as the eeriness surrounding him and thought to himself, *I know Jake was a good operative, but I'd still never trust him.*

Since he had given Ted Masters his motel phone number in Apache Junction, he was soon receiving regular calls from him for various delivery flights. Some of the calls were for additional supplies needed by Jake and Brenda. Rather than contact Yellowsnake personally, Jake preferred to call Ted when he had a list of needed supplies. And each time the enigmatic miner placed an order, he requested additional C-4 explosives.

While he and Ted talked, Yellowsnake couldn't help but share his curiosity as to what Jake was up to. "I don't know how any man could use as much C-4 as I've flown in to him. I know he was deadly using explosives in Nam but, for the life of me, I can't figure out what he's going to do with the hundreds of pounds I've already delivered. He's never said a word to me about how he intends to use it."

And now, after receiving another of Jake's customary requests for more explosives Yellowsnake felt, after five months, that it was time to get to the bottom of things. He decided that after this delivery, he wouldn't fly in any more C-4 until he was able to find out what the hell Jake had in mind. After all, with the large quantities he had stockpiled, he could surely blow up Fort Knox.

He set his trusty bird down on its familiar resting spot within Le Barge Canyon, and was met by Jake. As usual, the edgy miner had a sense of urgency in his voice and seemed eager to unload and get Yellowsnake out of there as quickly as possible.

The twosome carefully unloaded the volatile cargo. Yellowsnake couldn't stand the bizarre behavior a minute more. "Jake, what in almighty hell do you plan on using all of these explosives for? Do you realize how much of this stuff I've dropped off to you over the past six months?"

With a snide grin on his face, Jake proclaimed his intention. "I'm going to locate the Lost Dutchman Mine! In order to do that, I'll have to detonate a pretty good area, but I'm pretty damn sure I've narrowed down its location." Jake would elaborate no further. He was a reclusive and unpredictable man.

Weeks passed without Yellowsnake receiving a delivery call for Jake and Brenda. Not surprising, he read his newspaper one evening to finally discover what the shifty explosives expert had been up to. An article appeared on the front page of the Phoenix newspaper bearing a headline which read, **"Mad Man Tries to Blow Up Superstition Mountains."** Yellowsnake read on, confirming his suspicions regarding Jake's intent. "Crazy Jake Bennett, a recluse, was arrested yesterday, along with Brenda his mining partner. The two of them detonated C-4 explosives, destroying nearly three hundred acres of the Superstition Mountains. The pair were arrested by Federal agents and, after being taken into custody, disclosed their story. They claimed to have been seeking the legendary Lost Dutchman Mine, and had chosen to blow away the mountains of debris in hopes of revealing the fabled treasure."

"Adios, Crazy Jake!" said Yellowsnake to the newspaper in his hands. "I know damn well I won't be delivering you any more C-4. You've really done it this time. You'll be looking out through jailhouse bars!" Months later, Jake was sentenced to a lengthy term in prison and Brenda, his naive accomplice, was given a lesser sentence.

With the advent of 1976, and after more than six months of cooling his heels, Yellowsnake finally received the call he had been eagerly awaiting. It was from John Lincoln, announcing that the vacationing Comanche would be given a new assignment. Though they had talked casually on several occasions during the previous months, Yellowsnake never suspected his wise and respected leader would unload such an

155

unappealing assignment on him. The Colonel laughed as he spoke. "Snake, you'd better dig your longjohns out of the drawer! Since you've had quite a bit of time to play around, I didn't want you to get rusty and soft under the belt. The Company has decided to send you up to Alaska where you'll be doing some chopper observation work. You'll be spying on the Russians across the Bering Strait."

Yellowsnake drew a deep breath and wisely resisted the impulse to complain. He didn't relish the idea of the cold which lay ahead of him. "Colonel, what are you trying to do? Kill me with all of that cold weather?" The Colonel laughed, then fell into a more serious tone of voice. He went on to explain that he was still deeply entrenched in following the dangerous events occurring in Central America. Unfortunately, there was still nothing in the immediate future which would require Yellowsnake's presence in a warmer zone.

The Colonel knew Yellowsnake had no interest in politics and foreign affairs, let alone the devious actions of the politicians themselves. He put it simply. "I know without a doubt that sooner or later I'm going to be sending you into Central America. In the meantime, bear with it and go on up to Alaska for us...though you'll probably freeze your balls off!"

Yellowsnake was not inclined to question his leader's wisdom. He agreed to pack his duffel bag and be prepared to leave on a moment's notice. "We'll plan on picking you up a week from Tuesday," the Colonel said, "and when you arrive at our Alaskan headquarters, there'll be a Company chopper there for your use. Your assignment will be to stay in the air over the Bering Strait and get as close as possible to Russian waters. We're trying to determine exactly what their ships and submarines are up to. There has been a lot of quiet activity up there and we want to keep a close eye on their movements."

As surely as the sun had risen from the East, the following Tuesday found Yellowsnake seated on a Company jet bound for the barrens of Alaska. When he looked down at the frozen, horrifyingly frigid terrain below, he mused to himself. *Colonel John, I'll get even with you for this! Stop bitching,* he thought quietly, *the Company has a need for me here. I'll live through it.*

With little delay and without ceremony, he found himself aboard a Company helicopter. He was bundled in his insulated flying gear, shivering incessantly and wishing he could warm himself. His duty was monotonous and boring. The long tedious months found him flying day after day, with little variety in his prescribed routine over the Bering Strait. He kept his wits intact, and was always conscious of staying well clear of the invisible border of Russian waters. Sure enough, there was a lot of activity below, with ships and submarines often attempting to sneak into international waters unnoticed.

On this particular day, he was astounded when he saw the submarine off in the distance. It was huge. The sub was submerged and was trying to depart from Russian waters unnoticed. But it didn't escape Yellowsnake's eye. It was loaded to the hilt with missile bays. This monster was a new class of nuclear submarine, and it had to be reported to Colonel Lincoln right away. His commander was alarmed. The Colonel, with cautious concern in his voice, commended Yellowsnake for his sighting. Now, the Company would watch the sub and it's movements like a hawk. It was a new threat to U.S. soil and would no longer be able to escape the scrutinous eye of the American fleet.

Day after day, month after month, he faithfully reported the results of his surveillance on the sly Russians who were located only a short distance from the coastline of Alaska. He never failed to remind the Colonel he would be happier than hell when he was able to escape the frozen wasteland.

With a consoling laugh, the Colonel consistently replied, "I know you love it there Comanche, but I'll get you out as quickly as I can." During the long, cold months which Yellowsnake had endured in the barrens of Northern Alaska, he had managed to find a hobby which kept him amused and occupied. In the endless tundra, there wasn't much else to do with his free time. Since he had full access to the Company helicopter, he often ventured deep into the awesome mountains and valleys which had small streams running through them. There he searched for gold. He knew the precious metal lay in abundance throughout the unexplored area. From the air, he could easily locate a safe site on which to land his chopper and, with pick, shovel and pan in hand, he began searching out the remote creeks which held a good chance of bearing gold.

As he became more adept at locating gold, he found himself accumulating numerous large nuggets, flakes and a significant quantity of gold dust in a large leather bag. Whenever the other employees stationed at his outpost inquired as to where he was headed, he always told them he was going hunting, but not for animals.

His job of surveillance and spying on the Russians had become terribly boring and his twelve months in the cold Alaskan barrens seemed more like twelve years. Finally, in May, he received the long-awaited call from Colonel Lincoln. "Okay Yellowsnake, I think I've finally convinced the Company that you've spent enough time in the refrigerator, and they've agreed it's probably time for you to return."

Yellowsnake eagerly stuffed his few belongings into his tattered bag, happily ignoring all of his government issued cold weather gear. The task took only a few minutes and, all the while, his mind joyously celebrated his escape from the inhospitable, though remarkably beautiful wilderness.

He carefully calculated how much gold he had retrieved from the remote areas in which he had prospected through the long lonely months. He painstakingly weighed out each nugget and each pouch of flakes and dust, and estimated that he had amassed around sixty-five thousand dollars worth of gold. While carefully packing the heavy contents in his sturdy leather squaw bag, he had to admit that the past year had not been a complete waste. After all, he was returning home with something of value, and knew Ted Masters would quickly convert his gold into cash.

When the Company plane touched down on the Los Angeles airstrip, Yellowsnake breathed a deep sigh of relief. He looked at his skin, shuddering to himself at the sight of his once bronzed skin which had now paled to a sickly tone. His skin color was nearly that of an ordinary white man. *I'm not going to stay looking like this. I can't wait to get back into the sun and get my real color back!*

An hour later, he was aboard a shuttle hop en route to Phoenix, soon embracing the sight of Arizona soil. When he anxiously arrived at the motel outside Apache Junction, he was provided with the same room he'd stayed in a year earlier. He welcomed it's warmth and comfort more than anyone could have imagined.

He had no trouble reaching the Colonel, who was expecting his call. He greeted his boss with admonition. "Colonel, you can send me to hell, but please don't ever send me back to that place again. I can't take the cold!"

The Colonel chuckled, assuring him it probably wouldn't happen again. "Don't worry Snake, it looks like you'll be in limbo for awhile. Go ahead and have some fun and do what you please. We'll be talking as we always do, and I'll let you know when your next job pops up."

At the top of Yellowsnake's list of stops was a visit to the ever jovial Ted Masters. When he spread the beautiful yellow cache of gold across the desk, Ted's eyes glittered with delight. After he had negotiated a fair price and completed his sale of the gold which he had brought back from Alaska, Yellowsnake walked out of Ted's office with a check for nearly sixty eight thousand dollars. *A nice payday*, he thought, more than mildly proud of his accomplishment.

The following months found Yellowsnake receiving regular calls from Ted requesting that he and his Bell 47 fly supplies into the mountains to miners throughout Arizona. Gold values were on an upward spiral and now there were now more and more miners venturing deep into the mountains to work their claims. The miners were often loners who were reluctant to leave their rich claims and, as such, always had a need for more supplies. Because the conversations among the miners stayed in a tight circle, it had become a given that Ted Masters was the man to see if they needed supplies brought in.

If the weather permitted, Yellowsnake might be asked to fly a shipment of goods into the snow covered Bradshaw Mountains near Prescott. A few days later he'd be asked to shuttle supplies into the foothills of the Mazatzal Mountains. Each time he ventured into the air, he gained a deeper appreciation for

Arizona's vast beauty. He was keeping busy with his chopper and enjoying every moment of his time. The pleasure of his eight months in limbo seemed more like eight weeks. But as expected, the impending call from Colonel Lincoln arrived.

The warm breeze of 1978 had arrived, and with it fresh turmoil in Central America, specifically Nicaragua.

"Yellowsnake," the Colonel confidently exclaimed, "you're going to like this duty! The Company is sending you to warm and sunny Nicaragua. I know you'll love it, because it's nice and hot." Humoring him, the Colonel proceeded. "You've been sitting on your ass too long and need some action. Your assignment will be to enter Nicaragua undetected by everyone except a few high ranking rebels. We'll need you to meet and become acquainted with Daniel Ortega. He's one of the leaders of the Sandinista rebel movement going on inside Nicaragua. I know you don't give a damn about politics, and I won't even try to go into detail about the whole situation. But, you can take my word for it. Our government wants the current Nicaraguan government removed from power. General Somoza, Nicaragua's president, has tried to convince our government he is a good guy, and suddenly an ally of the U.S. But for some reason, our people in Washington want him out of power. So, your job will be to get close to Ortega and become acquainted with what his rebels know, and most probably don't know about jungle fighting and warfare."

"This assignment may get hairy," Colonel Lincoln warned, "because you never know from day to day who is going to do what. If the Sandinistas end up getting defeated in their revolution, you may find yourself running for your life. I have no doubt you can handle yourself, so you'll just have to wing it and be flexible day by day. The Sandinistas are a poorly trained bunch of fighters, and the Company would like you to try getting them whipped into shape so they'll have a decent chance of overthrowing the government. How do you like that can of worms?"

"Shit!" exclaimed Yellowsnake. "You sure know how to pick 'em Colonel! I'll get my bags packed and be ready to leave when you decide it's time."

160

The Company plane arrived in Nicaragua a few days later, cloaked in darkness. It didn't take long to discover the extent of turmoil the Central American country was experiencing. His travels took him far into the northern reaches of the strange new country before he was greeted by a high ranking official within the Sandinista movement. Yellowsnake was escorted to his modest, well-hidden quarters in the thickness of the undergrowth, where he spent his first night wondering uncomfortably if there was anyone in Nicaragua whom he might come to trust.

After he finished his breakfast the following morning, he was escorted to the headquarters of Daniel Ortega, the popular but politically questionable revolutionary leader of the rebel movement.

Daniel Ortega shook his hand and spoke in reasonably fluent English. "Señor Yellowsnake, we are pleased to have you join us in our fight. We are told you will help us get our revolutionary forces trained to fight guerrilla warfare."

Yellowsnake acknowledged Ortega's words, but his innards told him that maybe this wasn't where he should be. The situation was very unstable. Although he was not at all interested in politics, Yellowsnake had overheard various conversations that Ortega was, in fact, a believer in the Communist doctrine. He was leery of the whole situation, and wasn't ready to believe anything he heard coming from the lips of the rebel leader. However, Colonel Lincoln had given him his orders and he would carry them out as he always had. What amazed him more than anything was that the fervent group of revolutionaries had no Air Force. And, even more pathetically, they possessed only a few dilapidated helicopters, most of which were not even capable of flying.

He was even more shocked by the depth of inexperience and inadequacies burdening the rebels. Yellowsnake went to work carrying out the task for which he was so well-suited. Within weeks, and with the help of Ortega's rebel leaders, he had them grouped into a more organized band of potential fighters. He lamented to Ortega, however, how they lacked the experience to be any more than novice jungle fighters. Unfortunately, none of the troops had received any real training in jungle fighting or warfare, much less survival training to keep themselves alive.

Fairly soon, Yellowsnake had gained their respect and attention; they were beginning to realize what it meant to be real jungle fighters. Yellowsnake diligently instructed the rebels and with their officers interpreting his commands, they were soon performing rigorous tasks. He was on his way toward molding them into a more refined and skilled group of fighters. He forced them to make overnight marches through the jungle, hacking their way through the undergrowth as he had done for so many years in Vietnam. Under his watchful eye, he allowed them to sharpen their skills in the art of setting explosives and land mines. Like the Montagnards, they took great delight in hiding the deadly explosives in unexpected places. This maneuver alone would soon prove deadly to the Government National Guard troops who were always in hot pursuit of them.

Yellowsnake patiently demonstrated to the rebels how to properly position themselves as invisible snipers, carefully blending in with the surroundings of the jungle. He emphasized that if they followed his teachings, they might be fortunate enough to outwit the enemy and return with their lives intact.

Although he had met with Daniel Ortega on numerous occasions during the preceding months, their visits were usually limited to discussions on his progress with the Sandinista fighters. He told Ortega they were becoming highly skilled, and now he was showing them how to weave through the jungle, while tracking the enemy with only scant shreds of evidence to help them.

The jungle teacher was watching them with hidden delight. He could see the pride and satisfaction in their eyes, telling him they were finally beginning to grasp the elements of enemy tracking.

A couple of weeks later, while Yellowsnake was visiting with Ortega, the rebel leader presented him with a surprising request. Yellowsnake was more than slightly surprised when the crafty rebel delivered his interesting challenge. Ortega badly needed some air power support. He asked Yellowsnake, "If I provide you with the body, engine and all parts required to build a helicopter warship, could you do it? And, could you arm it to become a gunship which will hurt the government troops?" Until now, the Sandinistas had been limited to attacking the government troops with their ground fighters, absent of any air power assistance. "You're damn right I can," Yellowsnake chided confidently. *At least I think I can*, he pondered silently.

Yellowsnake smiled with anticipation, knowing that Ortega's request should not only be fun, but just as easy as jumping on a bicycle and riding it after many years absence. After all, once someone had learned how a helicopter was put together, he should be more than able to assemble one from the ground up. All of Yellowsnake's past experience told him that with his knowledge, it should be a relatively simple feat to build one. And most importantly, it came as a welcome challenge, because he had become bored with the burden of repeated training. "Yes, I believe I could build you a mighty gunship, Mr. Ortega. If you can get me everything I need and, above all, the necessary fire power, I'll make it a real warship." Ortega flashed a big smile at the gunship builder's assuring words.

The parts began pouring in from various underground sources throughout Latin American and, soon, the obtrusive Bell 205 Huey body arrived, followed by its powerful Dash 13 turbine engine. Now, the task of assembling the naked hull and its parts would begin. He was given the assistance of a few Sandinista officers who possessed an above average knowledge of mechanics. Yellowsnake, most confidently, was ready to assemble the formidable monster.

He spoke and gave directions through the Sandinista interpreters who remained at his side, detailing the various steps of assembly. Yellowsnake carefully inspected every part before it was fit into place. Five weeks later, the big day arrived. It was time to install the mighty engine. Within days, and with the crudest of equipment, the engine was carefully lowered into its permanent resting place inside the massive body. He proudly ran his fingers over the shiny black coat of paint which had been freshly applied to its smooth skin. Yellowsnake knew it was time to "fish or cut bait," as Max had proclaimed years earlier.

His eyes watched the chopper being fueled to its proper

level, then the fearless Comanche pilot climbed behind the control panel and fired up the mighty bird's engine. His senses reacted when he heard its burst of power as it ignited. He felt the rotation of the huge main rotor blade, then carefully manipulated the controls and within seconds, was airborne. The hulking machine was now hovering high above the gawking, wide-eyed workers standing below as he maneuvered it like it had been flying for years.

It suddenly sputtered and choked, as might be expected on its first test flight. The chopper hovered momentarily, then began its smooth descent to solid ground. Yellowsnake was filled with pride, and loving every ounce of his success! "You guys are not only good fighters, you're great chopper builders. Job well done, gentlemen! We couldn't have gotten this baby put together without everyone's help!" The workers' faces were beaming with joy, knowing they had contributed to a spectacular achievement. With some minor alterations, the nearly completed chopper was on its way to becoming a finely tuned and smoothly operating gunship.

The final, and most critical task of his exciting undertaking was to install the armament necessary to make it a destructive force. It could never reach its full potential until it was fully armed to maximum capacity with deadly rockets and machine-gun power. His years of war experience in Vietnam told him what it needed. He submitted his long list of desired firepower to Ortega, and within a few days, the eagerly awaited armaments arrived. Now, the deadly firepower was ready to be mounted on the nearly completed gunship.

When the forty-seven tightly grouped rocket pods and the machine-guns were successfully mounted to the huge body of the helicopter, Yellowsnake was ready to give the black beast a real test. His final run would include firing the rockets and other weapons to be sure it would prove as deadly and effective as he had predicted.

Once he had seated himself comfortably behind the sensitive controls, Yellowsnake lifted the craft smoothly off the ground and soon disappeared into an area well beyond the secret assembly location. He steadied the imposing bird, then fired the first set of rockets. Within moments, he had set the forest ablaze with fire and loud explosions, creating a path of devastation in every direction. He mused his satisfaction. *This baby is ready to go. I'd have been proud to fly it in Vietnam. If this won't stop the government troops, nothing will.*

Yellowsnake was satisfied with it's performance, and as he swept across the treetops back to the assembly area, he turned his thoughts to choosing a small group of potential pilots. He had built it, now they would have to fly it. After selecting the four most likely pilot candidates, he embarked on a vigorous program of teaching them to fly. They must be taught to fly the craft with the same careful skill which he had exhibited, and then safely return it to its resting place so it could fight another day. They were an awkward bunch, but he could see he was making progress.

The demanding flight instructor followed the tactics of his cousin Max years earlier. He guided the pilots through each intricate movement, aided by an interpreter. He knew it would be impossible from the standpoint of time, to ever teach them all of the tricks he had learned over the years. Nevertheless, he would teach them everything they needed to know regarding the chopper's delicate operation. His final job would be to school them in the fine art of firing the deadly missiles at the proper time.

Throughout the intensely grueling three month period, Yellowsnake relentlessly pushed the novice pilots until he felt confident that they could safely pilot the aircraft. He watched them perform, becoming even more assured that they were capable of completing a mission and returning with a reasonable degree of certainty. He had done all he could, now it was up to them.

The rebel leader was more than delighted with the achievement, and with a high degree of fanfare, Daniel Ortega ceremoniously presented the smugly proud helicopter builder with a Merit of Appreciation. The accomplishment of his task meant a great deal to Yellowsnake; ceremonies always tried his patience.

Two weeks after the ceremony, the deadly gunship began

proving to be much more than just a nuisance to the government guard troops pursuing the Sandinista fighters. The helicopter gunship was beginning to take its toll in great numbers, easing the strain on the rebels who, until now, had only been foot soldiers.

By late 1978, the Somozan government, which was gradually losing a grip on its power, began to crumble and would soon surrender control to the Sandinista rebels.

Yellowsnake had become leisurely as he performed his tasks, because he knew the end was in sight. His months in the jungle had deemed him a short timer in the confused, war-torn country. And most eagerly, he awaited a beckoning call from his Company leader.

Three weeks later, his wake up call arrived. "Yellowsnake, it's time to get your duff out of Nicaragua. The Company thinks you've been there long enough. Ortega gave us good reports on how well you trained his troops, not to mention that stupid helicopter you built for him. Get your underwear packed, we're sending a plane in to bring you home. Give me a call when you return, and we'll see what's in store for you. I'm still embroiled in this damnable mess concerning all of Central America and, believe me, your duty has probably been a hell of a lot more exciting than mine! It sounds like you've had all the fun. Mark my words, the whole situation down there is only going to get muddier. When you get back, we'll talk more."

Yellowsnake was overjoyed when his plane reached Arizona, the place he was now calling home. And he was back without so much as a scratch on his body. He headed straight for the comfortable motel outside Apache Junction to find everything just as he had left it. He breathed a comfortable sigh of relief after inspecting his cherished Bell 47 helicopter, resting peacefully at the small isolated airstrip outside of town.

The weary traveler unpacked his duffel and retrieved his knife and .357 magnum from where he had carefully stowed them, placing them in their proper resting place inside a drawer near his bed. Then, he dutifully called Colonel Lincoln to let him know he was safely back on U.S. soil. The Colonel had become increasingly involved in the unsettled politics of

Washington, and after hearing Yellowsnake's voice, he exclaimed, "Well, fearless warrior, how did you enjoy the warmth of the Nicaraguan jungles?"

"Sir, if you'd have been there to enjoy the luxury living and warmth of the sun along with me, it would have been a lot more fun!" responded Yellowsnake.

The Colonel got the gist of the message. "Believe me, son, I wish I could have been there. Things are not always a bed of roses here in D.C.! Now that you're back in Arizona, you'll have a few months on your hands to enjoy yourself and rest up. We're still dealing with the muddy mess in Central America, and don't have much for you right now. But, you know it won't be long before we ask you to go back to earning your keep!" The Colonel heartily wished Yellowsnake the best of relaxing times, and assured him he'd be in touch as soon as something was on the horizon. In the meantime, Yellowsnake was being ordered to "have some fun".

He was basking in sheer comfort as he lounged next to the pool just outside his room, sipping a cold Coke. He absorbed the warm Arizona sun with deep satisfaction. He dozed intermittently, pondering what his next move might be. Ted Masters seemed to be in touch with everyone in the outlying areas around Phoenix, especially those who needed something requiring an airplane or helicopter. In recent months, Ted had received calls from ranchers wanting supplies and materials flown into their sprawling ranches. It was the only way the highly inaccessible areas could be fenced, enabling them to confine their cattle.

His mind was comforted in knowing he was no longer transporting highly volatile C-4 explosives into Crazy Jake. Within days, Ted was giving him jobs flying in everything imaginable to the ranchers. He was perfectly content in performing the rancher's tasks, as it not only put cash in his pocket, but enabled him to venture further and further into areas he'd never seen.

It was a hot breezy day as he reminisced, and then with nothing better to do, he decided to take a trip back over the Superstition Mountains. He wanted to take a look at the area where he had delivered explosives to Crazy Jake. His Bell 47 swept over the Superstitions and when he neared the area around Le Barge Canyon, he sadly viewed the ugly devastation below. The tragedy had occurred after Jake planted and simultaneously ignited all of the C-4 explosives he had quietly accumulated. He looked down in disbelief, muttering within. *What a horrible mess that crazy bastard left behind! I knew he did a lot of strange things, but I never thought he would try to blow an area as large as that.*

Yellowsnake steered his airship somewhat aimlessly over the canyon, then a fleeting thought from his boyhood crept into his mind. He recalled the countless days he had spent on his parents' porch many years earlier, carving the intricately fashioned peace pipe. Although he was only fourteen years old at the time, it was his second endeavor to carve a most special pipe which would someday, be bestowed upon someone special in his life. The pipe was perfect in every detail, and would most appropriately signify character, achievement and dignity to its lucky beneficiary.

During his brief moments of thought, Yellowsnake had reached an irreversible conclusion. There was not a chance in hell that Crazy Jake Bennett would ever receive the pipe!

The treasured piece he had carved many years earlier would have to continue hibernating in its snug resting place a while longer.

If I ever meet anyone else named Jake, I damn well hope he's got more sense than Crazy Jake. It's too bad he lost his respect for the land and the people around him. He was a good mercenary, but I think he lost his soul somewhere along the line.

Without the benefit of a crystal ball to foresee his future, Yellowsnake couldn't have known at this reminiscing moment that there indeed would be another Jake in his life. Not another Crazy Jake. . . . . Jake Montana!

Yellowsnake felt distressed as he looked at the rock-strewn, crater-pocked expanse of acreage lying below. He wanted it out of his sight as he lazily steered his chopper, exploring in and around the many canyons and peaks within the mountains. In the back of his mind, he wondered if there was any truth to the

Lost Dutchman treasure legends he had heard, not to mention the dubious reports of rich gold deposits.

A few days later, the lure of legends past had drawn him back into one of the countless remote canyons deep in the Superstition's. The curious searcher had come looking for signs of gold which, for all he knew, was purely fictitious.

He had become a skillful gold panner during his time in Alaska, but this place proved different. As hard and diligently as he dug into the Superstition's nearly impenetrable ground, he found no signs of gold color. If there was any gold in the spooky mountains, it was probably treasure that had been buried by the Spaniards or Mexicans many years earlier when they were fleeing from the Apache Indians. In their frantic haste, they often buried their riches, or hid them within the boulder strewn crevices or caves. And most certainly, if the fabled Lost Dutchman's Gold Mine ever came to surface, it would be discovered by someone else, not Yellowsnake.

He was content with his new-found lot in life, and knew that during his tumultuous years he'd become financially secure with the dollars he'd tucked away. He had saved much of his Company wages, and had kept his profits from the gold he mined in Alaska. However, he knew it was only a matter of time until he received another call from the Colonel. His real security, though somewhat tenuous, was offered by his job.

He felt like a second sense was alerting him just as the expected call arrived. And even though he and the Colonel had talked casually on an infrequent basis, he knew this call meant business. "Yellowsnake, get back in the saddle! I know you'll be delighted, 'cause you'll be spending some time in Panama."

"Just a minute, sir, I'll dig out my map and see if it's anywhere near Alaska."

After they had traded their humorous jibes, the Colonel got right down to business. "It looks like your next adventure will be to assist General Manuel Noriega in Panama. Things are in a real shit turmoil down there. Their present leader, Omar Torrijos, is a dictator who's past being tolerated by the United States. The General has requested our assistance, and it looks like there's a slot for you. It's a lot like Nicaragua, because he has troops who don't know squat about jungle fighting. In the next few days, I'll call and give you more details on your job. In the meanwhile, enjoy your last days of vacation!"

Always true to his word, Colonel Lincoln had, within days, implemented Yellowsnake's latest adventure. His eyes were directed toward the southern horizon as he anticipated his arrival in a new and unsettled country.

On the ground, watchful eyes followed his stealth arrival outside of Panama City, then he was greeted by two Panamanian military officials, neither of whom he recognized. Before he even deboarded the plane, he was asked to present proper identification to them. He showed them his credentials, and after passing the scrutiny of the officials, he was escorted to the G2 Intelligence Headquarters of General Manuel Noriega. A swarthy looking assistant led him into the splendorous office of the General, where he was greeted by a sinister, imposing looking figure sitting behind a long formal desk.

The notorious General approached him and extended his hand in greeting. The suspicious warrior had already formed an opinion as to what the uniformed insurgent represented. His first thoughts were, *This guy is just as slippery as those greased pigs at Langley headquarters. I don't think I'd better give him my wallet for safekeeping.*

Yellowsnake had heard circulating rumors that the General was an exceptionally vicious and all too powerful leader of all of Panama's military forces. And as such, he had designs on becoming President and dictator. Although his political motives were cloudy at best, it soon became evident that the General had only one outcome in mind. His goal was to gain total control of the country. An assistant seated Yellowsnake in a velvet covered chair in front of the General's desk as Noriega announced he was happy to have Yellowsnake in his country. Yellowsnake would be acting as Noriega's personal advisor for the purpose of getting the General's military forces whipped into shape. They lacked training in the techniques of coordinated jungle warfare.

His fingers nervously rubbed the velvet chair covering, and one thought kept popping back into Yellowsnake's mind. His

170

wise and knowledgeable Colonel had warned him more than once that he should keep his eye on Noriega at all times. He could hear the Colonel's exact words. "We don't know a whole lot about this guy, and although he has always pretended to be a strong supporter of the United States, we know he's dirty. Besides being General, he controls the drug business down there. Stay alert. One of your jobs will be to keep a close eye on him and his activities, and let me know what he's up to on a regular basis. In the meantime, you're an invited guest in his country and, for all he knows, you're there to help with the training of his troops."

With the passage of time, Yellowsnake had become more and more disgusted with politics. The longer he was exposed to it, the more he realized the big picture was extremely fuzzy. He had never felt comfortable going through life without seeing clearly what lay ahead of him. And this assignment was no different. He would have to keep his eyes open and peeled at all times.

A few days later Yellowsnake found himself deep within the lower regions of Panama, absorbed in his lackluster job of training novice troops like he had so many times in the past. It didn't take him long to discover that Noriega's troops were a merciless, deeply dedicated group. And, they appeared to be following the General with blind loyalty. In spite of their dangerous allegiance, he was willing to ignore the uncertainties and proceed with his task of training the troops. There were many similarities with the months he'd spent in Nicaragua with Daniel Ortega. He found himself making repeated visits to Noriega's office, since the General was always anxious to hear of his army's progress in learning to fight as efficiently as American soldiers.

To complicate matters, there always seemed to be persistent rumors circulating that some of Noriega's subordinate officers were secretly planning to overthrow the General. This made him even more uneasy. He didn't want to get caught up in the middle of a coup. Sure as hell, he'd be mistaken as an ally and friend of Noriega and end up dead.

He persevered, doing what he did best, and as the months

flew by, Yellowsnake found himself becoming more personally acquainted with various government officials in important positions. There were very few of them that he could trust, so he had to be careful who he talked to.

Among those was the Minister of Antiquities, a cultured gentleman who seemed somewhat more refined than his counterparts. He appeared to have an element of honesty in his manner, and a sincere concern for the welfare of his countrymen. As the two became acquainted and spent more time together, it became obvious the Minister had heard of Yellowsnake's skills. In particular, he had heard about his ability to navigate through dense, uncharted jungle terrain and, most importantly, his ability to survive.

It was oppressively hot in late 1979, when Yellowsnake received a call from the Minister requesting that they meet for lunch to talk about a favor he wanted to ask of him. His curious nature led him to the dark, smoke-filled cafe in a small town nearby where he met the Minister. He listened to the Minister's strange request flow from his lips, while silently agreeing to undertake the highly unusual venture. The idea intrigued Yellowsnake, causing him to think it sounded more like fun than work.

Because of his important title, the Minister of Antiquities had become acquainted with the leader of a nearly extinct Indian tribe which inhabited a densely forested, and mostly unexplored area far to the south. The Indian leader had described an ancient ruin which he called the "Mountain of Bones". *Mysterious,* Yellowsnake mused. The leader and his tribe had never welcomed the incursion of modernized Panamanians, but had expressed a willingness to help the Minister. The antiquities expert wanted to gain a deeper knowledge of civilizations that had lived thousands of years earlier. In wanting to help, the short statured Indian leader had disclosed his story of the Mountain of Bones. It was a story like Yellowsnake had never heard before. It whet his appetite and, besides, he was ready for a change of pace.

According to the Indian leader, the Mountain of Bones was the site of ceremonial sacrifices which had taken place centuries earlier, deep in dense jungle areas once occupied by his ancestors. Their religious and ceremonial beliefs dictated that the ancient inhabitants perform frequent sacrifices to their Gods. Their sacrifices over the centuries had created a huge burial site for the unfortunate victims. "As I am told," the Minister confided, "the site is a very large mounded area which is now severely overgrown. The Indian leader told me the site contains several huge clay urns buried beneath it's surface. Each of the buried pots supposedly contains the bones of those who were sacrificed, along with their precious gold jewelry and ornamental possessions. He told me golden daggers were used to slay the poor souls, and were buried along with their remains," explained the Minister.

"What exactly do you want me to do?" asked Yellowsnake who was clearly fascinated by the story.

The Minister's plan was to provide Yellowsnake with a helicopter for air transportation to a point at which he could then travel by foot. At that location, he would be provided with burros by members of the Indian tribe. The Minister hoped that with some direction from their leader, Yellowsnake could locate the Mountain of Bones. After he had found it's location, Yellowsnake needed to remove the bones from the large buried urns, along with the gold artifacts and treasures which had been buried with each victim. His task was to carefully extract the contents of each pot and retrieve their valuable contents, then carefully pack them into panniers fastened to the burros. After Yellowsnake had completed his retrieval, he must then deliver them to the Minister for examination and retention by the Panamanian government.

"If you will accept this request, I'll make it well worth your effort," said the Minister. "I have been told that, along with the golden artifacts, there is an abundance of ancient pottery which should have substantial value. That being the case, I'm willing to pay you with all the pottery you are able to carry out with you."

Yellowsnake had quietly reached his decision. *What the hell,* he thought to himself. *I'm getting bored with nursing along Noriega's troops; they're pretty well trained now anyway. I'd*

173

welcome a break from the monotony. What have I got to lose?
I've got to stay here until Colonel John recalls me anyway, so I
might as well have a little excitement while I'm here.

Yellowsnake met with the Minister a few days later, and after receiving more accurate coordinates from the map laying on his desk, he was certain he could locate the Mountain of Bones. Once he got there and was able to get his bearings, he'd proceed by foot. A week later, he was strapped into the cockpit of an aging helicopter provided by the Minister. His renovated antique was headed toward a destination deep inside an unexplored and seldom seen jungle.

Before Yellowsnake's departure, the Minister had set up a meeting point for Yellowsnake to rendezvous with the tribal leader. Then, the leader himself would point out the general location of the Mountain of Bones they sought to locate.

Yellowsnake was thrilled with the change of pace as he arrived at the small clearing noted on the Minister's map. He looked guardedly in all directions as he carefully lowered the helicopter to the ground. There was no evidence of human life anywhere. He had no sooner opened the door of the chopper when he was greeted by the leader and three of his tribesmen. They had appeared out of nowhere. Each was carrying a long spear which could undoubtedly make a large and fatal hole in Yellowsnake's body, should he inspire their wrath.

The leader spoke little English, but only a few words were enough for Yellowsnake to gain a sense of direction toward the Mountain of Bones. The chief had a fearful look in his eye as he cautiously pointed in a southwesterly direction toward a dense, meaningless tangle of jungle. "Mountain...there. You no hurt. No take bones. We no go. . . " he said emphatically. Then, the leader and his accomplices turned and disappeared into the jungle, just as quickly as they had appeared.

Off to one edge of the clearing, the chief had pointed to four waiting burros which had been saddled with crude grass panniers. The panniers were meant to serve as giant saddle bags to transport the gold and silver riches from the area.

Yellowsnake secured the helicopter, unlashed the waiting animals and, not knowing what danger lay ahead, proceeded in the direction pointed out by the Indian leader. He adjusted his backpack on his shoulders, then grasped the rope which would lead the pack animals. He was ready to begin his trek. He had no idea how far he would have to travel to reach the Mountain of Bones, and would never know until he struck out along the centuries old path.

Before the day had ended, Yellowsnake had crossed six small streams, none reaching above his knees. And, all along the way, there were poisonous snakes of every color and size. He sidestepped and steered around them, hoping he wouldn't get bit and end up like the urn victims - dead! By dark, he was still without a clue as to the mysterious mountain's location. He struck a camp that night, relaxing next to his fire while resting his body in preparation for the next day. Much to his displeasure, he broke out canned rations for his evening meal. His wondering eyes stared contentedly into the coals of his campfire as he pondered what tomorrow might bring. He slept lightly that night. The snakes made him nervous as hell, and he didn't want one as a bed partner.

The loud squawk of the birds and chattering animals awoke him the next morning, telling him he'd slept long enough. It was nearly daylight and time for him to be on his way, so as soon as he reharnessed the grazing burros, he was underway. Although he still hadn't seen any signs of human life, he still felt more comfortable knowing his gun and knife were securely on his belt. Throughout his trek, he had a nervous feeling he was being watched, although if anyone was watching, they were as adept at hiding as he was.

The day was drawing to a close as he watched the sun drop closer to the towering tree line. Suddenly, he saw a mountain ahead which seemed to appear out of nowhere. Although it was not a towering fortress, it was the only mountain in the immediate area. When he and his animals reached the mysterious upheaval, which had probably never been seen by anyone but the mysterious Indians, Yellowsnake's senses told him he had reached his destination. It was evening, and he was ready to hobble his burros in a small clearing which looked like a good campsite. His curiosity urged him to take a walk in the general direction of the mountain just ahead. He soon found what he was looking for.

Elation hit him, for he had stumbled upon what appeared to be the ancient sacrificial site used for performing human sacrifices. The sight was unmistakably clear. Straight ahead of him stood a protruding, well defined white stone ledge, and below it, a scene which matched the Minister's description perfectly. Even though the ground was overgrown and tangled with vegetation, Yellowsnake was able to spot the giant clay urns which had been deeply submerged in the soil. Their perimeters were covered with dirt and stones, and there was no more than a few inches of their tops protruding above the surface of the ground. The urns had been carefully camouflaged so they would remain unnoticed by a casual passerby.

Yellowsnake paced off their measurements, finding each pot had a diameter of ten feet. He counted a total of twelve pots scattered about in a somewhat symmetrical pattern. The clay burial urns were filled with heaps of now whitened bones of their sacrificial victims. After two long days of trekking through rough terrain, Yellowsnake's weariness told him to hold off doing anything until the following morning.

After darkness had set in, he snuggled into his bedroll. He was tired and his eyes closed slowly as thoughts of his childhood took over his mind. His dreams drifted back to remembering the scrutinous eyes of his council Elders, examining every detail of the peacepipe he had carved before his acceptance into manhood. His day of judgment had arrived and the Elders had called him before them. They passed the pipe amongst one another, looking at every detail and symbol which adorned its stem and bowl. He had stood motionless before the council, his twelve year old body afraid to move. The senior Elder packed the bowl firmly with sweet grass, then lit the pipe, inhaling its first puff of smoke. Yellowsnake had held his breath, fearing the council would reject his effort. His fear was unfounded. After each member had puffed its contents, the pipe was judged worthy. They had accepted his pipe, and thus his manhood. The senior council Elder then welcomed him, and his manhood into their circle. Then, he spoke words which Yellowsnake would never

176

forget. "The making and acceptance of your pipe represents hard labor, pride and a strength of character which not every man possesses. When the forces of evil and injustice invade your domain, remember the pipe and what it means. Not only to you, but to your tribe as well." Yellowsnake had never forgotten, and never would.

He rose early, anxious to embark upon his eerie assignment. Removing the bones piece by piece, he piled them neatly along the side of their respective urn. As he dug deeper, he found exactly what the Minister had predicted. Within each pot were valuable gold artifacts and jewelry of the victims. He couldn't believe his eyes, for each time he reached into the deep holes, he discovered treasure scattered throughout.

The sunken urns were laced with golden nose rings and earrings, massive neck chains, bracelets and assorted ornaments. And within each pot he found golden daggers, which were apparently an important part of the gruesome death ceremony. The accumulation of gold and treasured artifacts he was taking from the ground would later prove to be of unimaginable value.

He had consumed four days and had successfully extracted, bone by bone, the entire contents of each giant urn. Just as carefully, he returned each bone to its original resting spot. Before he had completed his task, he had filled seven of the woven panniers which were strapped to the burros. The wise Minister had also accurately forecast the ancient pottery and artifacts which he said would be scattered throughout the area. The long-forgotten pieces had been skillfully crafted by an ancient civilization hundreds of years earlier. Now the craftsmen were no more than a bleaching mound of bones, left to rest for eternity.

He methodically gathered together as many of the pots and ornaments as the remaining pannier would hold, placing them in the basket. He exercised great care as he packed each of the delicate pieces with long, soft clumps of grass. Then he surehandedly positioned each piece to prevent any of the valuable pottery from being broken during travel.

He was satisfied that he had completed his mission, but had remained uncomfortably nervous while he worked there. He was well aware that the grounds were extremely sacred to the people who had lived there hundreds of years earlier. Even more unnerving, the site was equally revered by the Indian tribe which had directed him toward the area. Although the Minister told him they had blessed his presence, he was still uncomfortable being there. He had accomplished his feat, and though he was satisfied with his achievement, he hastily gathered his belongings together for a prompt return.

Early the next morning, he checked to see that the panniers were securely attached, then he hastily departed, driven by an urgent need to reach his helicopter as soon as possible. His senses had made him more than eager to depart the sacred area, and the longer he lingered, the more it spooked him. He had crossed two of the small rivers when he saw a quick movement in the tangled underbrush. It startled him. The fleeting figure was tall, much taller than the Indians who had pointed the way. And just as quickly, the figure vanished. That night, he sat nervously by his fire, keeping an eye out for the shadowy figure. Finally he dozed off, hoping he'd awaken without a spear through his heart. At morning's first light, he packed quickly and shoved off at a fast moving pace.

When he arrived at his helicopter well before sundown the second day, he was deeply relieved at his uneventful day. Without lingering any longer, he began loading the treasured cargo into the hull of his aircraft. Nearly two hours later, he was ready to lift into the air and deliver his horde of valuable goods to the Minister at his meeting place.

Suddenly, he heard the swish of moving air as the spear hurtled toward him. It hit the ground with a sharp thud, not more than three feet from where he stood. He looked up, then saw the two tall bodies standing just inside the thicket area surrounding the clearing. He jumped behind the chopper's body for protection, placing his hand on his gun. He peeked around the chopper nose and saw them still standing motionless. They had sent him a warning, and it was not a friendly one. He moved around the helicopter and jumped inside, keeping a wary eye on their whereabouts. Moments later, he was airborne. The Minister just shook his head in disbelief. He had no idea who

178

they were, or why they were there.

The Minister's eyes grew as large as saucers when he saw the golden treasure waiting to be unloaded from the burro's panniers. Under the scrutiny of the Minister, his workers carefully unloaded the gold and silver artifacts, placing each piece in a well-secured chest. Before long, the chests had disappeared from Yellowsnake's sight. The jubilant Minister didn't seem at all concerned about the value of the pottery and clay artifacts which Yellowsnake had retrieved as his payment. The humble Minister tried hard to express his appreciation, warmly thanking the jungle explorer for his successful efforts. The Minister cordially agreed to make the necessary arrangements for shipping his precious objects safely back to the United States.

Both Yellowsnake and the Minister were well aware of the obvious uncertainty and dangerous unrest mounting within Panama. The Minister wasted no time in arranging to have Yellowsnake's valuable objects shipped back to a safe resting place within Hotona's home.

A month later, and just prior to Panama's national elections, Yellowsnake received the call for which he had patiently waited. It was time for him to return home. He was ready to leave, and said his polite, though somewhat insincere good-byes to General Noriega and his staff. Thirty minutes later, Yellowsnake was safely nestled aboard the plane which would carry him back to the quiet and comfortable surroundings of Arizona, the place he now called home.

When he reached the warm, sunny surroundings of his humble retreat, Yellowsnake wasted no time in checking in with Colonel Lincoln. He was glad as hell to be out of Panama, explaining in no uncertain terms that all of the time he was there, he had felt extremely uneasy about his life and personal safety. Boss John warmly welcomed his friend back home safe and sound, telling him, predictably, to hang tight until the next chapter of their lives revealed what lay ahead.

Central America would have to survive without Yellowsnake's presence. He had experienced enough of Nicaragua's sunshine, and Panama's hospitality. If he ever saw either of the countries again, he wanted to see them as a pot-bellied retiree, adorned in bermuda shorts and a flowered shirt.

Chapter 11

Clyde Durham, Emmet Claggett and Monte

The much traveled warrior couldn't help but gloat with quiet satisfaction in knowing he had returned alive and unscarred from another successful assignment. The proud Comanche was more than pleased to return to the quiet solitude and beauty of the Arizona mountains. Although he was always proud of his accomplishments and, especially of being able to fulfill the assignments given by Colonel Lincoln, he hoped he wouldn't see Central America again in the foreseeable future.

He felt the warm, comforting breezes of spring, 1980, brush across his face, blowing his long hair in every direction. Yellowsnake was feeling the urge for another venture into the mountains. Though he had been out of contact with the everyday experiences of living in the United States, Yellowsnake had been aware of the crisis and turmoil within America's banking system. His concern, in turn, had caused him to become distrusting and fearful that he might lose his hard-earned savings which had been carefully invested by his mother.

He had always been self-sufficient, and had continued sending half of his Company wages to Maria, with the remainder going to Hotona. He knew his nest egg should now exceed five-hundred thousand dollars. He had heard about many of the banks that were on the brink of financial disaster and, more importantly, was aware that some had already failed.

Yellowsnake was gradually adjusting to what would be considered a normal life in America, but nevertheless found himself in the familiar office of Ted Masters, looking for something to keep him and his aging helicopter occupied.

Ted chuckled and greeted him warmly. "I hadn't seen your hide for such a long time I thought you were a dead man!"

Yellowsnake was never at a loss for words when he was among friends. "There's no way they're going to kill me in some country I don't even want to be in! Besides, you know it's almost impossible to kill a Comanche Indian."

"I know you're looking for something to do," observed Ted, "but about the only thing I know of right now is that, a couple of months ago, two feisty old miners came into my office looking for someone to deliver supplies to them in the Mazatzal Mountains. The locals around here call 'em the Matazals. They're a funny pair, but I think you'd enjoy their company. I know they sure would appreciate getting some supplies they need because, from what I hear, the country is rugged as hell."

"Sure, why not?" the eager pilot agreed.

"As far as I can determine, they have their camp set up somewhere up in Deadman Canyon, and from the looks of the Mazatzals on this map, it's nearly inaccessible on foot. Anyway, these two crusty old birds claim to know a secret trail leading into the canyon." He pointed to a spot on the large wall map hanging next to his desk, then spoke. "The best I can tell you is that they're somewhere around this spot right here. If you can find a way to fly in, I'm sure they'll reward you handsomely. You probably know, of course, you're not supposed to be in there. Some years ago the government declared that piece of land a national wilderness area and helicopters are forbidden. But hell, I don't think anybody would ever spot you in such a remote area and, if you want to take the risk of going in, go right ahead."

Yellowsnake was willing to stare risk squarely in the eye. He agreed that he might give it a try, and if things looked too dangerous, he would just pass on the idea. In the meantime, he'd fly over the area to check the situation out.

He knew it might be many months before he received his next assignment from Colonel Lincoln, and had plenty of time on his hands. He could put his time to good use by flying his helicopter and maybe have a little fun along the way.

Yellowsnake reflected on the brief description given to him of his new clients. *I don't know anything about those old miners, but I think I'll bring something along as a peace offering. If they have a list of goods they want me to fly in, maybe they'll be more comfortable knowing I'm a decent kind of guy.* So, before leaving town Yellowsnake stopped by a store, and figuring it was safe to assume that they probably smoked and chewed, he purchased both types of tobacco.

After he returned to the comfort of his motel, he scanned the area map covering the Mazatzals and reflected once again, *What a massive piece of real estate! This is a huge area. I can see why few white men have ever ventured back in there. There aren't many trails leading into the mountainous terrain. And those canyons could swallow you up.*

He adjusted his harness after climbing aboard his Bell 47, neatly tucking the two cans of Prince Albert tobacco, cigarette papers, and six pouches of Red Man chewing tobacco into his jacket. Yellowsnake was set to voyage into a largely unexplored area within the Mazatzals, and his destination was Deadman Canyon.

His faithful craft lifted off into the balmy winds which would carry him north around the edge of the Superstition Mountains, then he veered toward the treacherous-looking Four Peaks area. His journey was taking him north along the backbone of the dangerously protruding Mazatzals. He carefully observed his map as he flew over the restricted fly zone, realizing why very few men had even dared to venture in. His ship dropped down lower and lower as he approached the vicinity of Deadman Canyon. Then his eyes caught view of the faint remnants of old Spanish Conquistador trails which were probably formed hundreds of years earlier by the hooves of their horses as they searched relentlessly for gold throughout Arizona.

Although he was able to distinguish the outline of the trails hidden in the heavy underbrush below, all of them seemed to lead steadily upward toward the peaks of the mountains. And then, like they were barricaded, they seemed to stop. There appeared to be no continuation of the trails once they reached the upper pinnacles of the mountain.

Yellowsnake maneuvered his chopper high above what he was now certain had to be Deadman Canyon. He could see what was once a massive waterfall far below, dropping a couple of hundred feet from a high plateau to a much lower plateau directly below it. He had no idea exactly which direction he should point his helicopter relative to the location of the falls, which were now no more than a trickle. So, he decided the flattest area within the canyon was on the lower plateau, and would serve as a good starting point. Yellowsnake was unsure of whether or not he would be successful in locating the miners, but he had to start somewhere.

As his steady craft descended into the deep jaws of the lower canyon, he spotted a string of grazing burros near the edge of a thick stand of scrub oak trees. *This must be their camp,* he said to himself. *I sure as hell hope they don't start shooting at me because they think I'm a federal agent swooping into their canyon.* He circled the canyon in a graceful, sweeping and non-threatening manner, then settled his chopper skids gently on the ground near the area where the burros stood watching.

He grabbed the tobacco goods and placed them in a cloth laundry bag as he departed the aircraft, then slung the bag over his shoulder. As he approached the burros, he heard a shout. "That's far enough, stranger! What do ya think you're doin' here?"

Yellowsnake looked forty yards to his right and into the side of the sheer mountain face and saw the opening of what appeared to be a cave. The two old miners were standing in it's entrance with hands poised on their protruding pistols, ready to draw on him. Yellowsnake stopped in his tracks. He knew he was on their territory, and it would be wise for him to let them make the first move. He stood motionless, then slowly raised his left hand in a gesture indicating he was there in peace.

He watched with curious interest as the two bearded miners cautiously approached him. It was obvious what Ted Masters had been talking about. They sure were a crusty pair. The apparent leader of the two shouted out to Yellowsnake, "Who the hell are you?"

"I'm Yellowsnake. Ted Masters told me you might be needing some supplies. I'm here to see if I can help you out. I can fly my chopper most any place, and I deliver goods to a few other miners."

The wary pair looked at each other in silent agreement as to their trust of this stranger, then motioned for him to walk toward them. The uncertain pilot walked slowly in their direction, keeping a keen eye on the hands resting on their holsters. He reached them in seconds and, without speaking, carefully dropped the bag of goods onto the ground and extended his hand in friendship.

The strange looking miners were uneasy, but each of them firmly returned his handshake. The leader spoke. "You say Ted sent you down here? We didn't know he was gonna send anybody down right now."

Yellowsnake had the answer. "Yeah, I know, I just returned from out of town and was nosing around for something to keep me busy, so I flew over here to take a look." As the minutes passed, he was sensing that the two prospectors were becoming more accepting of his presence. Yellowsnake lifted the gray bag from the ground and handed it to Clyde. He accepted it hesitantly, then peered curiously inside at its contents.

"Well I'll be damned! Lookie here, Emmet, there's a slew of tobacco in this here bag. Hell, we're in good shape now." As he sat the bag down on the ground, the leader of the two introduced himself. "My name is Clyde Durham. And this here's Emmet Claggett. Me and Emmet been working this place for years and got to know Ted when we went to town and were needin' supplies. Since we're getting to be old farts, it's harder than hell to get our goods in by ourselves. That's why we went to Ted."

"Well, I'm just the man you want to see," said Yellowsnake. "I got the flying machine, and I can bring you supplies whenever you need 'em." His words were welcome news to their ears, and their eyes lit up with delight. Now they would have an easier time getting their precious supplies replenished.

They chuckled and whispered as they retrieved the valued tobaccos from the sack on their way back toward the cave. Then, after a few paces, Clyde hollered over his shoulder to Yellowsnake. "Come on into our hut and we'll talk a while."

As soon as he entered the dark, musty cave, he soon realized that this truly *was* the home of the two old miners. They appeared to keep a somewhat orderly house, in spite of it being a cave which had apparently been used long ago by the Spaniards. Their cooking utensils were neatly stacked along one wall, and the remnants of their fire smoked gently with wisps being drawn out the entrance of the cave. "This is one hell of a place you've got here," Yellowsnake complimented.

"Yeah, it does us okay," Emmet replied. "This place was put here by the Spaniards about three hundred years ago. When we moved in some thirty years ago, we found the skeletons of ten of their soldiers laying along that wall over there. We also found their armor, helmets and weapons that were left behind. All we can figure is that the Indians must have wiped them out, because the Spaniards were pretty good fighters, you know."

Both Clyde and Emmet stood a few inches over five feet tall on their tiptoes, reminding Yellowsnake of characters he had seen in old Western movies during his youth. Each of them had a forty-four, long barreled pistol strapped to his side, the barrels hanging nearly to their knees. *What a funny looking pair,* he mused.

Clyde, never one to mince words, spoke first. "You're an Injun, ain't ya son?"

Yellowsnake retorted quickly as he heard their words, "You bet your ass I'm Indian, and damn proud of it."

Emmet chimed in, "Indians are good people. The only problem Clyde and I had with anybody was white men through the years. Never had any problem with Indians." He went on to explain that during the past thirty years, there had been many attempts by other miners to follow them into the canyon. They obviously knew that he and Clyde had done very well extracting gold from the mountains. However, the twosome had been able to lose those who had attempted to follow them in.

Now it was Clyde's turn to speak. "You know, son, we've made our livin' here for thirty years, and don't want no trouble from nobody. But you know where we're holed up now, and I hope like hell we can trust you. We don't cotton up to anybody tryin' to follow us. It looks like maybe we can trust you, so if we make a deal with you to bring our supplies in, will you keep your mouth shut?"

Yellowsnake knew what had to be said, giving his solemn word that he would keep his mouth shut and never tell any man where the two were located. The longer they talked, the more

Yellowsnake sensed the two were becoming comfortable with his presence. Likewise, the more he talked with them, the more he liked them. Unquestionably, they were a heartwarming pair of eccentric old timers.

When Yellowsnake told them he would have to leave soon to make it out by dark, Clyde interrupted him. "Why don't you stay the night with us? You can eat at our fire, and get outta here tomorrow after first light. We'd like you to stay."

Emmet agreed wholeheartedly. "Yeah, what the hell. After we eat, we'll share some of that tobacco with you, and that'll give us a chance to put together a goods list of what you can bring back to us."

Yellowsnake was delighted to hear the ring of sincerity in their voices. He knew he had gained their confidence and, more importantly, their trust. "Sure, I'll spend the night. No one will miss me, and I can fly out of here in the morning like you said."

Later that evening, while he was sitting around their campfire with a warm full feeling in his stomach, Yellowsnake listened to an endless chain of fascinating tales. They told of how they had accidentally discovered the only passable trail into the forbidding canyon thirty years earlier. They had vowed to keep it a secret between just the two of them. The leathery pair had done well earning a living from the mountains. Over the years, they had become expert hard rock miners and had taken gold on a steady basis. They had also found rich placer deposits in the small stream running through Deadman Canyon.

Whenever they had gone into town for supplies, they had stopped and cashed in their gold, converting it to dollars for spending. Most recently, they had cashed in their latest accumulation at Ted Masters' shop. "We only take in whatever gold we need when we head into town," Clyde explained. "Me and Emmet have stashed away a lot of other gold around these hills where no one can find it."

As their distorted shadows danced on the smooth walls of the cave, the three talked into the night about things that were so near and dear to Yellowsnake's heart. Their mutual desire to live wild and alone in the wilderness, with only Mother Nature and God in control of their destiny–the three had more in common than they realized.

At dawn, Yellowsnake awoke to the pungent aroma of Emmet's coffee boiling over the fire. He lifted his stiff body from his comfortable mat resting on the floor of the cave, delighting himself in the scrumptious taste of Emmet's bacon and grits. Yellowsnake finished his meal, saying "I'd better get back in the saddle now and get the hell out before the Feds figure out I've been here. If you guys need some supplies, give me your list and I'll get back as quickly as you want."

Without hesitation, the lovable miners took a quick inventory of food goods and miscellaneous supplies needed to replenish their stores.

"Yellowsnake, Emmet and I have talked a bit and we figure we can trust you. So as soon as you can get our supplies, come on back in. We want you to know you'll always be welcome at our fire as long as our trust is never broken." Their words were music to Yellowsnake's ears, for he knew how it felt to distrust someone and live in fear of their betrayal.

As Yellowsnake walked out of the cave, he glanced toward the two fine looking horses standing hobbled near the burros. The two noticed his glance. Clyde spoke up. "That big brown one there, that's Monte. He's my faithful horse. The other one is Bigelow, and that poor animal belongs to a jackass named Emmet. He's not much of a horse, but he gets that old fart around. Monte could win a race on three legs any day if he had to."

"That old piece of crow bait of yours ain't worth a shit, Clyde, and you know it. He ought to be dog meat by now." Emmet had the last word on Clyde.

Yellowsnake was both humored and touched by the callousness of their words, for he had witnessed the obvious affection that existed between the two dear friends. Their arguments were incessant, but tempered with love in their hearts. There was no doubt they would remain steadfast friends until the day one of them died.

At the top of their needed items they had listed sauerkraut, link sausages and canned peaches. Emmet was quick to point these out to Yellowsnake. "Whatever you do, don't forgot those things. We really like 'em!"

After shaking Yellowsnake's hand as he prepared to leave the canyon, the two old miners smiled and waved. "Get yourself back real soon now, son. We'll be looking for ya'."

The dirt swirled wildly as the helicopter lifted off the ground and, again in a sweeping motion, circled over the floor of the deep canyon, soon disappearing from sight over the peaks of the imposing mountains surrounding the miners.

Three days later, the able and now anxious pilot returned to Deadman Canyon, packed to the gills with the valuable load of supplies his new friends had requested. And thoughtfully, he had brought feed for their horses. As soon as the Bell 47 had touched down smoothly, the anxious twosome began removing the valuable goods from the aircraft, each complaining to the other that he wasn't carrying his fair share of the load. The bickering brought a smile to Yellowsnake's lips. *I love those coots. Too bad there's not more of them in the world,* he reflected.

As his happy days passed into months, he found himself making frequent, albeit unannounced, trips into the treacherous Mazatzals, always remembering his friends' sauerkraut, sausage links and canned peaches. By now, he had found himself an admired and trusted friend of the pair. He sensed he could also trust them implicitly, realizing they were men of character who would not betray him. He had become absorbed with their honesty and sincerity, and more importantly, was welcome to sit at their campfire any time.

Prior to departing from one of his many visits into the canyon, Yellowsnake began saying his customary good-byes. Before he could finish, Clyde spoke, with a ring of authority in his voice. "Snake, come on over here. You've done a lot of favors for us and, even though we've paid you for your trips, there's something special me and Emmet would like to do for you." He handed Yellowsnake a short handled shovel and a large, badly dented gold pan, then the much shorter Clyde reached up and firmly grasped Yellowsnake's sleeve. Clyde tugged on his long arm, while awkwardly leading him in a direction which would take them across the dirt floor of the canyon toward the small creek. There was a wooded area next to the creek, and a mound of soft sand and gravel with a gurgling, shiny stream of water erupting from its surface. Yellowsnake looked at the two sheepishly, asking, "What next?"

Emmet spoke first as he pointed toward the spring. "Go over next to that spring there, and start diggin'. Me and Clyde are going to give you an hour to take out all of the gold you can find. So if you know how to pan, get over there and get your feet in the water. Start digging up that soft gravel and sand, and pan it out. When your hour's up, we'll let you get back in your whirly bird and go home."

Yellowsnake dared not question them as he walked over to the inviting spring which served as a submerged continuation of the small stream which trickled over the tall waterfall. He began digging as directed, placing each shovelful into the gold pan. As he crouched down, his hands reached the small pool of water lying at his feet. He began panning out the gravel and sand to see what lay at the bottom of the well worn pan.

He sloshed the water around, making the gravel and sand rise to the surface and tumble off the edge of the pan, then he saw with amazement what lay at the bottom. Before his eyes lay several small chunks of gold; mixed among the smaller pieces were two large nuggets. He shoved his hand into a large pocket on the back of his jacket, retrieving his leather squaw bag and began emptying the contents of the pan.

He now knew what that two miners were up to as he worked feverishly to make good use of his precious hour. Each time he placed a shovelful of dirty looking gravel into the pan and repeated the process, he was rewarded with beautiful, shiny nuggets. They were coming out in various sizes and shapes, along with a large quantity of flakes and gold dust.

Clyde and Emmet smiled wryly, and watched him from a distance as he diligently sifted through the sand and gravel. Generously, the hour became seventy minutes. With a look of satisfaction on their faces, they watched him retrieve the free gold lying within the gurgling waters of the spring, then approached him. "Have you got enough yet son?"

"Damn, this is fun!" Yellowsnake exclaimed in delight.

"I've never seen anything like this in my life!"

Clyde spoke up. "What happens is, the gold is coming up from under the ground and traveling up through this spring. When it reaches a certain point, it just lays there. Whenever there is some fresh sand and gravel coming up, there is always some gold buried just below. Once it's been played out, all we have to do is give it a few days to build back up."

An astonished Yellowsnake could only reply. "Now I know why you old wart hogs have been able to make a living all of your life. What a beautiful sight this is."

"Now remember, Snake, we let you pan this out because we trust you. And don't forget that if we didn't trust you, we'd damn well shoot you if you ever tried to take the gold without me and Clyde knowing about it," Emmet chided.

Yellowsnake responded with words that came from his heart. "This gold belongs to you two, and I would never touch it without your permission. Besides that, I don't need a hell of a lot. I've done okay for myself all my life, and you two deserve every bit of it."

When they heard his honest and reassuring words, the two miners knew that Yellowsnake was a man of his word. He could be trusted to respect the honor they had bestowed upon him by letting him pan from their rich pool of gold flowing from the ground.

A few days later, Yellowsnake found that after having placed his gold in the hands of Ted Masters, the value of his take during the generous hour was nearly three thousand dollars worth of precious metal.

The three knew that no further words needed to be spoken about mutual trust. It was now a given that they trusted each other with not only their fortunes, but their lives, as well.

When he returned to the comfort of his room, Yellowsnake felt content and at peace with himself. Although it had been ten months since his last assignment, he had stayed in close contact with John Lincoln. Lincoln had continued to tell him that there weren't any eruptions at the moment, but that he should rest assured there would be, sooner or later.

As he stretched out on his comfortable bed smoking a

cigarette, Yellowsnake still had an unsettled feeling about the much-publicized instability of America's banks. His poke had grown in size, and his investments were being carefully guarded by Hotona. He meditated at length, then reached a decision which he felt would make him more comfortable. If most of his investments and bank accounts were converted to cash and in his possession, he would feel much more confident. He'd come to harbor a deep fear that his bank would somehow fail and they'd grab everything he had. Moreover, he distrusted the bankers who ran the banks even more.

After finishing his breakfast the next morning, he picked up his phone and without hesitation, dialed the number of his parents. When he heard Hotona's welcoming voice clearly on the other end of the line, he relayed to her the events of the past several months. He eluded to a plan he had in mind before he asked her to close out a substantial portion of his investments and bank accounts, and transfer the funds to his bank in Arizona. She didn't question his wisdom, agreeing to see that the funds for which he had worked so hard would be transferred right away.

Within two weeks, the cash transfers had arrived at his bank in Phoenix. He had decided he would leave an adequate amount of cash on deposit, then told the cashier that he wanted the remainder of his funds, although unusually large, to be withdrawn and given to him in cash.

As might be expected, the request for the huge cash withdrawal nearly gave the bank manager a heart attack. "Sir, if you'll give us a couple of hours, we'll be able to gather up enough cash to honor your request, so if you wait patiently, we'll be happy to take care of you."

He knew that the sum of his large withdrawal would require an adequate bag in which to carry it, so he had brought his sturdy blue duffel bag along. By the close of bank business hours, he had withdrawn a lofty sum from the clutches of the bank, and still had a decent nest egg remaining.

Once the weighty transaction was complete, the edgy bank manager just had to ask the question. "Sir, if you don't mind, would you tell me what you're going to do with all that cash?"

Yellowsnake couldn't resist the temptation as he answered.

"Sure, I don't mind telling you. I'm going to deposit it in the Mazatzal National Bank."

The manager's eyebrows raised as he asked, "Where is that bank located?" Yellowsnake ended the conversation. "It's located someplace you've never been, and probably never will be."

Late in the evening, he returned to his living quarters with his inconspicuous bag stuffed to capacity with cash, and placed it under his bed right next to his gun. When he arose the following morning, he planned to make another, though unexpected, visit to the Mazatzals to see Clyde and Emmet.

Shortly after dawn, he was safely in the air with his blue duffel bag holding the large sum of cash nestled next to his pilot seat. Further back in the helicopter were strapped two large milk cans with lids which he had managed to round up from the owners of the motel. He had offered no explanation as to their intended use, and thanked the owners for helping him out. Dutifully, he kept a watchful eye out for a National Forest patrol plane which might be lurking somewhere in the area. Yellowsnake made his way back toward Deadman Canyon, all the while anticipating seeing his friends once again.

The instant he touched down on the now familiar canyon floor, he was greeted with smiling faces and waving arms by his friends. While he waited for the rotor blade of his chopper to come a complete stop, he crawled into the small cargo area and unlashed the two milk cans. He slid them along the floor of his chopper, then moved them to the open door, and while retrieving his duffel, put everything into position for removal. In a somewhat synchronized fashion, the two old miners walked toward him, both cussing and stroking their gray, haggard beards, asking what brought him here this fine, sunny day.

In a serious and businesslike tone, Yellowsnake explained that he had never trusted any banker he'd ever met, especially when it came to handling his money. Now, he distrusted them even more, given the all too frequent failures the banking system was experiencing. He had decided he'd be more comfortable if he had his hard earned money tucked away someplace he knew it would remain safe forever. Most importantly, it couldn't be taken away by the greedy bankers.

Clyde and Emmet quickly agreed with him. "Those sons o' bitches will steal you blind if you let 'em. I don't blame you, Snake," Emmet proclaimed . Then he continued. "I remember when my daddy lost his ass back in '29 when everything crashed. Those rotten bankers grabbed everything they could. They didn't give a damn about other people's money. The only honest banker is the one that knows you'll shoot 'em square between the eyes if he tries to screw ya."

Yellowsnake agreed, and wasn't going to take any chances. With a ring of confidence in his voice, Clyde spoke up. "Your cash will always be safe with us, because we would never do anything with your money, just like you would never do anything with our gold. What are you going to do now?"

"If it's okay with you guys, I think I'll try to put my money in these milk cans and bury it someplace where only the three of us will know it's hidden," explained Yellowsnake.

"Hell yes! Fill 'em up and we'll get 'em buried and no one will ever know, but us," replied Clyde, with Emmet's face showing his shared satisfaction.

As he transferred the bundles of American currency from his bag, it was only moments before Yellowsnake was stuffing with all of his might, the final package of cash into the top of the first milk can. "I think it'll only take one can, by the looks of things." He placed the lid on the can and, with satisfaction, gave the lid a powerful kick of his boot, setting it firmly in place.

After he had rounded up a shovel from the cave, he went to work digging a safe and suitable resting place for his depository can. He had located a very unusual looking rock not far from the small stream meandering through the canyon, then began digging a hole nearly six feet deep. With Clyde and Emmet standing by, watching him hurriedly prepare it's resting place, the three of them knew they shared another secret.

Suddenly, Clyde and Emmet were huddled close together, speaking quietly a few paces from the hole Yellowsnake was working in. Emmet spoke up as they returned to the deepening crater in which Yellowsnake was standing. "Snake, hang on there a minute. If it's okay with you, me and Clyde want to bury something there too. We've got quite a bit of stash around here, but over the years we've learned how to melt down our gold into bars. So hang on a minute and, if it's okay with you, we'll put our bars of gold inside your other milk can and bury it next to your cash."

Yellowsnake welcomed their idea. "That's fine with me. Go get it and I'll hold up until you return."

The two miners made no secret as to where this particular stash was located. They crept behind a large boulder near the mouth of the cave and, with shovels in hand, they soon were struggling with a large wooden box with rope handles on each end. They half carried, half dragged it back to the grave site in which Yellowsnake was standing. When they reached the hole, which was more than adequate to accommodate the two milk cans, the miners began pulling out small bars of gold which they had melted down into nearly pure form, from the badly weathered box. They methodically and neatly placed the weighty bars inside the milk can. Their task complete, the two of them grasped the can by its handles and gently lowered the vessel into the hole.

"We figure there's eighty or so pounds of gold in there, so in case everything goes to hell, we'll always have something to come back to. Besides that, we have a lot more stash we can always get to."

After making sure he had placed the milk cans in a firm, upright position, Yellowsnake placed several medium sized rocks around them to hold them in place. As the sweat poured from his brow, he climbed out of the hole and the threesome refilled the hole which had now become a secret resting place for not only Yellowsnake's horde of cash, but their precious cargo of gold as well.

They stood silently, knowing no stronger bond could exist among them after having placed such a valuable cache in a hiding place whose location they alone shared.

While he leisurely finished his cup of coffee and enjoyed the remnants of the morning fire, Yellowsnake decided it was time to head back to Apache Junction. He spoke his parting words to his cohorts, and reminded them he would be returning within the week with the supplies which he had by now, memorized. His instincts told him that any day now, he would be hearing from the Colonel, advising him that his next assignment had arrived.

The two miners stood with warmth in their hearts and trust in their eyes as they waved goodbye, knowing their Comanche friend would be returning soon. They knew that Yellowsnake was one to keep his word.

Soon after he had returned to the coolness of his air conditioned room, he again phoned his mother to let her know what he had done. "Mom, if anything ever happens to me, you will be the only one to know where my stash of money is. I buried it in Deadman Canyon and, other than my two friends up there, Clyde and Emmet, you're the only one who knows where it is. You can share my secret with Dad but, outside of the two of you, no one else will ever know I have this money. It will always be safe there."

Hotona acknowledged her son's concerns, asking him to come home soon for she hadn't seen him in a long time. He promised he would do so just as soon as time permitted, and provided he wasn't on an assignment somewhere halfway across the world.

Two days later, like clockwork, John Lincoln called, announcing there was another operation in the works, and that he should be prepared to leave within a week. Although it was too early to give him all of the details, it gave the Colonel great pleasure to inform Yellowsnake that this time he would be staying closer to home.

Yellowsnake knew that time was short and wanted to make one final visit back to the Mazatzals as promised. He boarded his helicopter which was loaded with supplies and horse feed and, as always, kept a wary eye out for the infrequent patrols of the National Forest Service around the Mazatzals.

The moment he dropped down into the canyon, Yellowsnake was greeted by the miners. Because they could hear his approach far in advance of his landing, they were always waiting anxiously for his arrival. While he unloaded their supplies, he explained he would be leaving shortly on another assignment, but would return to see them as soon as possible.

As he listened to the tone in their voices, Yellowsnake sensed that things were not quite right with Clyde and Emmet. There was obvious sadness in their eyes, and Clyde was nearly in tears. When he drew closer toward the two, it was apparent that Clyde was deeply distressed. "What's the matter, Clyde?" he asked. He could see the tears begin to stream down the cheeks of Clyde's weathered face as he sniffed and began telling his story.

"Poor Monte, he died last night. He was a faithful old horse and I dearly loved him," said Clyde in a quiet, grief stricken voice. "Even though he was getting on in years, he seemed to be in pretty good health. But last night he began having problems and by this morning, he was dead."

His heart was heavy when he heard the news, and Yellowsnake was nearly in tears himself. He knew how deeply Clyde loved his horse, and asked what he could do to help. "Do you want me to try to get you another horse? What can I do?"

"No," Clyde sobbed. "I'll have to take my time, because I'll be lucky to ever find another horse like Monte. But if you could help me out, I'd really appreciate it."

"Anything you'd like, just name it," said Yellowsnake without hesitation.

Clyde spoke. "Me and Emmet are getting so old, I don't think either one of us can dig a hole. If you don't mind, could you dig a hole for Monte so I can give him a proper burial?"

Oh shit, Yellowsnake thought. *This is going to be one hell of a job. But I love these two like brothers, and I'd do anything they ask.* Nevertheless, he immediately responded, "Sure, give me a shovel and I'll get to it. We'll see that Monte is buried in proper fashion. Where would you like him buried?"

Clyde was decisive as he pointed back toward the strange looking boulder lying near the small stream across the canyon. "I'd like to bury him right next to our stash," he said.

"Well, okay, but we'll have to figure out how to get him over there," Yellowsnake responded, realizing Monte probably weighed close to two thousand pounds.

After Yellowsnake had lashed a rope securely around the

massive body of Bigelow, they fastened the other end around the lifeless body of Monte. Slowly, the sure footed Bigelow dragged Monte across the canyon to the spot which would become his final resting place. Yellowsnake, with shovel in hand and driven by the undisguised sorrow on Clyde's face, began digging Monte's grave. Within hours and due to Monte's huge size, what had started as a hole, was becoming a huge chamber.

Five hours later, and sweating profusely, Yellowsnake had succeeded in digging a grave site deep and wide enough to hold the remains of Clyde's faithful horse. The threesome carefully maneuvered Bigelow into position, and after observing a moment of silence, they rolled the carcass of the beloved beast into the hole. When Monte landed in his final resting place, there was a mighty thump which echoed off the walls of the canyon. After he had removed the rope from Monte's body, Clyde stood at the edge of the hole with tears streaming down his face. "Goodbye Monte," he sobbed. "I'll see you in our next life." Filled with sadness, the three of them began burying the faithful steed which had served Clyde for nearly forty years.

After Yellowsnake had helped complete the unpleasant task of burying the animal which Clyde had held more dearly than anything or anyone outside of Emmet, he told the two he must return to Apache Junction to prepare for his next job. Unfortunately, he wasn't sure where it would take him, but in any case, he would return just as soon as possible.

Yellowsnake was cognizant of the fact that his two dear friends were approaching seventy years old, and he was fearful he might never see either of them again. His heart was sad as he bid them goodbye. With a smile on his face, Yellowsnake lifted off and looked back over his shoulder a final time at the canyon and small stream running along its edge. He knew he would forever treasure the time he had spent in the peaceful fortress. No other man, Indian or white, could ever emerge from the awesome canyon without acquiring a deep respect and admiration for it's lonely, serenely beautiful depths. More importantly, he knew whenever he returned, he would feel the cherished friendship of two people who had given this chapter in his life new meaning.

Although he knew that Clyde's heart had been broken by the death of his beloved mount, Yellowsnake could only hope that Clyde would regain his strength and find a new horse worthy of the precious old miner's friendship.

Chapter 12

Bandidos and the Green Eyed Latina

When he had finished showering and shaving, Yellowsnake stood before the partly fogged mirror inside his snug, Apache Junction retreat. A renewed awareness of his years struck him as he rubbed his fingers across the deep lines of war which had now become a permanent part of his features. He glanced down at the small, smooth, eagle claw fastened securely in place around his neck by a thin band of elk skin.

His willing acceptance of the deepening lines of life on his face sent Yellowsnake's mind wandering through his considerable cargo of experiences, some sad and some fond. His marriage to Maria had ended with regrets years earlier. But touching the smooth edges of the dangling eagle claw had awakened cherished memories of Clyde Durham and Emmet Claggett.

Like it was just yesterday, he clearly recalled the cave dwelling which Clyde and Emmet had occupied for so many years, and the moment Clyde had emerged from the cave with the eagle claw in his outstretched hand. He wanted Yellowsnake to take it as a token of their now binding friendship and at the very least, a reminder of the adventurous days they had shared in the Mazatzals.

Because the precious gift had carried with it a special meaning, Yellowsnake had vowed he would wear the eagle claw until the fateful day in which their circle of friendship was broken by the death of one of them.

He relished his thoughts of the countless times he had prospected for gold deep in the mountains, his mind hazily recollecting his adventure in extracting the treasure from the Mountain of Bones in Panama. Months after his departure from the war-torn country, it was widely reported that the raw value of the priceless relics was well in excess of two million dollars, and they were now on display in the Panama Historical Museum.

Abruptly, his flood of memories was interrupted by the ringing telephone.

He hurriedly wrapped a towel around his badly scarred body as he raced to answer the call which he knew was overdue. Colonel John was calling to give him the details of his next Company pleasure trip. The Colonel knew how deeply Yellowsnake had come to love the companionship of the mountains which surrounded him, and the freedom it offered him and his helicopter. His cheerful leader was pleased to notify Yellowsnake of his next duty detail.

"Snake, I think you're going to like this one! I know how much you love the warmth of the sun and, heaven knows, you've spent enough years out of the country, so here's what we have going.

"As you know, the drug traffic occurring between Mexico and the United States has increased dramatically. Our people are very concerned about bringing a halt to the free rein of the Mexicans and their running of illegal drugs into our country. This is really out of the Company's jurisdiction, but they would like to cooperate with the Drug Enforcement Agency. The DEA has requested a competent tracker to assist them in monitoring the movements of the drug caravans and shipments coming in from Mexico. The Company has agreed that, since we don't have anything pressing for you right now, we may as well lend you to the DEA. That certainly will justify your exorbitant paycheck, and will keep you in shape and primed for your next real assignment.

"You'll still be working for me and, of course, will continue to be paid by the Blue Ridge Corporation. But, on this job, you'll probably be working with the DEA agents on a regular basis, and your sole purpose will be to seek out and track the smugglers. After you've done your part, the DEA will step in and take care of the dirty work. They can make the bust, and you can go on with your next pursuit."

Yellowsnake had to admit that his handsome salary with the Company had ballooned nicely over the years. He chuckled saying he "supposed he should be doing something to earn his keep" and, of course, would do whatever the Colonel asked.

"Get yourself saddled up, Comanche, and go on over to our Company hangar at the Phoenix airport. From there, one of our planes will fly you to our San Diego field office. There's a DEA office there, and their people will give you the details. Best of all, you'll be able to maintain a life which resembles that of an ordinary civilian. With this deal, you'll be able to have many of your weekends off and be able to spend more time in your beloved mountains. So get your mind geared up and enjoy your last few days. We'll continue to talk on a regular basis."

He arrived at the DEA field office in San Diego smartly attired in the olive drab jungle wear he'd worn for so many years; now a new cowboy hat crowned his shoulder-length hair. He had retired his badly worn jungle headband a year earlier. As he quietly entered the plushly furnished office, the first thing he observed was the uplifted eyebrows directed toward him by several neatly dressed agents in tailored suits. He politely introduced himself to the receptionist, and was soon greeted by the field office Director who invited him into his private office. Observing the senior agent's freshly manicured fingernails and neatly trimmed hair, Yellowsnake listened to the Director explain the Agency's need for a highly trained tracker. They badly needed help bringing about the arrests of the drug runners who all too easily crossed the U.S. border. The chief looked coyly at Yellowsnake, as if he was a piece of coal which had been mixed with a collection of fine gems, then remarked, "Well, it looks like you're ready to go to work!"

"Yes sir," Yellowsnake remarked sardonically. "I didn't think it would be a good idea to wear my three piece suit, knowing where we're headed." Although his new boss had taken the liberty of providing him with comfortable quarters, Yellowsnake knew all of his precious free time would be spent in the familiar solitude of the Arizona mountains.

With the aid of helicopter and plane reconnaissance flights over Mexico, the DEA had been able to determine the general paths of travel of the drug cartel. Invariably, the difficulty arose in trying to follow their exact movements. Most often they were lost in the vast chasms and valleys which wove erratically through the mountains toward the U.S. border.

"We have the full cooperation of the Mexican government," the official explained. "Once you've arrived at certain jumping off points in Mexico, you'll be equipped with weapons, horses, a field radio and whatever you need to pick up their trail. Your objective will be to track them from start to finish so that we'll be able to make the arrest without fear of them retreating before they reach our border. Frankly, if it becomes necessary, we'd like you to create some fear in them while they're traveling, and keep them moving toward us so we can apprehend them.

"It seems like whenever they sense we are watching them from the air, they'll get off their trail and hole up until they feel it's safe to go on. Your job will be to keep them nervous and moving. This will ultimately make our job that much easier."

Although Yellowsnake didn't appreciate the limitation of involvement being placed upon him, he would nevertheless carry out his mission without question. He silently pondered the sure-fire cure he knew would end the problem once and for all; *Shit, if it was up to me, I'd kill the bastards right then and there. The DEA wouldn't even have to worry about making a bust up at the border.* However, it was not his job to reason how or why, it was simply his assigned task.

Within a few days, he found himself deep in the heart of Mexico and becoming familiar with obscure trails and routes leading toward American soil. Not by coincidence, they nearly always originated from the vicinity of Mexico City. Since the cartel "mules" preferred to travel in the darkness of night, he found himself doing most of his tracking well after the sun had set.

The work quickly became all too routine, although most of his tracking missions provided some level of excitement and intrigue. Several months passed and, more and more, he found himself deriving a mean-spirited level of satisfaction from the unnerving techniques he used to cause the bandidos a deep element of fear. His bag of tricks kept them uncomfortably aggravated and constantly looking over their shoulder.

It gave him selfish pleasure to silently creep into the thickets surrounding their crude camps, then create a commotion with a piercing bang on his metal messplate. Or even better, a sudden gunshot into the air. As a special treat, he occasionally terrorized them with a blood curdling Comanche war cry. He never had any fear of capture by the nervous caravan shepherds. He was always able to hide himself within the rocks, crevices and deep underbrush covering the mountainsides and ravines. He was like an invisible marauder, always lurking, yet never seen.

The plan was working as their nervousness kept them on the move, making their apprehension by the awaiting DEA agents nothing more than routine. *Damn, this is fun. It reminds me of going out at night and chasing down raccoons and possums. They're always looking for a place to hide, but know they can't escape my chase,* reflected the restless Comanche tracker.

While staying in continual communication with the DEA agents, who lay in wait for the wily illegals, Yellowsnake always worked hard to force his prey across the U.S. border. It was at the border that he took great delight in finalizing the relentless push which had driven them to that point.

His final moments of conquest often occurred at some unseen, though opportune location. At precisely the moment the DEA agents were making their arrest, he'd bellow as loudly as possible, "Congratulations! You've just been caught by Yellowsnake!" Like a wisp of smoke, the elusive shadow disappeared into the cover of the terrain, never once being seen by his victims.

For more than two years, most of his hours were spent on horseback tracking the cartel runners. His love for horses had reemerged, reminding him of their strong influence on his life as a youth.

On some occasions, his mission confined him to traveling on foot with his weapon, field radio and backpack. Yellowsnake always enjoyed his job more when he was able to climb aboard a strong, high-spirited horse who could make his job so much easier. By now, the DEA was racking up major drug busts with the assistance of his relentless pursuit of the Mexican traffickers. Even though his lengthy assignment with the DEA didn't always give him a great deal of satisfaction, he was proud in knowing he had helped slow the entry of insidious drugs into the United States.

As the Colonel had promised, his job with the DEA also allowed him the luxury of more reasonable working hours. The past two years had permitted him to make several visits back to Arizona, and his priority was always a quick trip to the mountains.

His last visit, however, had not been such a happy one. He was shocked and deeply saddened to learn Clyde Durham had died in the mountains. Emmet Claggett had called to let him know that his dear, trusted friend had died from the lingering heartbreak he had suffered ever since the death of Monte, his beloved horse. His voice was filled with sorrow as Emmet explained to Yellowsnake that he didn't want to return to the hills any more. He would probably spend his remaining years in solitude somewhere in Utah.

Emmet had notified Clyde's son, his only sibling after birth more than forty year earlier, of his father's death. The emotionally unmoved offspring had asked Emmet to see that Clyde was buried wherever he thought it best. When Emmet asked the son if he would like to provide his father with a headstone at his grave, the son replied with a tone of indifference, "No, I really don't care. You take care of it."

As Yellowsnake listened to the words which had been spoken by the cold, unloving namesake, he told Emmet, "I'm sending you five hundred dollars right away, and together let's make damn sure that Clyde has the finest headstone money can buy! If you need more, let me know."

"Don't worry, Snake, you know Clyde will have the very best, we're not hurting for money. He was like a brother to me, and the reason I'm calling you is that I know you share my feelings and would want to know." Emmet knew Yellowsnake would be deeply hurt if he hadn't called him. It had been a special love between the three of them and now the circle had been broken.

Yellowsnake realized an exciting and special era of his life had ended with the death of his friend Clyde. Emmet and

Clyde's exciting lives represented a real-life chapter in a folklore rich era which would never be forgotten.

With the approach of 1983 Yellowsnake received a pleasant change in his routine with the Agency. The Colonel had, sometime earlier, disclosed to the DEA that Yellowsnake was a highly competent helicopter pilot, and if they needed him for special chopper work, he would certainly be more than capable of performing the task.

The DEA was quietly delighted to learn that someone with his background and flight experience in remote, desolate areas, was available to assist them in their endless pursuit of the drug runners.

After he returned to San Diego following a two month rest back in Arizona Yellowsnake was assigned a sleek new Agency helicopter for use in his future endeavors. This time, however, he would be tracking the culprits by air in low level pursuit. He was known to be fearless when it came to flying in tight spots, and blanketed the movements of the illegal cargo carriers like a tight shirt. Whenever it became necessary, he withdrew himself and his helicopter back to a safe point, setting it down in some nearby secluded area. Then he would proceed on foot, continuing to harass the caravan while moving them in a direction which would drive them closer and closer to their downfall.

By the end of the year, his airborne chases had taken him farther away from the interior depths of Mexico. Now his efforts were becoming increasingly concentrated along it's coastline. In recent months, there had been a surge of shipping traffic which was suspected of carrying illegal drugs toward various points along U.S. shores.

The vessels he was tracking along the shores of Mexico and into U.S. waters were small to medium sized cargo ships, neatly equipped with helicopter landing pads. The swift choppers would then remove the illegal goods for delivery to widespread destinations. Yellowsnake, often accompanied by two DEA agents, used many unusual approaches to surprise and apprehend the unsuspecting boats. Often, after dropping down in nearly freefall fashion upon the illicit cargo, they'd jump onto the ship's rolling deck to make sure-handed arrests of the captain and his crew. Once they had made their presence known while in the air, the DEA agents often sent machine gun fire scattering across the bow of the ships, announcing their intent to board the craft. As soon as the skids of his chopper were placed firmly upon the ship's landing pad, Yellowsnake's primary mission was fulfilled. The sometimes dangerous task of completing the arrest was out of his jurisdiction.

Although he had assisted the DEA for nearly three years, Yellowsnake never felt like he was working for them. From the day he was temporarily assigned to them, the Colonel had made it absolutely clear to DEA officials that Yellowsnake was only "on loan" to them. As such, he was treated with the courtesy and respect afforded an independent contractor. In the most competent manner possible, he was simply performing a badly needed task for a sister agency needing his skills.

With the Christmas and New Year's holidays only days away, it was time for him to take some time off and return to Arizona for another short rest. While he was there, he would take time to undergo his annual physical examination, as required by the Company.

His energy level always rose when he saw the sober face of the Superstition Mountains. And snugly moored in it's shadow was his most favored helicopter, waiting for its next mission.

He was unpacking his duffel in the warmth of his room when he remembered the parting words of Emmet Claggett. "Yellowsnake, when you decide to return to Deadman Canyon, I want you to know that the milk can holding me and Clyde's gold is all yours. Clyde would want you to have it and, besides, I have a hell of a lot more than I can ever spend myself. So don't forget! It's all yours when you return."

Sadly, Yellowsnake now had no desire to return to the depths of the Mazatzals, because Clyde Durham and Emmet Claggett were no longer there. After convincing himself that he had no other pressing matters to take care of, and knowing Christmas was only a few days away, he figured he might as well get his physical exam out of the way.

He parked his pick up truck outside the low profile, adobe

style clinic which the Company had recommended for obtaining his physical. When he entered through the darkly tinted glass doors, he walked briskly toward the long gray counter which nearly hid the blond head sitting behind it. He hadn't bothered to stop at the receptionist desk as he banged his knuckles on the counter asking, "I'm here to take my physical. Who do I see?"

The obviously irritated medical assistant sitting behind the counter fired back, "You'll never get to see anybody if you don't quit banging your damn knuckles on the counter." With an authoritative tone in her voice, the green-eyed sprite asked, "What's your name, anyway?"

Just as sharply he replied, "Yellowsnake," just daring her to push his buttons further than she already had.

With a thrust of her invisible dagger, she asked, "And does Yellowsnake have a last name?"

"Yes, but it really doesn't matter. If you'll look in your records, you'll see I'm filed under Yellowsnake."

Judging by the sharp tone of her voice, and sensing that she was probably never at a loss for words, he thought to himself, *I'll bet she's the meanest bitch that ever crawled out of a bed roll. Maybe I shouldn't rattle her cage too much. She sure is cute, though. Maybe she's just having a bad day.*

After she stretched up on her tiptoes to retrieve his medical chart from the high shelf, the five foot, three inch, fireball returned to the counter. "Now Mr. Yellowsnake, if you'll be so kind as to cool your jets, I'll get you into the doctor's office in just a few minutes."

He stood there, not only amused, but intrigued by her abrupt behavior, then asked, "Well, what's your name?"

"Liliana", she replied.

Yellowsnake had chosen to know more about her, so he persisted. "And does Liliana have a last name?"

Without cracking a smile, she had a ready answer. "Yes, but it really doesn't matter. You'll find that I'm filed under Liliana."

With this dangerously playful exchange of words, he knew that the field of battle had been firmly established, and was certainly level.

He couldn't help but admire the trim, feminine figure of

Liliana as she escorted him into the doctor's office. His mind was at work as it occurred to him that the lovely escort might well become his next target. A few minutes later, the gray-haired doctor stood in awe, looking at the nearly naked torso of his Comanche patient. He couldn't hide his astonishment at the assortment of scars which covered Yellowsnake's body. "You undoubtedly have more knife scars and bullet wounds than anyone I've ever set eyes on. I'm surprised you're even sitting here before me."

Yellowsnake chuckled inside, for he knew he had a story which was much too long to tell, and would refrain from elaborating on how he had received them. Following his lengthy two hour exam, the doctor proclaimed Yellowsnake to be in good health, saying he was in fine physical condition and able to continue working for the Company another year.

After he slipped on his faded jeans, cowboy boots and plaid flannel shirt, Yellowsnake reentered Liliana's domain and was greeted by her flashing eyes. As light as a cat on his feet when an instinctive move was needed, he quickly popped the question. "Liliana, how would you like to go out to dinner tonight?"

He felt the sting of her arrow piercing his gut as she replied, "I don't know. How would I?" And then, breaking into a wide and gentle smile, she spoke with a comforting sincerity in her voice. "What exactly did you have in mind?" Since he rarely spent any of his leisure time in Phoenix, he replied, "I don't know. I guess I'll leave that up to you."

Not at all ashamed of the sporty new pick up truck he had purchased a few months earlier, he picked her up promptly at seven o'clock. She was pleasing to his eyes, and was dressed in a sleek, yet comfortable looking emerald green dress and high heels.

Now friendly foes, the two of them sat in the lush and dimly lit surroundings of Christy's Steakhouse, Liliana sipping her wine demurely while he nursed his glass of beer. To their mutual astonishment, they felt profoundly at ease with each other and soon became intimately acquainted. Only hours earlier, they were wishful fantasies in each other's minds. Before the evening had ended, Liliana had come to know the entire life of the well-traveled warrior. Likewise, he had become warmly intrigued with the beautiful young lady in his life. Liliana was fourteen years younger than Yellowsnake, and after her birth in Argentina, had received an extensive education in various parts of the world. And now she had, for many of the same reasons as Yellowsnake, chosen to live in Arizona.

Liliana spoke six languages fluently and, in each instance, cursed like a drunken sailor. For the first time in many years, the blood in his wandering spirit was beginning to heat up. It seemed as if he had once again met his match, for he was deeply attracted to the feisty, green-eyed Latina.

The holidays brought a new meaning of happiness to Yellowsnake's heart, for now he was with someone for whom he really cared. They had come to realize that each knew what they were seeking in life and shared common goals. Most importantly, they were beginning to care for each other very much.

Within a few fleeting weeks, the high-spirited Liliana had consented to become his wife. A long forgotten sense of joy was once again filling his heart, and he knew he was ready to forge ahead into life with his eager companion. In time, she would prove to be a powerful, driving force in the tumultuous years to follow.

After their simple, unceremonious wedding in Santa Fe, the two lovers embarked upon a trip of pleasure which had long ago escaped Yellowsnake's desires. The passionate fires of love had returned to fill his body, and he felt the warmth of her words as she vowed to dedicate her life to his life. Now she was his wife, promising to faithfully follow him no matter where life's path took them.

Throughout the deeply passionate days of their honeymoon, she unleashed upon him her pent up desire for fulfillment and lasting love. They reclined as one passionate body in the quiet, posh confines of their honeymoon getaway. They were safely surrounded by the snowcapped mountains which served as watchful sentinels, ready to warn them should the outside world attempt to invade their intimacy.

When the twosome returned to Phoenix after a whirlwind

honeymoon, Liliana convinced Yellowsnake they should find a more suitable and conveniently located home near Phoenix. Though he could not fully understand how Liliana could be less than content to live in Apache Junction, he was agreeable to finding a new home base.

When Yellowsnake arrived back in his sparse, yet comfortable motel room for his last visit, he gathered his meager belongings, and bid farewell to his accommodating and caring landlord. He sneaked one last glance over his shoulder at the cloud shrouded and forever mysterious Superstition Mountains, then headed westward toward his new home near Seven Springs. Now, it didn't really matter where he hung his hat. He had Liliana at his side.

Chapter 13

Resurrection

Within a few months, Liliana proved to be the adhesive factor in Yellowsnake's life. Each of them had become nicely adapted to their new and loving life, and the quiet retreat of Seven Springs offered a mutually convenient home base from which they could continue their individual pursuits.

They agreed there was no good reason for Liliana to quit her job at the clinic and, of course, Yellowsnake had become a permanent fixture with the Company. He had gone back to his routine helicopter assignments, chasing and harassing drug runners along the coast.

Even though he was spending much of each week working out of the DEA headquarters in San Diego, the comfort and speed of his Bell 47 helicopter brought him home effortlessly for weekends. The contented pair were able to build their nest of happiness, just like any ordinary working couple. With the aid of her gourmet chef mother, Liliana soon added twenty pounds to the long lanky frame of Yellowsnake. Without a doubt, marriage was agreeing with him.

Much to Yellowsnake's disgust, Mexico's 1984 drug traffic had increased dramatically along the coastal waters adjoining the United States. His flight was always commanded by at least one DEA agent, and Yellowsnake found himself landing on suspected drug-carrying vessels with increasing frequency. And rarely, did the DEA agents miss making the bust they were after.

As Yellowsnake guided his chopper down toward the 190 foot, paint-peeled black trawler below them for a closer look at the ship's landing conditions, the DEA agent was convinced that the non-descript boat was carrying a valuable shipment of illegal cocaine and heroin. The CIA's informants, working deep in the heart of Mexico, were seldom mistaken when notifying the DEA agents of scheduled drug departures. The aircraft dropped closer and closer to the boat, then Yellowsnake's accomplice

213

announced over his loud speaker that he was a DEA agent. He was going to board their craft, and was advising the captain that his ship was now in U.S. waters.

After he set the chopper down softly on the pad of the gently rolling ship, Yellowsnake looked at the DEA agent. "Do you think you'll need any help?"

"No, this is a small ship. There shouldn't be any problem at all." However, the agent was heavily armed, knowing he had a definite edge in defending himself if something unexpected arose.

While the DEA agent sat in the seat next to him and fumbled with his seatbelt, Yellowsnake had already unfastened his belt and opened his door in preparation for boarding the ship. The agent had taken a few moments before unbuckling his belt to be sure his automatic weapons were fully armed. During those moments, Yellowsnake had eased out of the chopper while its main rotor blade continued spinning at a very high speed.

Tragedy had been lurking, totally unseen by the two unsuspecting agents, when it struck like a thunderous bolt out of the sky. An employee in the ship's pilot room had control of the ship's cargo boom, and knew the entire crew faced imminent arrest and the ship confiscation. With fear in his heart, the crewman activated the lever to raise the boom from its resting place below deck. Within seconds, the giant boom made lethal contact with the whirling rotor blade. It hit him with the impact of a speeding train crashing into a concrete wall, then the world went black for Yellowsnake and his companion.

The boom had caused the blade to become a tangled mass of steel, with the tip bent into a downward angle. In a split second, the blade had completed its rotation and struck Yellowsnake directly in his face. The lightening-like blow was so intense it nearly severed his entire face from the nose down. During the same split second, the blade shattered the plastic cockpit bubble of the helicopter, cutting through its thin shield, gruesomely decapitating the unsuspecting DEA officer.

Throughout the horror of the few seconds which had now placed Yellowsnake on the brink of death, a backup DEA chopper had been hovering a quarter of a mile away. The instant they saw what happened, the backup agents immediately dropped down for a forced landing on the deck of the still-moving ship. It was an awkward touchdown as they positioned their skids on the boat's main cargo hold door. They hastily deboarded, one of them keeping his automatic rifle fixed on the startled captain and crew. The other agent ran directly to the badly mangled helicopter. It took him only a glance to realize the seriousness of the situation. In a moment, the backup agent had retrieved his cellular phone, calling for an emergency evacuation team.

Since the mishap had occurred near San Diego, it took less than ten minutes for the emergency helicopter medical team to arrive. By now, there was scarcely room for the hospital craft to land and retrieve the critically injured Yellowsnake. The emergency chopper was manned by three highly-trained medics who, within seconds, had determined that the DEA agent's life had ended. It was of utmost importance to get Yellowsnake to the San Diego Hospital if there was to be a thread of chance in saving his life.

Blood covered the deck of the ship like a red blanket, splattered from gunnel to gunnel. While two of the medics strapped Yellowsnake to a flight gurney, the third attendant placed his hands around the nearly severed remnants of Yellowsnake's lower face, trying to hold it intact. To make matters worse, his neck was oddly contorted. They knew their options, and the medics sensed they had no choice but to move him. If they waited any longer, the brave pilot would be dead and there would be no further urgency.

They arrived at San Diego Hospital within minutes. Soon a large contingency of medical staff was on hand to do everything possible to save Yellowsnake's life. They frantically cut off his clothes and removed the blood-covered eagle claw from around his neck while wheeling him into the emergency operating room. The downed Comanche's body was splattered with blood from head to toe.

The doctor evaluating his vital signs looked in his eyes, and spoke with candor. "I doubt if this poor guy will make it. The question is, where should we begin? He has multiple problems and they are all severe." The crack surgical team had quickly brought his bleeding under control, and were infusing fresh blood. They worked feverishly to stave off brain death from loss of blood and oxygen.

Each specialist stood by awaiting his turn, acting with skill and precision. The radiologist's jaw dropped as he reviewed x-rays of Yellowsnake's neck. "I can't believe this man is even alive. He has seven crushed vertebrae in his neck."

The lead surgeon stepped forward. "Damn, this guy is missing most of his right jawbone. This is a real mess." After scanning Yellowsnake's entire body and looking at the x-rays, yet another specialist remarked, "Would you believe this, he's got four teeth lodged in his lungs?"

The clock ticked away the hours while the skilled team of specialists labored intensely at the frustrating task of stabilizing Yellowsnake's trauma and keeping him alive.

Nine hours later, the exhausted team exited the surgical suite, shaking their heads in disbelief of what they had witnessed. Against all odds, the tough Comanche lying in surgery was still alive, offering no medical reason for breathing at all. For the moment, they had done everything humanly and medically possible to save his life.

During the frantic moments of madness, Liliana was notified of the tragedy and given scant details of Yellowsnake's condition. Within an hour, she was aboard a private plane en route from Phoenix to San Diego, accompanied by her mother.

And, most appropriately, Hotona and Jimmy were notified of the tragic incident which demanded their urgent presence if they hoped to see their son while he was still precariously alive. They departed immediately for his bedside.

Softly weeping, Liliana absorbed the technical information the doctors shared with her regarding the massive injuries to her husband's body. "Frankly, we believe in being honest around here. He's not out of the dark yet but, for the moment, he's at least alive. People with his level of trauma seldom survive this long. Your husband is a lucky man. His vital signs are still shaky, but we're giving him heavy transfusions to keep him stable, and the next twelve hours should tell the tale. For the moment, I think you should try to get some rest, and come back first thing in the morning."

Throughout the lonely night, the mangled warrior somehow remained alive. Early the next morning, the chief surgeon reappeared and expressed his troubled thoughts to Liliana and her concerned mother. "Liliana, we're happy to report that Yellowsnake is still alive. But, you should face reality in knowing there is extreme likelihood that if he lives, he has probably suffered some irreversible brain damage. With your medical background, you understand what that means."

Liliana felt utterly helpless as she and her mother sat for hours next to Yellowsnake's bed. His body was unresponsive to stimulation, and there was no movement to indicate he was even alive. Only by seeing the rhythmic movement of the respirator pumping oxygen to his lungs, did they believe he was still with them.

During the early hours of Yellowsnake's tragic encounter, Hotona and Jimmy had arrived at Yellowsnake's bedside and, were soon warmly acquainted with Liliana, their son's new wife. Although time had not allowed them to meet each other, Yellowsnake's accident had brought them together and a family bond quickly formed. Liliana took an instant liking to Hotona, and Hotona likewise knew Liliana was a wonderful addition to her son's life. Through their following weeks of vigil, the two families shared intimate stories, each coming to know more about Yellowsnake and his violent life.

They maintained a continual vigil for three days, seldom sleeping, and eating only when necessary. They felt absolutely powerless as they watched the labyrinth of tubes attached to his body feed him and maintain his bodily functions.

Late in the morning of the fourth day, the chief surgeon joined them in Yellowsnake's room. "It's remarkable that your husband is still alive. None of our people can explain how he was able to pull through! But now, he has passed the most critical point of survival, and his vital signs suggest he will continue to remain alive. Unfortunately, his prognosis is impossible to predict."

In the waiting area, an unfamiliar figure suddenly appeared, and standing nervously, his eyes searched the room for a person named Liliana. The agitated stranger was none other than Yellowsnake's trusted leader and friend, Colonel John Lincoln.

Shortly after the tragic mishap had occurred, Colonel Lincoln had been notified of his comrade's horrible accident. For the last three days, he had monitored the life-and-death struggle of his friend by telephone and through Company officials. The Colonel had seized his first opportunity to leave Langley, and his jet had flown him straight to the bedside of his friend. His body language reflected his deep concern as he approached Liliana and her mother sitting on the overstuffed couch in the waiting room.

They glanced up at the distinguished-looking stranger as he extended his hand. "Liliana, I'm John Lincoln, Yellowsnake's friend."

His words brought a smile to Liliana's lips. "I'm so happy you're here Colonel. I've heard a lot about you. I'd like you to meet my mother." After they had all shaken hands, the Colonel sat on the edge of the leather couch near the two of them, asking that he be given all of the details of the tragedy.

Liliana explained she had not been told much about the mishap, but understood that had Yellowsnake not stepped out of the helicopter, he surely would have been decapitated along with the unfortunate DEA agent.

The Colonel, seeking to comfort the two women, spoke from his heart. "You know Liliana, it doesn't make much difference at this moment and it seems rather meaningless, but Yellowsnake would be proud in knowing that the DEA agents apprehended the ship's captain and crew, and they're now detained and charged with drug smuggling."

Liliana sensed, much like Yellowsnake had so many years earlier, that the Colonel was a man of his word, and one who could be trusted. She felt more than comfortable talking with him as family, and was eager to share the events of her and Yellowsnake's recent marriage. The Colonel didn't have to speak any words, for it was obvious by his reaction that he was a very caring man. And, most importantly, she sensed that he would not let his faithful friend down, no matter what he had to do.

Colonel Lincoln wasted no time in finding the chief surgeon who had spearheaded the miraculous effort to keep his friend alive, and was soon talking to a staff of seven specialists. He directed them to do everything humanly possible to not only keep his friend alive, but everything they could to restore him to his original self. Liliana could overhear only a few of his hushed words.

"This is a priority case, and you are authorized to do whatever it takes to put this man back in one piece. If you need authorization to do anything out of the ordinary, you are to call me immediately at Langley."

John Lincoln spent many hours during the next few days sitting with Liliana and her mother, sometimes in the waiting room, sometimes at Yellowsnake's bedside. His heart was talking, and the Colonel spoke as if Yellowsnake could hear his words. "Come on old buddy, you can make it."

The Colonel bid the two women goodbye, telling them regretfully that he had to return to Langley. "Don't worry, we'll be talking regularly from here on out. There are a lot of decisions we'll have to make. I'll be back as soon as I can. Liliana, rest assured that even though things seem hopeless, and this appears to be a tragedy you can't endure, the Company will make sure that Yellowsnake and you are properly taken care of. I'll make sure of that."

The next two weeks dragged as his family continued their vigilance at the hospital. Throughout the long hours, Yellowsnake lay in a deep coma, his bandaged head and face looking like an Egyptian mummy. His face revealed only small mouth and eye openings, and tubes protruded from all the crevices of his body.

The consoling surgeon, who by now was on a first name basis with Liliana, welcomed her presence at Yellowsnake's bedside. He spoke with a guarded, but optimistic tone, explaining that her husband's vital signs were becoming more stable. "If we're going to attempt reconstruction, we had better do it soon."

Liliana tried bravely to keep her lip from quivering as she spoke. "Doctor, I trust your judgment, and will do whatever you say because you have kept him alive so far. Do whatever you need to do to put my husband back in one piece."

With an infinite amount of detail, the doctor laid out his recommendations. "Although we have him stabilized, our first priority will be to start repairing his face as well as the crushed neck vertebrae, and then extract the bone fragments and teeth that are lodged in his lungs. After that, we'll have to call in a plastic surgeon to begin reconstructing the lower half of his face. That, in itself, will not be an easy task. Although we were able to salvage the main material from his face, there has been such extensive nerve damage and bone destruction it appears we'll have to remove bone from his hip, and fuse his jaw into shape. We'll use his bone combined with a steel plate in order to rebuild his face. We're conducting brain scans and although there is some detectable damage, there are indications it's functioning. Unfortunately, there's still only a remote chance of reasonable recovery."

Now the intricate and dangerous task of reconstructing the badly disfigured face would begin. Soon the skilled surgeons were forming a new bone structure supported by steel to create what was once the figure of his face. Yellowsnake was mercifully unconscious during the entire ordeal, not knowing that he would need to undergo many future operations to repair various parts of his neck and face.

The skillful doctors went to work, delicately fusing bone sections to his badly fractured neck vertebrae, then binding the fused areas with wire to hold them in place. Then began the arduous task of removing the broken teeth and shattered fragments from his lungs.

It was painfully slow but, like a jigsaw puzzle, his mangled face was returning to a remarkably good likeness of his old self. His lips could be reattached, but the doctors knew he would have very little feeling in them. The right half of his face now included a two-inch steel plate to replace the missing bone which was once his jaw.

Week after week, the delicate surgeries continued. And week after week, Yellowsnake continued to live. His body, which continued to breathe, never failed to bring a look of amazement to the doctors' faces, and the entire medical staff attending him.

Although Hotona and her husband could stay for only a week at a time, they were never gone for more than a few days before returning to visit their gravely-ill son.

Nearly three months had passed and the team of doctors were becoming concerned that Yellowsnake might remain in his coma indefinitely. They knew his chances were dismal to begin with, but had hoped that as his body stabilized, his consciousness might return as well. They had tried everything they knew to bring his mind from its long sleep, but thus far, they had been unsuccessful.

Throughout the tedious and nerve wracking weeks, Liliana and her mother had resided at the hospital family quarters, never far from the fallen soldier.

At this point in their vigil, the doctors felt compelled to tell Liliana, Hotona and Jimmy that Yellowsnake's future did not look good. "Frankly, if he doesn't come out of his coma soon, his condition may destabilize and throw him into complete reversal." Their words were alarming.

With good reason, the entire family was being asked to accept the possibility that Yellowsnake's life might be coming to an end. However, a look of determination blazed brightly in the eyes of Hotona. There was no way she was going to accept the imminent death of her son.

As Hotona looked into Liliana's eyes, a resolutely defiant mother spoke. "Liliana, I must leave now for a few days, but Yellowsnake's father will remain here while I'm gone. There is someone I must see."

Hotona had listened to the doctor's gloomy forecast of Yellowsnake's deteriorating condition, and had earlier sensed that his time was indeed growing short. Her mind had been flooded with thoughts of urgency. She knew it was imperative that she now visit the Yaqui medicine woman, Shahana, her long-time friend.

She offered no further explanation as she gathered her belongings and left.

Many years earlier, when Yellowsnake was a small boy,

Hotona had explained to her inquiring son that there were many things which conventional medicine could heal. However, there were also many things modern medicine alone could not do to heal a man's body and, equally important, his spirit. She told him that no matter what he learned throughout his life, he must never forget the mysterious healing power of the spirits.

With the aid of a small commuter plane that could carry her out of Phoenix, she arrived at a neighboring town outside the border of the Yaqui Indian Nation. An old friend living nearby the town agreed to drive Hotona to the home of Shahana.

The lonely brick hut, set well apart from the other villagers, had not changed in appearance. After Hotona thanked her friend who had so cordially agreed to wait while she spoke to Shahana, she knocked on the weather-beaten oak door. As it slowly opened, the deep brown penetrating eyes of the woman whom she had not seen for many years, met her gaze.

Strangely, while Hotona detailed the account of Yellowsnake's tragic mishap, she could sense by looking into her old friend's eyes that the wise medicine woman was already aware of the tragic occurrence. Shahana listened intently, but said nothing.

Before Hotona was able to complete her urgent request for Shahana to join her at the hospital, the old woman had quietly moved to her adjoining room. She had begun packing a few belongings for the trip which lay ahead of her. Included in her bag were three leather pouches, the contents of which Hotona dared not ask. Shahana motioned that she was ready to leave, and an hour later, the two arrived at the small airport. Hotona was not surprised when she discovered that Shahana had never flown in an airplane. And furthermore, Shahana had no intention of flying high in the sky in the "iron birds" which had flown over her hut. She respected Shahana's wishes. Hotona agreed to her friend's request that they ride in a more safe and dependable way. After thanking her chauffeuring friend, they were soon aboard a bus, bouncing along the monotonously long road headed in the direction of San Diego.

The bumpy bus stopped only at brief intervals to allow the passengers to stretch their legs, then continued through the long night. Shahana had spoken few words during the ride, and late the next morning, the weary travelers entered the hospital waiting room.

Hotona wasted no time in introducing Shahana to the family members, and a handful of doctors who had noticed them enter the waiting room. Hotona briefly explained the reason for Shahana's sudden visit. "Shahana must see Yellowsnake now, for there is much to be done." Shahana's dark eyes flashed as she smiled only faintly at the doctors. She grasped Hotona's arm for support as they walked slowly toward Yellowsnake's room. Around Shahana's shoulders was the same brightly colored, though now faded shawl she had worn for more than fifty years.

They quietly entered Yellowsnake's dimly lit room. Shahana seated herself comfortably close to his side, then reached into her dark bag, gently removing the three leather pouches. There seemed to be a mysterious confidence about Shahana as Hotona remained silent, curiously watching her every move. Then Hotona saw Shahana's dark eyes looking over her shoulder toward her, as if to say, *"You must leave me now, for what I have to do, I must do alone."* Hotona knew that her brave son's fate was now in the hands of Shahana. The doctors and nurses could never understand. But she did.

After she had closed the door quietly behind her, the concerned mother retreated to the hospital waiting area, knowing it might be some time before Shahana would return from Yellowsnake's bedside.

The next four hours would forever remain a mystery, for only the spirits of hundreds of years past knew what was transpiring within the confines of Yellowsnake's room. Yellowsnake's door finally opened, and Shahana, looking weary, shuffled slowly toward the anxiously awaiting family, and most curious doctors. She had a look on her face which revealed she had undergone an enormous undertaking. When Hotona and Liliana reached her side, they grasped her elbows before she nearly collapsed.

Wisely, everyone listened as Shahana spoke in barely audible tones. "Yellowsnake is not yet ready to join his ancestors who are beckoning him. He was born with a determined spirit which will not leave him at this time. His will is strong, and he still has much of his life to live. Within seven days, he will return from his deep sleep, and be with you again." The doctors politely restrained themselves. Her prophetic words were totally unrelated to their science of medicine, but they could feel Shahana's remarkable presence, and it gave them pause.

Shahana had become very tired. She whispered to Hotona that she must leave soon, for she would be comfortable only in the warmth of her hut. Shahana rose feebly to her feet, then adjusted her warm shawl as she looked the doctors squarely in their eyes. "When he awakens, the eagle claw which now lays at his bedside will be forever gone. In it's place, will be seven feathers of a golden eagle."

Her prophecy had reached everyone's ears, and with few final words, she bid the family members and doctors farewell. She was clearly anxious to return to her home in Mexico.

Soon after they were comfortably seated aboard a bus destined for the return trip, Shahana and Hotona began their trek along the same winding bumpy road, leading them back to the heart of the Yaqui nation. Daylight had not yet arrived when they reached the familiar brick hut of Shahana. She had spoken very few words during their long trip, letting Hotona know that she wouldn't be comfortable until she was back on Yaqui soil.

Hotona held a deep concern for the seemingly ageless medicine woman, reflecting that Shahana must now be well in excess of one hundred years old. No one, including her own tribal members and friends, knew exactly how long she had lived during her present life. Many believed, however, that she had lived many previous lives before this one.

After she had made herself fairly comfortably on the woven padded mat which she had placed beside Shahana's bed, Hotona was soon asleep.

The sun had fully risen, and it was late morning when Hotona was suddenly awakened by a cough, one which carried with it, a death rattle. She rose quickly to see what was happening, then noticed that Shahana's eyelids were only slits, neither open nor closed. Hotona grasped the feeble woman's leathery hand before she heard Shahana cough a final time...and then there was silence. The stress of Shahana's most important visit to Yellowsnake's bedside had taken its toll.

While she observed the look of peace upon her friend's face, Hotona believed that Shahana had reserved her body's precious remaining strength for the critical hours during which Yellowsnake needed her help. With the wisdom of a medicine woman who possessed many mystical powers, Shahana had bestowed upon Yellowsnake her last ounce of life.

Hotona had a clear knowledge of Yaqui traditions, and knew Shahana would have to be buried very soon. She would stay until her dear friend had received her sacred ceremonial rites, and was certain her spirit had been safely entrusted to her forefathers. As soon as the brief, though solemn burial ceremony had ended, Hotona knew she must make her way back to Yellowsnake's bedside.

While Hotona was gone, the highly trained doctors had privately scoffed while they talked about Shahana's voodoo sounding prophecy. However, sadness engulfed the waiting room as Hotona described the last moments of the remarkable woman's life. As they listened to Hotona's story, no one in the quiet waiting room, including the doctors, made any attempt to unravel the mystery of Shahana and her visit.

Colonel Lincoln had kept in close contact with Liliana throughout the ordeal. Each time they talked, she gave him an update on Yellowsnake's condition. He explained in greater detail the progress of the important matter he was attending to on Yellowsnake's behalf. From the onset of Yellowsnake's mishap, the Colonel had set into motion a carefully conceived plan of negotiation. His plan of attack would result, hopefully, in a substantial cash settlement in recognition of not only Yellowsnake's career-ending injury, but his many years of loyal dedication to the Company's needs. The Colonel had become as highly skilled as a Philadelphia lawyer in the art of negotiation for, unfortunately, much of his life and Company duties dealt with the distasteful world of politics.

During one of his most recent visits, the Colonel had left the hospital dubiously convinced that Yellowsnake's long-term prognosis was dim. Aside from full recovery, he and his family's greatest need would now be the long-term financial security which the government could well afford. Since the accident, Lincoln had met with the Claims Settlement Committee within the hierarchy of the CIA on several occasions. He had, at an earlier date, presented Yellowsnake's wartime accomplishments, along with a comprehensive summary of the tasks which he had faithfully completed for the Company. The Colonel was slowly but surely making a case which the Committee would be compelled to acknowledge.

Although the Committee was sympathetic from the onset, they were not willing to agree on a reasonable settlement. They were taking the position that, after all, Yellowsnake was an employee of the Company and therefore knew the risks involved. However, the Colonel would not accept their reasoning or logic regarding the value of Yellowsnake's service. He had persistently reminded the Committee that they should consider themselves fortunate in many respects, since it appeared Yellowsnake was never going to regain consciousness. The Colonel minced no words as he reminded the Committee members that Yellowsnake had seen much of the unsavory dealings of the Company. Now, given his prognosis, he would never be able to expose the covert activities which had been ordered by the Company, not to mention the ugly atrocities he had witnessed during his assignments.

"And gentlemen, let me remind you that everything he witnessed during his long and dedicated years with the Company, was sanctioned by the Company!"

After many long intense meetings with the Committee, he was beginning to get their attention. They were finally realizing that they were, in fact, fortunate that Yellowsnake had not regained consciousness. The Colonel was drawing upon all of his acquired skills as he began his negotiation for what he knew would be an unreachable settlement. However, this was only a starting point. "Gentlemen, given the wartime service record of Yellowsnake, and all of the productive and dedicated years he's served the Company, I believe the Committee should approve a three and one half million dollar cash settlement to fulfill its obligation to Yellowsnake."

Many of the Committee members shook their heads and rolled their eyes at his outrageous request. "This is totally impossible. There is no way we can justify granting such a large settlement to just an ordinary Company employee."

The Colonel fired back at the passive Committee. "Sirs, Yellowsnake was not just an ordinary Company employee, and if you'll look closely at his record, I think you'll agree with me. We've all lost count of the number of successful operations he faithfully completed, not to mention the number of times he personally saved my life. And I tell you most emphatically, gentlemen, if Yellowsnake is not treated with the highest possible consideration, you can consider my resignation to become effective with your denial of his claim to a fair settlement." The persuasive Colonel had put the stubborn Committee on it's toes, but they continued to display their indifference to the issue of fairness.

"We believe a settlement of seven-hundred and fifty thousand dollars would be a more than adequate sum of money to agree on." With like indifference to their callous counter-offer, Lincoln retorted that their suggested settlement was only a fraction of the value of the services Yellowsnake had provided. The Committee was reacting, and listened as Lincoln proposed that perhaps a more acceptable amount would be two and a half million dollars. Again, the Committee choked on the mere thought of having to pay such an exorbitant sum for ordinary services rendered. They huddled privately, then agreed to take the matter into consideration, promising to meet with him very soon. John Lincoln had backed the Committee into a corner, and he could sense a successful mission nearing it's end.

When the Colonel phoned Liliana at the hospital two days later, and shortly after Hotona's return, he asked for an update on Yellowsnake's condition. "I'll be down to see him soon, but I wanted to find out how he was doing and bring you up to date on what I've been doing." The Colonel described the critical point he was at in his serious negotiations with the Claims Committee.

After listening to the Colonel's depiction of his effort to make things right, Liliana told him about Hotona's cheerless trip to Mexico, and the death of her dear friend, Shahana. The Colonel's kind words were understanding, as he added his blessings. "You know, Liliana, I've come to know Yellowsnake very well through the years, and although he has never been a religious man, I know without any doubt, he's always had the spirits in his corner. Even though I don't understand the ways of the Yaqui or Comanche Indians, I'm sure there are forces far beyond my knowledge which will bring him through his ordeal." He gave her his reassurance that he would remain in close contact, telling her he'd call when he knew the final outcome of his nerve-wracking negotiation with the Claims Committee.

Four days passed, yet there was no apparent change in the fallen warrior's condition. The doctors were becoming increasingly pessimistic as to his chances of ever recovering from the severe blow to his head. They had silently dismissed Shahana's witch doctor prediction that Yellowsnake would regain consciousness before the end of the seventh day.

With an undeterred vigilance, Liliana, her mother and Yellowsnake's parents had remained steadfastly confident, each taking turns at his bedside. Since her return from Mexico, Hotona's eyes had held a renewed confidence. She, better than anyone else in the room, knew the powers of the spirits and especially, the powers of Shahana.

It was early in the morning on the sixth day, and after the family had finished breakfast in the hospital cafeteria, Liliana first returned to the waiting area. From there, she went directly to Yellowsnake's room. Then suddenly, the attending nurse heard a frightening shriek and rushed to his room, not knowing what had happened to the motionless patient under her care. When she entered his dimly lit room she nearly fainted, for when she looked at Yellowsnake, she could see his eyes were open. He was peering blankly toward the doorway in which she was standing. Liliana was next to his bed, holding his hand tightly. She was nearly breathless, still not believing her eyes.

Though he lay motionless, the warrior's eyes were now open, and through the clearness of their blue color, his mind was escaping from the dark world in which it had been trapped. As she rushed down the tiled corridor, Liliana quickly caught the attention of the family. "Come quickly! There's been a miracle!"

The entire family converged on Yellowsnake's bedside, and their tears of joy were flowing freely. There was a look of contentment in Hotona's eyes, as if she had known all along that Shahana's prophecy would be fulfilled. Hotona bent over and looked closely into his blue eyes. Then she gently kissed his cheek. "My dear son, I knew you'd come back to me." While he quietly watched from the opposite side of the bed, Jimmy grasped Yellowsnake's tube-riddled arm, holding it tightly to his chest. Though he was a man of few words, everyone in the room could read his thoughts. He too was not only grateful, but relieved.

Not many minutes passed before the room was buzzing. The skeptical doctors had entered the room and were gasping in disbelief, for they couldn't believe what they were seeing. Defying all odds, Yellowsnake had indeed returned to their world. Without saying so, everyone knew there was some higher authority responsible for saving his life, and awaking him from his deep coma. Of course, the doctors had performed all of their skilled medical maneuvers and techniques to save his life. But now there was rising certainty in the eyes of those gathered in his room that only one person was truly responsible for his return to the living world. And that authority was, without any doubt, Shahana, the mysterious one who had given her last moments of life to ensure his life would continue.

Through all the tumultuous excitement taking place within the walls of his small hospital room, a most remarkable occurrence had gone unnoticed. During the joyful moments of pandemonium, one of the doctors had become noticeably quiet, a somber look overtaking his face. As he pointed toward the nightstand next to Yellowsnake's bed, he was staring in disbelief. Everyone was alarmed at the doctor's sobriety and stopped to look. Nearly out of site behind the small bedside lamp, was the final element of confirmation that Shahana's prophecy had been fulfilled. As if arranged by an interior decorator, there were seven golden eagle feathers spread in a semi-circle. And most significantly, the small eagle claw which

229

Yellowsnake had worn around his neck for so many years, had vanished.

Suddenly, the air of skepticism and disbelief which had prevailed among the doctors had become an unexplainable phenomenon which they could no longer deny. Medical science had played an important role at every critical turn in his recovery, but only one mysterious spirit had passed through Yellowsnake's near-lifeless body. The experts had been presented with a new challenge to their thought processes, and they alone had to come to grips with what they had witnessed.

When the Colonel was notified of the sudden turn of events, he elatedly boarded the Company plane, arriving at the hospital within hours. He looked intent, and with a smile on his face, the wise leader exclaimed, "If anybody could ever make it through the valley of death and back into the world of the living, it would be Yellowsnake. For some reason, I felt deep down inside he would pull out of this."

Taking Liliana aside, the Colonel described his final and triumphant meeting with the Claims Committee less than twenty-four hours earlier. Not withholding his disdain, he said, "The Claims Committee is a bunch of cold-hearted individuals who really don't give a damn about anything except the operations of the Company. But I've done my best to see that a fair and just settlement was agreed upon for the benefit of Yellowsnake and you. I didn't know anything so miraculous as this would happen and I demanded that the Company agree to my final offer of $1,600,000. They were reluctant, but they caved in. So I'm happy to tell you that you're going to have enough money on hand to live a decent life. On top of the settlement, the Company has agreed that for as long as he lives, Yellowsnake will be provided with the best medical attention money can buy, at no expense to you."

Liliana was overjoyed as she wrapped her arms around the trim waist of the Colonel, thanking him for his unrelenting effort to see that her husband had been treated fairly. The Colonel had a tone of overall relief in his voice as he told her that he must return to the never-ending world of turmoil at Langley, but would stay in close touch. If there was a downturn in

230

Yellowsnake's condition, she was to call him immediately. They grasped each other's hands in a warm and now meaningful grip, knowing each had done everything possible to keep their mutually dear friend alive and well.

The Colonel's parting words were new to the ears of Liliana. "Perhaps Yellowsnake has never shared this with you, but many years ago he and I made a deal. I told him that if he would see that I got through Vietnam alive during our war years, then I would see that he was taken care of the rest of his life. I know he never understood what I meant, but I always knew that as long as I lived, I would do everything in my power to see that my promise was kept. As you probably know, he saved my life on more than one occasion, and I believe now that I'm one step closer to keeping my end of the deal."

She knew nothing of the details of the unwritten agreement they had reached long ago, but Liliana felt the Colonel had indeed done everything a friend could do to help a fallen comrade. And since she now possessed knowledge of their well kept secret, Liliana deeply respected him for trying to keep his end of the unwritten pact. She could see that the now bloodied pact had become an important part of each of their lives, and knew that if Yellowsnake could speak, he would surely agree.

And Liliana now felt with commanding assurance that Lincoln, if called upon to do so, would willingly add his letting of blood to their strange, though now understandable contract of survival.

Chapter 14

Happy Jack

The helicopter accident had taken its toll in many ways. Not only had it dramatically impacted Yellowsnake's life, but it had also affected each member of the immediate family who ended up spending many months by his side.

After having become more closely acquainted with John Lincoln, Liliana had acquired a deep confidence in the wise Colonel. Although he was out of sight, he was never out of touch; his concern for Yellowsnake remained steadfast.

The Colonel had extended all of his political and negotiating prowess toward seeing that his friend would be properly cared for during the remaining days of his uncertain life. He explained in great detail to Liliana how a Federal judge in San Diego would administer the secret trust being established on Yellowsnake's behalf. The presumption of the Claims Settlement Committee within the CIA hierarchy, accompanied by supporting medical opinions, had led them to conclude that most of Yellowsnake's remaining days would be spent in a private care facility. He would most likely remain comatose, and no longer posing a threat of exposing the Company's clandestine activities.

Four days had passed since the injured warrior first opened his eyes and showed an indication of returning to the world of the living. While Liliana and her mother sat at his bedside, both of them suddenly noticed something different was happening. Yellowsnake's eyes were beginning to move from side to side and, on occasion, blink. He looked first at Liliana, and then toward her mother. His eyes shifted to every corner of the room–though he never spoke a word. The doctors had watched him from the onset of his mishap. And now, after observing his eye movement, they were even more stunned. It was far more than they had ever expected.

Even so, they knew it would be not only months, but

probably years before he would accomplish the painstakingly difficult physical therapy and rehabilitation which lay ahead. Throughout the entire nightmare, Liliana had quietly dedicated her life to Yellowsnake's recovery. She had permanently moved out of her home in Seven Springs weeks earlier and, with her mother, had taken up residency in a small apartment near the hospital.

Two days later, after the first signs of movement had appeared in Yellowsnake's eyes, the locked door within his mind began to slowly open. Liliana was sitting faithfully at his bedside, silently reminiscing about the many dangers her husband had faced. Suddenly, she was struck with alarm as she watched his arm begin to quiver then lift slowly off the bed. Although the lower half of his face was still tightly wrapped down to his collarbone, she was startled as his lips also began to move. Yellowsnake was beginning to make indistinguishable sounds. There was a sense of urgency in his eyes as they blinked with rapid movement, then he slowly turned his head a few inches in each direction. His weak voice began muttering and stammering muted words which, only to him, had great meaning.

Liliana listened intently as she bent over his still body, placing her ear close to his lips. She could barely distinguish his whispered, though frantic words. His arm had lifted ever so slightly off the bed, his index finger pointing toward the wall directly ahead of him. "Shahana! She's here. Do you see her? Do you see her? She's here," he whispered.

A chill ran through Liliana's body, for she knew with a quick glance over her shoulder that there was no one in the room other than herself and her mother. Nearly unable to contain her joy, she responded wisely. "Yes, sweetheart. I know she's here. She's always been here."

Liliana could never have imagined how correct she was. Of course she hadn't seen Shahana, but Yellowsnake had! Shahana's image had appeared before him as he laid motionless, staring blankly from his bed. Her soul healing presence had placed her above the foot of his bed, still dressed in the ancient clothes that had adorned her frail frame from many years earlier. Her long gray hair was smooth and shiny, and her eyes sparkled

234

even more. Yellowsnake could feel her warm smile penetrating his injured body, and felt a strange warmness within. Was it her strange healing powers that were flooding every part of his body? She was speaking to him, not with her words, but with her spirit. Her message was clear. His body would become healed, and his spirit would live many more years before joining those of his ancestors. Her invisible image had silently pierced his inner barrier, burning into his eyes and heart.

Shahana had made her presence known to him alone, and the story of her remarkable appearance would not be shared with anyone until several years later.

Throughout the long and tiring months which followed, the tedious and intricate surgical procedures continued as Yellowsnake was slowly, but surely, being restored. The doctors didn't attempt to hide their amazement, and were beginning to believe they had a better than average chance of restoring him to some semblance of normality. Each day, more and more words were flowing from his lips, and as his face continued it's healing, he began enunciating his words more clearly. Dreadfully, however, the attending psychiatric staff was of the opinion that although his badly injured body stood a fair chance of recovery, his brain had probably suffered some damage.

He had no recognition of written words, much less the ability to write, and didn't seem to remember anything prior to his fateful accident. He had been placed in a rehabilitation wing of the hospital, now being guided through the arduous task of regaining his senses and, hopefully, some remnants of his memory. Liliana, an endlessly patient person, spent every available hour telling him in her most sensitive way about the tragedy which had struck him, offering only brief glimpses of his previous life.

He was now well into the second year of his sheltered life inside the hospital, and never having seen the light of day outside its walls, Yellowsnake was slowly regaining fragments of his shattered memory. Though minutely small, each returning thought was a piece of the scrambled jigsaw puzzle. His memory flashes were triggered by a particular word or story told by Liliana, which in turn caused a brief instance of recall. Even though Yellowsnake was many miles away from complete recovery, he was making progress.

As the end of his second year of internment at the hospital approached, Yellowsnake's daily physical therapy program now enabled him to walk, although feebly, and move with a limited range of motion. The doctors were determined to thwart his weakened condition as they submerged him into a strenuous program to bring his body back to full strength. Their ultimate goal was to somehow get him released from the hospital, and into an environment which might help heal his mind.

During her lengthy stay at the hospital, Liliana had spoken regularly with John Lincoln, keeping him posted. From the onset, they had agreed it was in Yellowsnake's best interest for him to continue his rehabilitation without Lincoln's untimely intrusion. When the time was right, the Colonel could reenter his life and, hopefully, resurrect their long relationship.

For nearly three years, Liliana's life had been focused on her firm commitment to caring for her husband's never ending needs.

Finally, the long-awaited day arrived. The doctors smilingly announced they had done all they could for their Comanche patient, and were ready to release him into the personal care of Liliana and her mother. They warned Liliana that he would have to maintain a very strict schedule of follow-up visits to the hospital, but he was now free to spend the remainder of his life in her comforting care.

She had dreamed about this moment, and had long ago decided it would be in his best interest to move him to a remote location somewhere within the boundaries of Arizona, which he so dearly loved. Her arbitrary judgment told her that a comfortable and secluded setting could be found near the village of Happy Jack.

Within days, Liliana, her mother and Yellowsnake were en route to Happy Jack, driving toward the mountain village which would serve as their new refuge. The small, comfortable, log cabin which she had leased could provide them a secluded setting, ideally meeting his needs. The three acre ranch was located high on the Mogollon Rim, a serene setting which could offer his weakened mind a chance for recovery.

His progress was painfully slow, but day by day Liliana was consciously relinquishing her control over his fragile life. With a certain amount of anxiety, Liliana allowed him to stand unattended outside while she shopped in the small stores near Happy Jack. Often, she'd return to find him gone, wandering aimlessly nearby, and desperately trying to return to the spot where she had left him.

Liliana was strong in perseverance and refused to become distressed by small and inconsequential incidents. During the succeeding three years, she schooled him with relentless dedication, and succeeded in teaching him to read and write. And all the while, she persisted in forcing him to regain small pieces of his distant memory. Slowly, her efforts were beginning to bear fruit, for now she could now see the light of happiness returning to his eyes. Her greatest joy by far was that Yellowsnake was beginning to recover greater and greater chunks of memory, which she feared had been lost forever.

By 1990, their life together was beginning to resemble that of a normal couple. Although his memory had been badly shattered, he had unexplainably never forgotten what it took to tame a wild horse, ultimately earning it's love and loyalty.

Happiness had returned to their lives, and they had grown comfortably attached to their mini-ranch, deep within the mountains near Happy Jack. Yellowsnake's newest devotion was to Zack, a mountain horse which he had purchased a few months earlier. Zack, a formidable steed, had become an integral part of his life. Next, he acquired Gaucho, a constant companion for Zack, which in turn brought a double dose of pleasure to his life.

The sturdy quarter horses, as handsome a pair of horses as he had ever seen, resembled massive mountains of rippling muscle and were always on call for their master's next command. Yellowsnake devoted all of his waking hours to training the fine beauties, watching them become steadfastly adept at performing any task he lay at their feet.

His dedicated horses also opened up a new path of freedom for him, for he was now spending many hours each day riding deep into the mountains with his hunting rifle, often bringing back fresh game for their table. Time had become the best medicine for healing his badly injured mind. He had become dedicated to his own self healing, and was approaching a threshold of personal independence.

Like in years past, he sought something to keep himself useful and sharp. Polishing his native skills became his next venture. Within months, he was guiding elk hunters into the mountains in search of game. The word had spread quickly that if a trophy hunter wanted to go hunting for elk and have a more than average chance of success, they should hire Yellowsnake to be their guide. This in itself, pleased him greatly. Throughout his many years of rehabilitation and recovery, he had, fortunately, been mercifully spared the burden of total recall of his violent years of loyal service to the army and the Company. Subconsciously, he had chosen not to allow the dangerous and ugly memories back into his conscious mind. Fate would intervene, however, and in the waning days of 1990, a new disruption entered his life.

It was a frosty December morning when he was in his small barnyard feeding Zack and Gaucho. Suddenly, he noticed an official looking car enter his driveway. As he approached the stranger, he was joined by Liliana. In moments, they were being introduced to Mr. Madison, an agent with the Federal Bureau of Investigation. They were somewhat startled, and neither he nor Liliana had any idea why this suspicious-looking government official was standing before them.

Liliana politely invited him in for a cup of coffee, and the two listened intently as the FBI agent began unfolding a story of fear and brutality. Agent Madison spoke with a sense of seriousness and urgency in his voice as he carefully described the events of previous days.

"Two nights ago, a murderer by the name of Billy Starr escaped from the prison down in Florence, and now he's on the loose," explained the agent.

Starr had been convicted of mutilating a six year old child and, subsequently, a number of other people while on a killing spree. He had been apprehended and placed in the Florence prison on a temporary basis, awaiting transfer to more secure confinement in California. Once there, he was expected to be tried and convicted on separate charges, and sentenced to death.

However, the crafty killer possessed a keen knowledge of the rugged terrain throughout most of northern Arizona. And now, most amazingly, he had managed to escape his confinement and was presumed to be headed toward Happy Jack. The scant information the FBI had gathered during the past forty-eight hours indicated he had fled on foot and, somewhere along the way, had stolen a horse. His injured horse had been found abandoned along the east slope of the Mazatzal Mountains, and it looked like he was traveling on foot, headed in a direction which would steer him into Happy Jack.

"But how does that concern us?" asked Liliana.

As one might expect, the nervous FBI agent had all the answers. "Once we learned of his escape, we immediately began a search through our extensive files and those of our Washington contacts to find someone capable of assisting us in our search for him in this rugged mountain region. Whenever we have a situation like this, we don't try to exceed our limitations, especially when it comes to tracking. And he's someone who probably won't leave many signs of travel. We have people standing by to apprehend him, but before we can make the extraction, we need your help in picking up his trail and tracking him to a point where we can make the arrest."

Yellowsnake and Liliana were dumbfounded as they looked at each other. Finally, Liliana spoke with a sharp tone in her voice. "We don't want any part of it. We're happy with our lives the way they are."

Before Yellowsnake could agree with her, the agent quickly pointed out that he had already received prior approval from several sources, including the Federal Judge in San Diego who was administering Yellowsnake's secret trust. "Apparently, your physical and psychiatric reviews indicate you are capable and competent to assist us. That being the case, we specifically requested your assistance. Your medical record says you've had a rough time of it, but we badly need your help."

Yellowsnake, through instinct alone, had never allowed his

tracking skills to escape from his damaged mind. He harbored an obvious reluctance, but agreed that if he didn't have any choice, he would assist the FBI in their search. "If I go with you and pick up his trail, and can get close enough to him, do you want me to bring him back dead?"

Agent Madison was adamant as he spoke. "No, that's totally out of the question. Our objective is to bring him in alive, and transport him to California for his murder trial. After he's convicted, he'll be executed."

His peaceful life had been rudely interrupted, for once again Yellowsnake was being given an unsavory task. The job, much like his DEA assignments long ago, had its limitations. FBI Intelligence had determined that Billy Starr's path would sooner or later lead him into Jack Canyon, desolately located about 40 miles from the quiet village of Happy Jack.

Yellowsnake didn't dispute their assessment, and with equal candor regarding himself and the FBI, he agreed that he was probably the only candidate with an intimate knowledge of Jack Canyon. "Here are my conditions. I don't give a damn about the five hundred dollars a day you're going to pay me, but I'll need my horse, Zack, and my dog, Bandit, who'll help me get the job done."

Bandit had been laying close to Yellowsnake's feet when his ears perked up at the mere mention of his name. The mixed breed Australian Dingo was devoted to Yellowsnake's needs. "Just so you know, I'll be carrying my .357 magnum and fighting knife. And just in case something goes wrong, I'll have a 30-30 rifle packed on my saddle." The FBI agent didn't argue the point, agreeing to Yellowsnake's terms and knowing that now, time was critical.

Early the next morning, and over the pleading objections of Liliana, Yellowsnake and the agent were headed in the direction of Jack Canyon. They were hauling Zack in his trailer, and Bandit in the back seat of his truck. As they neared a dead end on the rough two-track trail leading to Jack Canyon, they pulled over and parked.

Agent Madison laid out his area map on the hood of the truck, carefully detailing their method of attack. Although Jack

Canyon was a long, winding and treacherous canyon, Yellowsnake was told to proceed southeastward as far as necessary on horseback until he reached a point where he was able to pick up Billy Starr's trail. No matter how far his travels took him along the mostly unexplored canyon, he was to keep riding until he picked up Starr's trail and could drive him back toward the direction of Happy Jack.

Yellowsnake had no doubt about his ability to pick up the vicious killer's trail, it was simply a matter of where. Zack had been saddled up, and the saddlebags strapped across his back were packed with food, ammunition and a map of the surrounding area. Yellowsnake and his companions had everything they needed to survive in the barren wilderness.

Agent Madison equipped him with a two-way radio, and he was given a prearranged set of communication times and arrest rendezvous points. During his trek, he would need to continue communicating with agent Madison. Madison's plan was that at the FBI's preestablished checkpoints, he would have his agents waiting until Yellowsnake had flushed Starr into the open where he could be captured.

Madison's agents were going to hide and lay in wait until Starr reached their extraction point, then surprise him with their highly orchestrated plan of arrest. Yellowsnake's gut feeling told him that the plan sounded much too simple. In any case, he'd do what agent Madison requested.

After checking his gear one final time, he mounted Zack and was headed in the direction of Jack Canyon, fully prepared to ride for as long and hard as necessary to pick up the killer's trail. He knew he'd have to travel a long way just to get started, so his first and second day on the trail passed uneventfully. By the third day, he had traveled many miles along the steep edges of Jack Canyon, heading further and further away from Happy Jack, and ever closer to the northern reaches of the Mazatzal Mountains.

That night, after he selected a campsite in a remote, well-protected side canyon, he sat by the warmth of his fire. He sensed an uneasiness in his stomach, telling him he wasn't far from Billy Starr's trail. Madison had given Yellowsnake a small shred of Starr's clothing, and he was carrying it tucked away in his saddle bag until it was time to give Bandit a whiff of what he was looking for.

Before dawn the next morning, Zack was carrying him toward his target, with Bandit on his heels. Yellowsnake inched closer and closer to the main corridor of Jack Canyon, then stopped to retrieve the small bit of clothing. He knelt on the ground, holding it before Bandit's nose. "Okay boy, let's go to work! It's time to find this guy."

Bandit seemed to understand every word from his master's lips, his ears perking up as he began sniffing the ground intently. When they reached the canyon floor, the threesome began their intense search for signs of Starr. They had now fully reversed their direction of travel, and Bandit's alert nose reaction was telling Yellowsnake to head northward toward Happy Jack.

Not an hour had passed before Bandit's sharp bark caught Yellowsnake's attention. He knew his dog had found something which would lead him in the direction of Starr. The farther they traveled up the canyon, the more excited Bandit became. Finally, at ten o'clock in the morning, Yellowsnake stopped to call agent Madison.

When he received Yellowsnake's message, agent Madison replied, "Okay, if you think you're getting near him, keep heading up the canyon and try to drive him up to Checkpoint `A', which I marked on your map."

Yellowsnake's keen eyes spotted the footsteps firmly imprinted in the sand along the edge of a creek running through the canyon. His prey was not far ahead. Bandit's ears were peeled back as he stopped abruptly, signaling his master that there was danger ahead. Yellowsnake pulled his binoculars from his saddlebag, carefully scanning not only the floor of the canyon, but its sharp declining banks. Finally, he saw what he was looking for.

There, little more than a quarter of a mile ahead, the killer was skillfully maneuvering through the rocks, appearing to know exactly where he was headed. "I've got him in sight," Yellowsnake radioed to agent Madison. "Hang back. Keep him in sight, but keep him moving in our direction," Madison directed.

Yellowsnake readied his .357 Magnum as he peered ahead. He could see the floor of the canyon, and it's sides were heavily forested with pinion pine and scrub oak trees. Like a shadow, the fleeing figure had disappeared into the thickness of the trees and undergrowth, presumably moving closer to the first designated point of apprehension. Yellowsnake again radioed a message. "He should be in your area. Have you got him in sight yet?"

"Hold on. I'll check to see if anybody's spotted him, then I'll call you back," said Madison.

A few minutes later, Madison returned Yellowsnake's call, expressing an even deeper concern for what was happening. "He hasn't passed in front of our people. We don't know where in the hell he is."

"Damn," Yellowsnake scolded, "I put him right in front of your noses. Now what?"

Darkness was rapidly approaching when agent Madison declared they had better call it quits for the day, and wait until tomorrow before they resumed their chase.

Yellowsnake had chosen not to move any further toward the unpredictable killer. He made camp in the rocks that night, deciding he would forego the luxury of a fire. He knew the ruthless killer wasn't going to have a fire, and might double back to take his life.

The wary tracker crawled out of his bedroll into the cold air the next morning, wolfing down a bit of food before he passed on a chunk to Bandit. He wasted no time in saddling up Zack, who had grazed leisurely throughout the night. It was time to get back on Starr's trail.

Soon after their last communication with Yellowsnake the previous night, the embarrassed agents admitted they had been foiled by the slippery maneuvers of Billy Starr, and had moved farther up the canyon to Checkpoint 'B'. Once he heard where the agents were, Yellowsnake proceeded with caution. He began weaving his way up and down the sides of the mountain slopes until he again picked up the fleeing killer's trail.

During the night, Billy Starr had moved with the craftiness

of a fleeing mountain lion, continuing on foot, slowly making his way up the canyon. The FBI team had lucked out for he had stopped to rest, and had not yet reached the second checkpoint.

It was shortly after noon and although he hadn't seen Starr for several hours, Yellowsnake knew he wasn't far away. Suddenly, a gunshot rang out in the clear air. As the bouncing echo of the gunshot reached his ears, Yellowsnake quickly radioed to see if agent Madison and his boys had made their bust. Madison woefully exclaimed, "Our guys spotted him and shouted for him to stop, then fired a warning shot over his head. Since then, they haven't seen him."

"Shit! If you see him, why in hell don't you just shoot him and get it over with? You may never catch this guy!" Yellowsnake disgustedly accepted the fact that they had totally screwed up, and another day had ended with Starr still on the loose. The results of the third day, however, would prove even more disappointing. The tired tracker had done his job diligently and by the FBI's book, and now, he was becoming more than irritated that the FBI hadn't done theirs. Although they were well-trained, highly skilled agents, they were woefully overmatched by the rugged terrain and formidable obstacles laying in their path. They were losing the battle of wits, and Yellowsnake knew it.

In their eagerness to follow established procedure, the small band of FBI agents had given up their chase for the second night in a row, moving upcanyon to Checkpoint `C'. Yellowsnake kept his eyes sharply peeled, while Bandit kept his nose to the ground as they continued their search long into the uneventful third morning.

Suddenly, Bandit sounded a shrill bark and came to a sudden halt. He looked upward toward a ridge on the adjacent mountain peak, his nose in the air. Yellowsnake glanced upward, and could see that the well-adapted killer had nearly reached the top of the ridge. The slippery killer took a few more strides, then passed over it's edge, falling out of sight.

He shot off an urgent message to agent Madison who, by now, was more closely accompanying his handful of apprehenders. "You'd better get moving up the side of the mountain off to your left, because I just saw him pass over the ridge, and if you don't move now, you're going to lose him."

The agents were way out of their element, never expecting they'd have to make a fast climb over the rugged ridge high above them. Most foolishly, they elected to find an easier route which would still place them in front of Billy Starr's projected path of travel.

"We're not going to try to chase him over the mountain," agent Madison replied. "Instead, we're going to move up the canyon and find an easier trail to take us over the hump. At that point, we should be able to pick him up."

Yellowsnake had finally had enough. The limits of his tolerance had been tested by the entire fiasco, and bonehead maneuvers of the Bureau. He then declared in an unmistakable tone, "Agent Madison, you've received all the tracking you're going to get from me. You're on your own from here on out. I'm headed back to Happy Jack."

A feeble reply reached his ears. "Yellowsnake, I'm sorry our plan didn't turn out the way we thought it would, but I'm going to keep our agents on his trail. I'll see you back at your ranch." Hours later, the shamefaced agent apologized profusely for the gross bumbling of the entire affair. "It's our fault, and I know we should have done a better job. Unfortunately, that dangerous maniac is still on the loose."

Yellowsnake, without saying, knew the hapless agents were well outside their comfort zone, and stood little chance of catching the skillful killer. Two weeks later, the Sedona News proudly announced that, following a long and fruitless pursuit, Billy Starr had finally been apprehended at a small motel outside of Sedona, and after a relentless pursuit was being brought to justice by the FBI.

"What a farce," he barked at Liliana. "Those dumb bastards could have finished the job in one day but, like I told you, they had to do it their own way."

Yellowsnake had become acutely aware that the dangerous interruption had forced him to recall some unpleasant memories of his past, but he willfully set them aside, returning to his comfortable life in Happy Jack. He no longer craved the

245

perilous adventure which had necessarily dominated his former life. His first thought was to turn his back on the whole experience. Now, the only things really important to him were his wife, his horses and faithful dog. Nothing else seemed to matter anymore.

The experience had served as a harsh reminder that there was now a lot more to life than living on the edge of disaster. He was willing to leave that task up to the new adventurers, those who needed the excitement in their lives.

He was out of the game.

Chapter 15

Old Faces, New Places

The happy ranchers were feeling their lives once again returning to the level of comfort they had become accustomed to before their uninvited visit from the FBI. Yellowsnake and Liliana firmly agreed that turmoil and terror had no place in their lives.

Liliana, up until a year earlier, had been the only one to speak with Colonel Lincoln. Each time he called, she had let him know about Yellowsnake's progress and gradual recovery, and each time, he was more and more pleased with her report. Although John Lincoln had waited patiently for the right time, he was eager to see his loyal friend again.

Liliana had sensed the time was right, and had guardedly encouraged Yellowsnake to speak with the Colonel by phone so that they could slowly become reacquainted with each other. Although large pieces of his memory had returned remarkably well, his thoughts, especially where it concerned his war torn years were hazy at best. And likewise, his mind was telling him, absent of many details, that he had a close relationship with the Colonel.

Within the ever expanding boundaries of his recall, he had recovered enough memory to remember that the Colonel was a person he had trusted and admired.

The luxury of his recovery time, and the healing solitude of the mountains had also permitted Yellowsnake and Liliana to see his parents on a more frequent basis. Hotona and Jimmy were comforted knowing their son had, for the most part, returned to a normal life.

His healing mind had also allowed him to remember those who had been so important during his long years of recovery. High on his list was the person to whom he owed deep appreciation, Liliana's mother. She had been Liliana's rock, the foundation which kept Liliana afloat. The long ago warrior and his devoted wife had adjusted nicely to their sheltered life in Happy Jack. Unfortunately, the thing which bothered Yellowsnake more than anything else was the extreme cold which swept in unpredictably, causing him to curse his discomfort. "Damn it, Liliana, I love it up here, but it seems like I'm cold all the time."

He was smart enough to always dress properly for the weather, but he was never comfortably warm until he huddled close to the blazing fire in their fireplace.

Whenever he wasn't engaged in guiding some enthusiastic group of elk hunters deep into the mountains in search of their trophies, he found himself being called to help out a few ranchers in the area with their cattle operations.

He loved his life, sometimes feeling more and more like a rugged cowboy out of some John Wayne movie. Along with Zack and Gaucho, and his tireless dog Bandit, they were spending their delightful days chasing and rounding up stray cattle for the ranchers who lacked the time or the means to bring them home. Life couldn't be any more satisfying, and he had come to cherish its simplicity.

The richest reward to emerge from his simple lifestyle was that he could set aside his present task and do whatever he chose, whenever he chose. He indulged himself deeply with his new found luxury of doing only pleasurable things, those which brought him joy and satisfaction.

Hotona's loving command that he and Liliana visit them for a few days had prompted them to climb aboard their sleek new pick up truck, carrying them back in anticipation of sitting in the familiar surroundings of his parents' kitchen, swapping tales.

While the two spent hours reminiscing with his parents, and sharing some of the memories he was continuously recalling, a thought occurred to Yellowsnake. *While I'm here, I think I'll take that peace pipe I carved when I was a kid back to Happy Jack, while I'm here, I might as well bring the Mountain of Bones pottery which Mom has stored away for me.* He knew Liliana couldn't wait to have the pottery adorn her cabinets, and Yellowsnake knew the pipe still needed a master.

They warmly embraced his parents goodbye, then Liliana

and Yellowsnake anxiously returned to the comfort of Happy Jack, for their impatient horses and dog wouldn't tolerate their absence for long. The priceless pottery he'd retrieved so many years earlier was carefully packed away, along with the delicately etched peace pipe, which would now rest in their home. The impatient animals heralded their return with barks and whinnies. The devoted followers let their masters know with no uncertainty that they were overjoyed at their return.

A month later, Yellowsnake was in his dusty barnyard, carousing with his horses as he prepared to gain their fond attention with a load of sweet feed. He was suddenly startled by the slam of a car door which had quietly entered his driveway. The unannounced, and all too familiar figure approaching him stirred a surge of joy in Yellowsnake's heart.

The friendly face stood before him, and then his brain triggered a realization that it was his long lost friend, John Lincoln. He was wearing sun glasses, a neat plaid shirt and trim blue jeans. The deeply tanned figure extended his arms, wrapping them tightly around the body of his Comanche friend. "Old warrior, I couldn't wait any longer to see you. I know you and I have talked only once over these past months, but Liliana and I have talked many times, and we finally agreed it was time that you and I got together." The caring tone of the Colonel's words hadn't changed and, most importantly, his voice reinforced even stronger his sincere concern for Yellowsnake's welfare.

The reunited trio sat comfortably around the smoldering remnants of the warm fire which had burned brightly in the fireplace, talking for hours about the many experiences they had shared during their long tumultuous years. Much to their surprise, the Colonel revealed that he had retired from the Company more than two years earlier. He had chosen to keep it a secret until he was able to see both of them in person. Until now, neither Yellowsnake nor Liliana knew anything about his move. And, like the two of them, he was enjoying the luxury of retirement at his farm in North Carolina.

Yellowsnake, during his most recent years, had become more conscious and appreciative of the rewards which had resulted from John Lincoln's diligent effort, namely, his fierce battles with the CIA Claims Settlement Committee. The Colonel had fought hard to see that he was properly compensated and provided for throughout the remainder of his life. "Colonel, I think it's time I admit that you've kept your end of our strange deal. I realize now, that you gave me a life that only I could have been happy with, and I'll confess, from the time we talked years ago, I never really understood what our deal was all about. But I know you put your butt on the line for me, and now I know we've each kept our part of the bargain. Liliana told me how you went to bat for me when everybody thought I was going to end up a brain-dead vegetable. My memory isn't perfect, but I do know you've made every effort to keep your end of our deal. I think that now we can call things even."

The expression on the Colonel's face was unmistakably clear, for he was not only relieved, but happy to hear Yellowsnake's declaration. And then, a lightening-like decision engulfed Yellowsnake. He excused himself from Liliana's and Lincoln's presence for a moment, then bounded up to the bedroom. From high up on a shelf, he retrieved the carefully stored peace pipe which had laid in wait for so many years until the perfect moment arrived.

When he returned to the living room, he stood proudly before the Colonel, trying to look like a fearsome Indian chief presenting one of his warriors with a victory gift. Yellowsnake reverently handed the Colonel the peace pipe which heretofore, had not been smoked. The Colonel was astonished, and marveled at its beauty. He had never seen anything like it in his life. "Colonel, I carved this pipe with my Comanche knife when I was only a teenager, and promised to keep it until I was able to present it to someone worthy of it and what it represents. You're one of only a few with which I've had close ties over the years, and you're the only person I know who is worthy of owning this pipe."

The Colonel was speechless as he watched Yellowsnake pack its bowl with sweet smelling tobacco. The proud warrior placed a match above it's smooth edge, instructing the Colonel to puff on it, for a peace pipe would never be suitable for it's intended purpose until it had been smoked by its giver, and its receiver. Yellowsnake knew he had made the right choice. The Colonel, without saying so, knew full well the pipe's meaning, and what it represented. He didn't need to ask of it's purpose, and that was important to Yellowsnake.

The three elders showed their respect for time honored tradition as they shared puffs off the ceremonial gift, now entrusted to the Colonel's care. Neither of them knew when they'd see each other again. The Colonel and Yellowsnake grasped arms, each promising to call regularly. Although there were many miles of mountains and forest between them, they'd remain friends until each had joined their forefathers.

Both of their lives had, at one time many years earlier, hung precariously in balance. In Yellowsnake's heart, no greater friendship could exist without each being willing, in their own way, to sacrifice themselves for the other. The slate was clean, and there was nothing left but their friendship.

Following the Colonel's warm departure, the arrival of winter and its cold winds had brought no sunshine to Yellowsnake's mood. More and more, he had come to dread the long months of uncomfortable cold which accompanied winter. Yellowsnake and Liliana seemed to be on a mutual wavelength, for it took only moments for them to agree they were ready to seek a warmer climate in Arizona.

Since their annual lease had nearly expired, they set out in search of a warm peaceful setting somewhere near the Valley of the Sun. Neither of them wanted to live in Phoenix, nor did either of them want to be too far from the valley's comforting heat. By process of elimination, they found themselves intrigued by the quaint, old western town of Cave Creek. It suited their needs perfectly, since the days were warm and the evenings cool and comfortable.

This time, however, they'd construct a home of their own design, and build barn accommodations more than adequate to house their faithful animals. They doggedly sought out every piece of available acreage before finding a site which would be perfectly suited for their new home.

Six months later, the proud homeowners admired their newly

completed home, accompanied by their animals' echo of contentment in their new surroundings. Their friendly new neighbors seemed to gravitate toward Yellowsnake and Liliana, and before long, they were surrounded with friends eager to help whenever they were needed.

Liliana was more delighted than ever with her new surroundings, and happy knowing she was much closer to her mother who had stood by her so faithfully throughout Yellowsnake's recovery. The body-warming heat of the Arizona skies, together with the warmth of their new friends, was giving life a new meaning, and they were cherishing it.

One evening, after they had finally settled into their new home, Yellowsnake was lightly dozing while comfortably reclined in his leather chair, when suddenly he remembered something. He jumped to his feet as if he had been stuck by a thunderbolt. He nearly gave Liliana a heart attack as he exclaimed, "I'll be damned, Liliana. I've remembered something!" And, heretofore that something had never been disclosed to Liliana.

Yellowsnake's memories always seemed to return at the strangest times. "I was thinking about Clyde Durham, Emmet Claggett and Monte, when all of a sudden it came back to me. I've got a milk can full of money buried in Deadman Canyon. And it's right beside Clyde's can of gold! I can't remember how much money was in it, but I think I buried it around the same time I buried Monte."

The memory intrigued him. Although the milk cans containing the unknown quantity of cash and gold was not critical to their financial security, it was something Yellowsnake couldn't get off his mind. Because the long lost occurrence had now become a certainty in his mind, he was being presented with a new pursuit. Most challenging, however, were the critically important details which were still deeply buried within his injured mind.

His returning thoughts told him Deadman Canyon was located deep within the Mazatzal Mountains, but he had no idea which overgrown and treacherous trail would lead him into the heart of the deep canyon.

Yellowsnake focused his hazy memory, trying to recall Clyde's words from many years earlier when they stood on the floor of the canyon. Clyde had pointed out that there were eight trails up to the main mountain range before reaching Deadman, but there was only one trail which would lead a man and his horse all the way into the depths of the canyon. At the mountain's summit, all other trails would end abruptly.

He thought, wistfully, about how exciting it would be to once again fly a helicopter over the forbidden flying zone blanketing the Mazatzal Mountains. But reality told him that if he was ever going to see the depth of the canyon again, it would be on foot and horseback. His tragic accident years earlier had ended his helicopter flying days, and he wasn't anxious to invite any interactions with the Feds. The value of the cache was not even an issue. He was financially comfortable, and needed only the adventure the search would offer. But, the challenges of finding Clyde and Emmet's lost trail, and searching for the milk cans of booty they had buried together, now that held the new Yellowsnake's interest.

For the next six months following his startling recall, Yellowsnake and his new neighbor, Ray, spent many long days and nights in the mysterious mountains, searching for a trail into Deadman. The obscure trails demanded skillful riders who were unafraid of the many dangers posed by the ancient paths. Each path was more dangerous than the last, and only one would lead them into Deadman. Their attempts were filled with renewed hope, and with each attempt, they returned empty-handed. Every time they set upon a new trail, they invariably, just as Clyde Durham had said, reached a dead end. Their futile quest continued for months, as they tried time after time to discover the mythical trail. They knew that when they found it, the path would lead them over the impassable backbone of the mountain standing boldly in their way.

Not only was Yellowsnake thrilled with the adventure of his new challenge, he was even more thrilled knowing a precious memory had reentered his mind. Clyde and Emmet's lives would forever remain locked in his memory, and their past adventures moved his spirit each time he thought of them.

Whenever the relentless riders returned from one of their fruitless expeditions in search of the uncertain passage, Yellowsnake often lamented to Liliana. "Well sweetheart, there's one thing for sure. I know the milk cans will always be there, because no one but me could ever find them. Even if someone did stumble into the canyon, I'm the only one who knows where Monte's buried. And if somebody finds their way into the canyon before I do, it'll probably be because they crash landed their airplane. If they get in there alive, they'll be even luckier if they come out alive. Deadman Canyon has a way of dealing out it's own measure of misfortune. That's how it got it's name."

Chapter 16

In the Footsteps of Peralta

Nineteen ninety-four was ushered into Arizona with sweeping winds and driving rain. Yellowsnake found himself with an abundance of time on his hands, able to do things on his own leisurely schedule. And delightfully, he was spending more and more time in various parts of the mountains. The ageless sentinels offered him a friendly sanctuary in which to visit the spirits. He happily continued his tireless search for the evasive placer gold which he knew lay hidden in many of the remote canyon areas nearby. In and of itself, the discovery of gold was not as important as the thrill of the search.

He looked disgustedly at the rain clouds overhead as he stood in the barnyard late one morning during the early winter months. Yellowsnake was tending to the chore of nailing new horse shoes on Zack and Gaucho. He winced as he bent over, holding the front leg of Zack while preparing to nail on his last shoe. He quietly cursed his aching back. The sound of the slamming door reached his ears, and he looked over his shoulder to see an unfamiliar truck in his driveway. He dropped Zack's hoof and set his hammer aside, walking toward the stranger's truck to see if he could help him. "Yeah, I hope you can," the stranger replied. "I spend quite a bit of time around here, and get into the mountains whenever I can. I was wondering if you could tell me how to get up to the old abandoned Silver Dragon Mine?"

The stranger's question brought a smile to Yellowsnake's face as he pointed to the North. "Yeah, it's easy to find. Just follow the dirt road over there and it'll eventually narrow down to a rough two-track, and when you reach the end of it, you'll know it. When you get that far, park your truck and look up over your left shoulder. You'll see the covered up entrance to the mine."

The stranger was delighted, for he had finally found

someone who knew what he was talking about. The stranger extended his hand as he introduced himself. "I'm Jake Montana, and I appreciate your help."

As a fellow miner, Yellowsnake was happy he could offer a helpful tip as he reached out to shake Jake's hand. "My name's Yellowsnake. So you like to prospect for gold too?" Jake's eyes lit up, and he wanted to talk some more. "I sure do. Whenever I'm out here for a few months every year, that's all I do. I like to go gold panning and prospecting because it gets me out of the house, and away from the swarms of people around this area."

"Damn, I love to do the same thing," Yellowsnake confided. In moments, the two prospectors knew they had something in common.

"When you pan for gold, where do you go Yellowsnake?"

Yellowsnake was more than happy to share his knowledge. He described the many trips he had taken into the far reaches of the Mazatzal and Bradshaw Mountains and as far west as Wickenburg.

"Shit!" Jake exclaimed. "Those are the same areas I've worked whenever I've gone out searching." Their ears were tuned sharply as they shared their secret discoveries of small gold flakes, dust and nuggets. A destined friendship had been struck, and soon Jake Montana and Yellowsnake were seen heading into remote areas of the mountains. They were toting their shovels and pans, en route to an exciting new search for gold.

Their discussions were endless as they traveled the rough two-track trails in Yellowsnake's jeep, each sharing the common thread of interest which runs through the veins of all gold prospectors. Their probing conversations soon brought one certainty to a head! If you were a prospector, you never ignored the possibility that hidden treasure may lay somewhere nearby. After all, the Spaniards and Mexicans had prospected all of Arizona hundreds of years earlier.

To pass the time during one of their long bumpy rides into the Bradshaw Mountains, Jake began reeling off a story which had been passed on to him years earlier. The story had come from a down and out hard luck miner named Ernie. It seemed that Ernie had spent many years during his youth and early manhood living with the Pima Indians much farther to the South. During Ernie's time with them, they had taken him into their confidence and, in doing so, had shared with him a very intriguing story. Interestingly, Jake had come to consider the story more than just a legend. He had concealed his interest, and had felt all along it warranted a closer look. Most stories were nothing more than legends, but he sensed this one might point the way to where the Mexican and Spanish explorers had hidden a treasure.

Just the mere mention of the word "treasure" brought a look of excitement to Yellowsnake's eyes. Ernie had grown old, and was nearly unable to walk the steep mountains any longer. His poor health aside, he was more than willing to share with Jake his copy of an old treasure map which had been given to him by the Pima Indians. Not so coincidentally, Jake had a copy of the treasure map in his backpack, and had waited patiently to show it to his Comanche companion.

Upon hearing Jake's mention of the map, Yellowsnake immediately pulled over to the side of the trail, turning off his engine. "Let's have a Coke, and let me take a look at your map."

For many years, Jake had maintained a keen interest in not only searching for gold, but in gaining knowledge of the ancient explorers' travels. And even more importantly, he searched for events which might have caused them to hide their treasure. He had taken the time to read multitudinous books which provided a somewhat detailed account of how the Spaniards and Mexicans operated, especially when it came to drawing their maps.

The Mexicans, and especially the Spaniards, always drew their maps in a symbolic fashion. The scrawled maps, many dating back more than 400 years, always noted certain landmarks, trails and unusual shapes of mountain terrain. There were three key symbols which remained paramount in their art of map drawing; the most critical symbols, indicating the presence of gold or buried treasure, were very simple. The three unmistakable symbols were the numeral seven, the numeral eight and, most importantly, a symbol carved in the shape of a "heart".

The heart was by far the most important symbol. It clearly

represented to the reader of the map, that if he was able to discover the whereabouts of heart, he would be standing very near to gold or buried treasure.

Yellowsnake was now living with a memory which was only a fraction of his earlier years. He faintly recalled that during his youth, he had heard a story very similar to what Jake was describing. Jake, who hadn't spent nearly as much time in Arizona as Yellowsnake, had studied Ernie's map on numerous occasions, but hadn't been able to figure out the location of the drawing, based on it's symbols.

Yellowsnake studied the map closely, then suddenly became aroused. "Damn, there's something on this map that I recognize. And that something is Four Peaks." Jake had been looking over Yellowsnake's shoulder and spotted the symbol which his new friend was pointing to on the map. He quickly agreed. "You know, I think you're right!" They were bubbling with anticipation. Yellowsnake knew that he and Jake had a serious mission ahead of them.

They spent the day digging around the cold waters of an unnamed creek. The pair had gleaned their typical small pittance of gold flakes and dust, but were nonetheless happy with the hours they had spent together.

The day had ended and the two gold searchers headed toward Yellowsnake's ranch, when out of the clear blue sky, Yellowsnake resurrected a long forgotten event. "You know, years ago I knew a guy named Crazy Jake, just like your name." Jake Montana stared at Yellowsnake, not too anxious to be confused with Crazy Jake. He too, had heard the story.

"Yeah, it seems to me I read something in the paper about him. Wasn't he the crazy bastard who blew up the Superstition Mountains?"

"He sure as hell was, and I was the one who gave him the C-4 to do it. Now I'm sorry I ever flew that nasty shit into him. He did a hell of a lot of damage."

Jake Montana knew nothing about handling C-4 explosives, let alone blowing up the mountains. The two Jakes didn't have anything at all in common! A week later, the game plan had been fully formulated. Yellowsnake had decided the best way to

258

venture into the area would be on horseback. And what better means than Zack and Gaucho to carry them into the rugged terrain which lay ahead.

Four Peaks, which loomed north of the Salt River, represented the south end of the Mazatzal Mountains, and were coincidentally, not far from the Superstition Mountains. The Superstitions, in turn, had become well-documented as the area through which not only the Spaniards, but Mexican explorers had traveled in their search for gold.

Yellowsnake had determined that their route would follow a nearly impassable trail. From there, they would need their sturdy mountain horses as they headed into rugged and nearly impenetrable terrain. The trip was on. They followed what was now just an ancient foot trail, finally reaching a small creek within the canyon area they were seeking. Their eyes scanned the eerie silence of the canyon walls, and they knew they couldn't venture any further on horseback. They would have to set out on foot, equipped with backpacks.

After securely tying up Zack and Gaucho in an area where they could graze comfortably, Yellowsnake and Jake wove their way down the narrow canyon floor over which the crystal clear water of the small creek was running. Suddenly, they found themselves at an impasse. Just a few feet ahead of them, the creek bed had unexpectedly become a waterfall, dropping to a depth of more than twenty feet. On each side of them lay mountain slopes which were reaching steeply upward, creating a treacherous picture of improbable access.

However, undaunted by small obstacles, Yellowsnake challenged Jake, "So, do you think you can follow me up the side of this mountain cliff? I think that if we could reach the top of that ridge, we can get closer to the area I believe we need to be in."

Although he was four years older than Yellowsnake, Jake had deemed himself as fit as any other explorer, and would never back off from a challenge like that. "Comanche, if you can make it, I can sure as hell make it," Jake countered.

The Comanche mountain climber was blessed with long lean legs which could carry him in careful steps up the side of the mountain wall. He began nudging himself closer and closer toward the formidable ridge above them. While Jake was not enjoying the advantage of extra long legs, he stayed in close pursuit. He carefully followed each footstep and handhold that Yellowsnake had used as he climbed higher and higher. The mountainside had become dangerously steep.

They had passed the point of no return on their way up the mountainside, and Jake had stopped momentarily to look downward at what was now the narrow thread outline of the creek.

The fearless leader stopped to catch his breath, and was six or seven feet above when he realized that Jake, with a certain degree of concern, had a problem which had not confronted Yellowsnake. Due to his shorter legs, Jake was not able to reach the next foothold and, likewise, the next hand hold necessary to carry him upward. Jake growled, explaining his dilemma. "All right Big Cheese, now what are we going to do? I can't step downward, so there's no way I can possibly retrace my steps. I can't get up to where you are, so what do you suggest?"

Yellowsnake chuckled as he lit a cigarette. "We'll figure something out. What the hell, you can always jump off the side and get down real quick if you want to," he said laughing. He realized this was not a good time to be funny. Jake didn't see much humor in the solution. Yellowsnake took a more serious look at the situation. He concluded that there was only one means of solving the problem, and that was to help Jake advance his movement upward and out of the danger zone.

Like a poker player who had been dealt a bad hand, Jake wasn't so sure he liked the idea at all. "Here's what we'll do," Yellowsnake commanded. I'm going to remove my backpack and, as you can see, there are two shoulder straps which look like they're pretty damn strong. This is a fairly new backpack. What I'm going to do is brace myself, and try to lay backward to make sure I won't slip, then I'm going to sling the backpack toward you. When the straps reach your hands, you grab them and I'll pull you up out of that crevice."

"Shit! You've got to be kidding. And what if the straps break?" Jake moaned.

Never without a quip, Yellowsnake bellowed, "Well, if you've got a better idea, let me know white man. I'd say you're between a rock and a hard spot right now." Jake knew there wasn't any really safe solution to the crisis, so he agreed to place his life in Yellowsnake's hands.

Jake gathered his courage, took a deep breath and said a short prayer as he prepared himself to catch the shoulder strap when it reached his hands. Yellowsnake laid back at nearly a forty-five degree angle from upright and, bracing his feet firmly in small ledge cracks with his heels, he said, "Okay, here we go." With his long arms, the confident rescuer catapulted the empty backpack over his head and downward toward Jake's hands, which were still clinging to the rock handholds.

Jake's timing was precise. He was being driven by the strong flow of adrenaline shooting through his body. He released his hands at the exact moment the flying shoulder strap arrived. He grabbed it securely, hanging on for dear life. Yellowsnake very carefully began inching his way up the slippery cliff side, causing Jake's feet to become suspended in midair. With all of his strength, he hauled his mining friend's body up and over the perilous point. Though it had taken only three or four minutes, the ordeal seemed an eternity to Jake. He scowled his approval of the hair-brained tactic as he rested safely on the upper reaches of the ledge. Jake had a relieved smile on his face, and was breathing hard as he sat next to a smiling Yellowsnake.

The two mountaineers sat enjoying a smoke, remarking at the beauty of the canyon below. They agreed they had to find an easier way off the mountain. Twenty minutes later, they reached the top of the ridge, which had been their destination all along. They sidestepped stones and loose gravel as they walked about a quarter of a mile along the mountain's boulder-strewn spine. Soon, they reached the junction of another deep canyon entering from another direction.

"This is awesome, " Yellowsnake remarked. "I'll bet there hasn't been anyone up here in a hundred years." The two gingerly detoured around an ancient Mesquite tree lying ahead of them, and peered across the wide adjoining canyon. Both of them had spotted something which caught their attention. Across the deep forbidding canyon, and carved high on a precipice were obvious symbols, undoubtedly left by Spanish explorers. The Spanish predecessors had chiseled deeply into the smooth rock face of the canyon wall the image of a church cross. And beside the cross were two oval shaped engravings which represented a pair of eyes looking in another direction. The searchers proceeded further, knowing their daylight would soon vanish. The inhospitable and forbidding canyon offered no further clues as to which direction they should follow, much less what they should be looking for.

Being novices in this new arena of adventure, both agreed to retreat and call it a day. They'd regroup in the comfort of home to figure out more precisely what the hell they were doing! After searching around, Yellowsnake discovered a new crevice which would allow them a more gradual descent from the treacherous mountain, and back to their waiting horses.

Three days later, Yellowsnake's new found adventure was abruptly interrupted when he received an urgent call from Hotona. Her distressed tone of voice revealed her concern over his father's recent heart attack. Jimmy's attack had greatly damaged his heart and now there was some uncertainty as to how long he would live.

Yellowsnake and Liliana packed a few belongings and hastened to reach his side. The concerned son looked at his father's nearly colorless face and agreed with Hotona. Judging by his ailing father's appearance, Jimmy probably wouldn't live much longer. Yellowsnake felt the end was near as he sat quietly at Jimmy's bedside. Suddenly, his father began to speak in a weak voice.

Jimmy had sensed his time was preciously short, and was saying whatever came into his mind. He was fading quickly as he whispered audibly in Yellowsnake's ear, "Son, don't forget your can of money up in the mountains. You know, you've got five-hundred and sixty thousand dollars up there." Until that solemn moment, Yellowsnake's damaged memory had not permitted him to recall the sum of cash he had buried years earlier along with Clyde Durham's can of gold. Within the hour,

Jimmy had died a peaceful death. Yellowsnake had lost another link in his lifeline.

While Yellowsnake was gone, Jake Montana made good use of his time. He probed tenaciously for information regarding Spanish gold and buried treasures. In due process, he found himself talking to Leo, an old friend he'd met years earlier. Leo himself was a gold prospector and treasure seeker. He was born part Cherokee, and like Yellowsnake, had spent his earlier years roaming around the Superstition and Mazatzal Mountains, and any place that showed signs of color. However, Leo possessed a special talent which Jake had witnessed, and was intrigued by.

Leo had become an expert dowser, which was a new and foreign term to Jake. "Dowsing," Leo explained, "works like this. You take two metal rods and shape them in an L-shaped configuration. The long side of your L is your dowsing wire, and the short side is the handle which will enable you to hold onto the wire. While holding these wires in a perfectly horizontal position in front of you, and grasping the handles very gently, if you walk in a straight line, the rods will indicate when you have passed over a number of things. For example, a dowsing rod will tell you where water is located, or it may even tell you where your lost wrist watch is lying. But I've learned one thing. Dowsing rods will also react strongly if you have passed over metallic objects or something buried deep below."

"Intriguing," Jake thought. While his eyes watched Leo demonstrate their use, he listened as Leo told him how the rods were fashioned from wire coat hangers. Jake became not only fascinated, but extremely interested in seeing how they worked. Soon, he was getting surprising results using the dowsing rods himself, following the instructions Leo had given him.

They stood around idly while they talked in Leo's shed, then suddenly Leo came up with a brilliant idea. He knew that Yellowsnake and Jake were searching for buried treasure somewhere up in the mountains, and wanted to assist. "Here, let me do something that might help you. At least we can give it a try. If you can give me a detailed map of the area where you're searching, we'll try something different."

Jake, without asking why, retrieved a detailed topographical area map of the mountainous area containing their target. Leo laid it out on his large table and went to work. He gently grasped the single dowsing rod, and went into a trancelike state of concentration. He quietly asked a question with his words directed toward the rod. "Show me where the treasure is located that Jake and Yellowsnake are looking for."

From the corner of the map, the dowsing rod began its horizontal rotation across the detailed topography, finally stopping over a specific area. When Leo saw this, he drew a light pencil line following the direction of the rod. He was satisfied it was working and moved to the other three corners of the map, performing the same identical ritual. Soon, by triangulation, the rod had indicated from all four corners, the location of something. Maybe it was a treasure. Neither of them had any way of knowing what the rods were telling them.

Jake was amazed as he asked, "Can I try doing the same thing?" Leo agreed.

"Sure, give it a try," he urged. Jake placed his own dowsing rod on the corner of the map exactly as Leo had done, then nearly fell over when he saw his own rod had stopped on the same pencil line that Leo had drawn. The novice dowser followed Leo's example, proceeding to each corner, asking the same question of the rod. Minutes later, Jake was nothing short of astonished. His own dowsing rod had coincided exactly with all of Leo's pencil line marks.

They gave each other a dubious look, for it was obvious that not only Jake, but Leo as well, was amazed at the outcome of the experiment. It was mysterious, the way the dowsing rods had performed in a concise though magical way. Leo admitted he had not attempted the feat more than twice. Each previous time it had been done to locate much broader targets, one being a burned out cabin site. He confessed that he had no idea why the rods had reacted the way they had.

They chit-chatted a few minutes longer, then Jake finally left, thanking Leo for the exciting experience he had shared with him. Jake was thinking more and more about the sobering event he had witnessed, and he wasn't about to let it rest.

After Yellowsnake had sadly completed the task of placing

his father to rest near Hotona's home, he and Liliana returned to Arizona from their unhappy trip. Although his father had not been a driving force during his formative years, he would still be sadly missed by Yellowsnake.

Within days of returning from Oklahoma, Yellowsnake received a call from Jake. "Hey, Comanche, are you ready to go at it again?"

Yellowsnake gave him his quick reply. "You bet! What have you got in mind, Carpet Bagger?"

"I'll come over to your place. I've got something interesting to show you." When he entered Yellowsnake's home, Jake anxiously retrieved the large map from its protective folder, spreading it over the kitchen table.

Yellowsnake scratched his head as he listened to what had occurred between Jake and Leo during his absence, and the weird results after they dowsed the map. "I've never heard of anything so crazy!" he cried. He stood looking at the map, musing over the prospect that there might be any shred of accuracy in the triangulated lines. His mind was vague as he recalled his childhood. He had not only watched his grandmother use willow sticks fashioned much like the metal dowsing rods, he had seen her find water for various wells throughout the reservation. He was amazed at her powers, for she had never failed to find a deep hidden pool of water for some family needing to drill a well.

"Bullshit, there's no way you can find buried treasure with dowsing rods, let alone find treasure with lines drawn on a map," he guffawed.

"Okay," Jake said. "I'll believe you for the moment, but in the meantime why don't you try something. Here, use my dowsing rods and see what answer you come up with."

The skeptical Yellowsnake followed the same prescribed ritual and was dumbfounded by the results. He had held the single dowsing rod over the map, asking it the same question as Leo and Jake. He watched the rod lie directly over the lines drawn earlier. Undeniably, three separate people had now arrived at the same conclusion.

Jake was beginning to get his attention, and Yellowsnake

was becoming more intrigued by what he was witnessing. He asked, "What would you like to do?"

Jake suggested that if they could use the horses, they should once again travel deep into the mountains. Only this time they had to travel further north because the lines on the map indicated they were four miles from where they should be. "What the hell," Yellowsnake exclaimed, "I've done some stupid things before. Besides, it should be fun and we'll have a chance to ride the horses."

Jake agreed to wait for a few days until Yellowsnake had settled himself from his return trip, and waited patiently until his still skeptical partner gave the word. "Okay, let's load the horses and get up to where you want to go." As they prepared for their next journey into the strange and forbidding mountains lying fifty miles away, Jake suggested, "Why don't we stop by Leo's shed? I'd like to introduce him to you."

"Okay," Yellowsnake agreed. "I guess we've got plenty of time. Besides I'd like to meet this guy who's got your brain all twisted up into thinking you can dowse a map."

They quietly arrived at Leo's hut, and as they entered through his doorway, their startling entry brought Leo to his feet. Leo looked at them as he scratched his head, and with a shocked look on his face, he looked intently into Yellowsnake's eyes. "Haven't I see you before?"

Although Yellowsnake was surprised, he politely responded to Leo's unexpected question. "I don't know. Have we met before?" A long forgotten past was emerging, and both were sensing what was coming to the surface.

"Didn't I fish you out of the Mekong River a long time ago?" Leo asked. "Devil be damned, I think you did!" Yellowsnake exclaimed. "What's your name anyway?"

"Well, back in those days, the handle I went by was Cherokee Meredith." Yellowsnake faintly remembered the event, as he excitedly blurted, "Damn, I think I remember you now. You and your Navy SEAL buddies pulled me off the shore of the river when Charlie was chasing me." The reunited counterparts shook hands, marveling at how small the world had become, especially the world of former jungle warriors, gold

266

miners and treasure seekers.

"You know," Leo continued, "it was a coincidence that I was even on that rescue boat. Being there was not part of my normal duty. Until that trip up the river, I was usually a shooter. I was like a sniper, except it was my job to pop North Vietnamese high ranking officers. Usually, my job would have resembled your tracking job. There were a lot of times when I'd be hidden in the jungle for days on end before the time was right for me to pop my target. Then I had to run like hell, just like you. The day the message came in that our SEALs needed to pick you up, I volunteered for the trip. I was loose at the time, and the word was that the boat might be ambushed during the trip. They said they could use a shooter to help them out, and there I was. I hate the water, but I was willing to make the trip."

There wasn't a peacepipe to smoke right then, but the three of them smoked a cigarette, and drank a beer in remembrance of the fateful day.

Yellowsnake chuckled, "I'll be a son of a bitch, who would have ever known."

While Yellowsnake thanked Leo for his brave effort in rescuing him so many years earlier, Jake was engrossed by their conversation. He respected the moment, yet he was anxious to get back on the road and head for the mountains.

Now, everyone's interest was peaked by the new mission. Leo pissed and moaned that "if he didn't have to work he'd join them on their adventure", then he bid them "adios" as they resumed their odyssey toward the unpredictable mountains ahead.

The anxious pair picked up the same rock strewn two-track trail they had followed earlier, and soon reached a point where they could go no further except on horseback. They saddled up the eager horses, loaded their equipment into the saddle bags, strapped on their revolvers and knives, and were off. It was time to begin their search for the triangulated point on the map which Jake carried in his backpack.

This time, however, they would have to travel more than four miles in the opposite direction following the bed of the stream running through the canyon. They headed north, weaving their way along the floor of the canyon, zig zagging around massive boulders strewn everywhere, led by the sturdy and discerning Zack.

For the moment, they were in no particular hurry as they stopped every few minutes to admire the beauty surrounding them. Although both had spent countless hours in the mountains, they never ceased to marvel at their rugged beauty. They advanced northward before they reached the area which should place them very near the triangulated spot they were looking for.

Yellowsnake had become an astute map reader during his war years, and soon recognized by looking at the topographical lines on the map that they were very near their target. They wove their way a couple of hundred yards further, then Yellowsnake stopped. "Let's tie up here and give the horses a rest. We can go on from here by foot." They checked their backpacks to see that everything was secure, and carried as little weight as possible, knowing they had to journey on foot.

They were underway for more than an hour and Yellowsnake had taken the lead, when suddenly he stopped. He raised his hand in a halting fashion, his keen eyes directed ahead. "Jake, take a look up there." He pointed over his right shoulder, his finger signaling Jake to look at a rock strewn pile of rubble. Jake wasn't exactly sure he knew what he should be looking at. "What do you see?"

"What I see is an old abandoned mineshaft covered with rocks. I think we're in the right area." By now, the relentless searchers were experiencing a rush of excitement, knowing that if there was a mine, there may be something else hidden near its location.

Jake had volunteered to be their mule when it came to carrying their tools. He had strapped the cumbersome shovel on his backpack in case they wanted to look for anything hidden below the surface of the ground. They stood before the rubble strewn mouth of the long abandoned mine, wisely concluding there was no sense trying to poke around it's rock-barricaded entrance. It would probably take days, even months to open up the mouth of the shaft.

Yellowsnake kept scrutinizing the surrounding area, making mental notes and drawing some very definite conclusions. His years of tracking had taught him to judge how old a trail was, and when it had last been traveled. "I can tell you, this trail leading up to the mine is more than two hundred years old. I don't have any doubt that the Spanish explorers were probably up here, and I think the Mexicans followed them later."

Jake unbuttoned his shirt and stripped down to his bare back, ready to go to work. He didn't doubt Yellowsnake's proclamation as he looked around, agreeing that the trails and overgrowth looked very old.

"Okay, Jake, what do you want to do now?" Yellowsnake questioned.

"Hell, I don't know. We're here, but I don't know what we're supposed to be looking for. Are we looking for buried treasure, buried gold or what?"

It was time to ponder their next move as they sat on a large boulder and surveyed the area. Jake said, "Sit still. I'm going to try something." He retrieved his metal dowsing rods, then began wandering around somewhat aimlessly in front of the mouth of the abandoned mine. He dropped one of the rods to his side, and holding the other rod horizontally still in front of him, Jake asked the rod a most profound question. "Okay, show me where the treasure is buried outside of this mine."

Slowly, and to the astonishment of both, the dowsing rod began its steady rotation, moving closer and closer to Jake's left arm. Suddenly the dowsing rod stopped and remained motionless. Jake began to follow the direction in which the rod was pointing, walking slowly behind the pointing rod. While he was walking, he positioned the second dowsing rod, so that now both rods were pointing in the same direction, side by side. They were directing him on a straight line.

After about twenty paces, the two dowsing rods suddenly crossed abruptly. Jake backed up a few paces, then repositioned the rods in a side by side manner in front of him, and walked in the same direction. Once again, the rods quickly crossed, forming the shape of an "X".

Jake was totally bewildered as he turned his head toward

Yellowsnake. "Snake, I want you to do the same thing." He was not believing what he had seen, but the skeptical dowser agreed to Jake's request. He grasped the dowsing rods and followed the same line of movement as Jake. He became even more amazed, for as Yellowsnake reached the identical spot, his rods suddenly crossed, forming an "X". Both were deeply mystified as they stood motionless and asked, "Why did the rods cross at this particular point?"

Jake didn't have an answer to their question, so he began circling the spot at which the rods had crossed. The spot was very distinguishable. It was the resting place for a large flat rock, about three feet in diameter. "Why did the rods cross here?" Jake again asked, as he slowly circled the gray rock. Excitedly, he yelled as he nearly jumped out of his boots. "Take a look at this, Snake. Here's why the rods stopped here."

Yellowsnake walked around to Jake's side, then his eyes grew as large as saucers. Before them, imprinted faintly on the large flat rock was something remarkable. They bent over to take a closer look and ran their fingers along its outline. They knew what they were looking at. It was a large numeral **"7"**. Within moments, they had each drawn the same conclusion. More than a century earlier, the etched numeral had been imprinted on the rock by someone possessing the talent to impregnate the rock with an intensely rich red dye which had penetrated the rock's surface. Even though it was badly faded, the numeral was unmistakable.

Within a few seconds, Jake had pulled a camera from his backpack and was taking pictures of the remarkable find. They knew what they were looking at, but were asking the same question. "What's here? Why is the seven on this rock?"

Yellowsnake then noticed something which only an experienced tracker would recognize. The small rocks which were laying carefully positioned around the upper edge of the curious rock had been placed there intentionally. Their arrangement was not a natural looking formation. After Yellowsnake had given Jake a mini-lesson in rock reading, the two of them became even more excited knowing this particular disguise was created by man.

270

Jake declared his intent as he picked up the shovel lying on the ground. "Okay partner, let's go to work digging and see what's here."

Yellowsnake knelt next to the flat rock while Jake placed the point of the shovel into the dirt just above it. Yellowsnake gave the order. "Go ahead and start digging, and I'll watch." In Jake's experience, Yellowsnake had never been one who favored being on the long end of a shovel, swearing the handle would never fit his hands.

Jake hurriedly dug into the soft dirt packed behind the otherwise inconspicuous rock, commanding, "Be sure to look at everything that comes out of the hole as I dig."

Yellowsnake nodded his agreement, watching Jake, shovelful by shovelful, removing the uncluttered, nearly pure dirt which lay behind the large rock. Ever so carefully, he dug as Yellowsnake watched. The shovel had now reached a depth of nearly eight inches, when suddenly it's point sounded a sharp thud on something lying below. Now more excited than ever, Jake kept removing dirt from the hole, taking care not to throw anything out which might offer them a clue. When the shovel point once again struck the rock, they saw its surface peeking through the dirt. Like a magician about ready to pull a rabbit out of his hat, Yellowsnake reached into the hole with his long, narrow fingers and gently removed the object which the shovel had struck.

As Yellowsnake held the object in his hands, it was judged to be nothing more than a simple rock. "Oh, it's only a rock," Jake barked, "Go ahead and throw it aside and I'll keep digging." Yellowsnake fingered the odd looking rock which was approximately ten inches long, looking closely at its shape. Then, and to his own amazement, he saw something which very few men would see in their lifetime. The hand fashioned, ten inch rock had been sculptured to resemble the shape of a heart.

When he turned the rock over, a most startling sight reached his eyes. A treasure map was clearly etched on the back of the rock. Together, they had spotted its unique shape, noticing the absence of dirt clinging to its surface. It was a clear indication that it had been secretly placed within its resting site. The soft

271

dirt which Jake had removed had been spread neatly over it's surface to hide it's resting place.

The blood raced through the treasure seekers' veins for incredibly, they had something very exciting resting in their hands. Clearly inscribed on the clean flat surface of the rock were some conspicuous symbols. However, the most remarkable symbol was the clearly etched shape of a 'heart'. The telltale heart was a sure indicator they were standing very close to something buried beneath the ground's surface.

They were still disbelieving as they examined the stone map closely. By using simple logic, they were able to determine that the four arrows going from the point of the heart in different directions was a road map to more than one cache. The first arrow clearly indicated the location of the long abandoned mine. The other three arrows were pointers to caches which lay buried nearby. The map was indeed specific, for etched below the heart was a clearly inscribed square, representing a burial box.

The map was delivering a clear message to them. The heart was telling them there was gold nearby, and the heart had even been colored to a golden hue. The inscribed box indicated that whatever was buried, was first placed inside a box. Most importantly, the arrows were pointing to natural objects which lay less than a hundred yards away. The two treasure hunters decided to follow the shorter and most obvious arrow pointing the way. Jake, carrying his shovel, walked toward a huge boulder which didn't seem to belong where it was placed. Though unattractively gray in color, the boulder contained an unmistakable message. Within it's huge body, a section had been carefully hewn out, forming a cavity in the shape of a triangle. And within the cavity, an entirely different colored section of stone had been inserted. The inserted stone was gold in color. Had they indeed found what so many thousands of treasure seekers before them had sought? A lot of questions were beginning to surface.

Was their discovery really a buried treasure map placed there more than a century earlier? Had it been buried there by one of the last members of the Peralta family, the famous explorers who had followed the ancient trails of Spanish Conquistadors?

272

Without proof to the contrary, the discoverers were firmly convinced they had stumbled upon one of the legendary Peralta buried treasure sites.

For hundreds of years, countless old prospectors had searched for hidden treasure, but seldom was there ever a reported discovery.

The sun was quickly dipping toward the horizon and the two men agreed that if they pursued their intriguing discovery right now, they'd never get back to their faithful tethered horses, much less home, that night. The pair confidently agreed that the treasure would wait, and with a higher sense of responsibility toward their animals, they'd return with supplies and tools as soon as possible.

As darkness closed in, the weather turned. Yellowsnake's old Vietnam injuries were further aggravated by the cold. His neck was hurting, and his headache was getting worse. Meanwhile, a strange feeling had come over Jake. He was not a superstitious man by nature, but he had the knack of sensing when things were not quite right.

"Snake, I've got this feeling that someone or something is watching us. I don't know why, but I've had this nervous feeling in my gut that something's in the rocks up there." Yellowsnake's blue eyes flashed up toward the jagged ridge above them. Then, they heard small rocks rolling, causing an eerie echo in the canyon. Was the sound caused by man, or was it just Mother Nature playing tricks?

Yellowsnake put his hand on his pistol butt, his jaw tightening. "I think you're right. I don't like what I just heard up there." The thunder rumbled overhead, and a sudden flash of lightening got their attention. "Let's move quick and get the hell out of here. Our treasure will keep." One thing was for sure. This was not a good time to have someone lurking in the rocks high above them. If someone was watching them, they would undoubtedly be carrying a gun. Yellowsnake and Jake would leave for now, but they had the advantage. Their stone treasure map was safely tucked away in Jake's backpack. They knew where the mysterious discovery might take them. No one else did.

As they walked back toward their horses, they were both reaching the same conclusion. The stone map was sending them a mixed bag of directions to follow. They were going to have to spend some time studying the strange rock before they did too much more digging. What's more, the two knew that the ancient gold seekers were crafty in their map making.

Jake and Yellowsnake agreed that they would wait until things had settled down and the time was right for another trip. They made a pact, vowing to return the following autumn to complete their intriguing mission. And, next time, they'd be better prepared for possible intruders. Yellowsnake would see to that! For the first time since Yellowsnake's loss of his dear friends Clyde and Emmet, he knew he had found a capable and trustworthy friend to join him in his search for the milk cans buried in Deadman Canyon. That pursuit, too, would have to wait.

Their anticipation of the next adventure haunted the days and nights that would follow. What surprises would it hold? What dangers? Would they find gold? How much? Would someone else get there first? Their questions taunted their thoughts, but, they alone held the map which would lead them on the path of discovery.

The adventure which had started only hours earlier was, for the moment, coming to an end. Yellowsnake sat watching, while Jake carefully filled the shallow hole which had revealed the stone map. He was covering the diggings with rocks to disguise its presence. Yellowsnake's tired and hazy mind was becoming flooded by the multitude of events which had passed through his life. His thoughts had returned to the days of his early childhood and, subsequently, the day he had visited with Shahana before entering the Army. He felt comforted, for his injured mind was clearly recalling her strange prophecy.

The wise old Yaqui medicine woman had shared with him her crystal clear visions. She had prophesied that Yellowsnake would live a long and perilous life and ultimately, enjoy prosperity. He had experienced all of her predictions. Had her prophecy been truly fulfilled? He was immersed with an unwavering conclusion that the wise old woman had foreseen his path of travel and accurately foretold the events of his most extraordinary life. Creator's blessings, along with Shahana's presence had seen him through some of life's toughest moments. Now, her indisputably true words were cast in stone, forever etched in his conscious mind.

"You will have many hard and perilous days ahead of you, but you will survive to live a long life with much happiness and good fortune. The spirit of your forefathers will shield you from death, and when your spirit is struggling to join those of your ancestors, I will be there when you need me. You will see me no more in my world, but I will see you in yours."

There was one question which Jake had been wanting to ask Yellowsnake for quite some time. As the two of them were driving away from the forbidding mountains which sheltered the mysterious canyon, Jake asked "Did you ever see Shahana again?" Yellowsnake had a warm glow in his eyes as he smiled. "Yeah, I see her every now and then."

Yellowsnake's heart had become softened by his life's experiences, and years earlier he had quietly thanked Creator, who, along with Shahana's help, had cast out the beast which had dwelt in his spirit so many years ago.

He could rest peacefully now and forever more, for the beast had been slain.

A strange prophecy.

Strong medicine!